MW01679577

DON'T DIE BROK

IMPORTANT NOTICE

This publication is for educational purposes only, and is designed to provide authoritative information with regard to the subject matter covered. The publisher and author are not engaged in rendering legal, accounting, investment, or other professional advice. If such advice or expert professional assistance is required, the services of a competent professional specialist should be sought. The publisher and author hold no invested interest, except through client accounts, with any corporation or institution referenced within this publication. We do not endorse nor attest to the accuracy of products, material, or services provided by them. Investment performance is not implied nor guaranteed. Never invest unless you understand the underlying investment concept and are willing to accept the associated risk. Reproduction of this publication, in whole or part, in any form or manner, is explicitly prohibited without the written consent of both the publisher and author. Information referenced herein is subject to change without notice. Investors retain sole responsibility for all gains, losses, and taxes associated with their investment portfolio.

We suggest readers study this material from cover to cover before investing one single penny. Never rush into an investment blindly. Never invest against the market momentum trend. Strategies found throughout this book are the suggested starting point in the formulation of a wealth building plan. The plan should be modified as necessary to meet specific individual investment objectives.

A liberal unit price discount is available on this product to qualified corporations, clubs, schools, churches, book dealers, independent salespersons, and fund raiser organizations. Discount pricing information may be requested in writing from the Publisher.

G Howard Gunn: Publisher/ Author.

Printed in the United States of America by BookMasters, Inc.; PO Box 2139, Mansfield, OH 44905-9099.

Cover photography courtesy of Deanna Lynn Gunn.

Library of Congress Catalog Card Number 96-95052.

ISBN 0-9657753-0-5.

G. Howard Gunn
370 Lakeshore Drive; Swan Lake
Stockbridge, Georgia 30281
(1-770-506-9592)

DEDICATION

This book is dedicated to my wife Jean Ann Lyons Gunn.

A *special friend* since 1965.

Thank you for bearing with me throughout the years it took to research and publish this material.

ACKNOWLEDGMENT

Special Thanks To

Mr. H. Ray Belcher
Ms. Deanna Lynn Gunn
Mr. Leonard Jacobowitz
Mrs. Teresa K. McClellan
Ms. Nancy Ann Johnson Terry

<u>and</u>

to all who contributed in making this publication possible. Without your assistance, perhaps thousands of American children and parents alike would have never experienced the opportunity to achieve financial freedom. Children, in particular, now have available an important asset management tool. If properly utilized, it could enhance their wealth building strategies for 25, 50, or even 75 years hence; so they, like previous generations *Don't Die Broke.*

IN MEMORY

Mr. Leonard Jacobowitz passed from this life on May 20, 1997. Our thoughts and prayers are with him and his family. The investment strategies and friendship he shared with his closest friends will be everlasting in the hearts and minds of those who were lucky enough to have known him. To a dear friend, we bid a sad farewell.

TABLE OF CONTENTS

The stock market is clearly an agiotage paradox. It can be as simple or complex as the investor makes it to be. The market is in a constant state of change and has indeed changed dramatically since its origin. The average person putting money into the market place of today are fooled into thinking they are investors. The opposite is most likely to be the truth. They often become a victim of their own greed! Divestors are simply unaware they are being manipulated to benefit someone other than themselves. They will continue to be divested of wealth until they understand how to play the game. We will introduce investors to the game players. Henceforth, there will be few excuses for our readers to be victimized by greed!

In this chapter, investors are introduced to several investment strategies which have historically proven to offer superior investment total returns. For the strategies to succeed; however, the investor must be mentally and financially prepared to accept the risks associated with success. Ironically, a local checking account is often more risky than equity investing. Wealth building mandates a long term personal objective to increase net worth year after year. Avoid attempting to recreate the system. To be successful, merely walk the path of those who have built fortunes through the strategies we share. While walking the path, keep alert for hazards designed to stop you.

Don't Die Broke is based upon years of research. Many hours have been used searching for a successful wealth building strategy useful to the average person. The strategy is not a "get rich" scheme, but is actually a way of life. We can change our lifestyles to the betterment of all Americans. *Don't Die Broke* will help fulfill Senator Doles dream to "Wake up America" by sharing important information essential to achieving the important objective of not dying broke. Why not die broke? You can't take it with you, many have scoffed! The answer to the question is as close as our children. Take a close look into their eyes. After realizing our generations usage of mother Earth is nothing more than a loan from all subsequent generations, to the reasonable person, the answer will come!

Wealth building does require a starting point. A "zero mile post," so to speak. We have provided within the Appendix crucial worksheets, an optional pledge, a distribution offer, and the opportunity to share with others personally authored informative material. It is very important to always know your personal net worth value, cash flow demands, and income sources. We encourage investors to reproduce for future use the Appendix worksheets. Consider them your "zero mile post."

Alphabetic listing of important subject matter.

FORWARD

" No great thing is created suddenly, anymore than a bunch of grapes or a fig. If you tell me that you desire a fig, I answer you that there must be time. Let it first blossom, then bear fruit, then ripen." Epictetus (C55-135)

" He is poor whose expenses exceed his income." Jean de La Bruyere (1645-1696)

" Nothing is better for you than something you don't like." Leonard Jacobowitz (Investor)

" There is no security on this earth. There is only opportunity." General Douglas MacArthur

" What is too often missing from a wealth building strategy is the average person. Most middle working class Americans are excluded from the strategy because they have been wrongfully lead to believe, they don't belong. Include yourself without anyone's permission. Seek an education. Get a job. Learn debt management. Eliminate wasteful spending. Network skills. Invest wisely. The track record of building wealth is as old as humankind. Unfortunately, the majority actually believe they can not succeed. Accepting the lie of despair to be true, they will take the easy road to the poorhouse only to die broke. Those wishing to succeed can, once they understand the game rules." George H. Gunn (Investor, Author)

" If a speculator is correct half of the time, he is hitting a good average. Even being right three or four times out of ten should yield a person a fortune if he has the sense to cut his losses quickly on the ventures where he has been wrong." (Source unknown)

" Lies. Half Truths. One sided stories. Whether you're buying a new car, investing your money; or, checking into a hospital, you're being secretly manipulated by shrewd spin doctors who slant the truth to fit their hidden agenda." Martin Edelston, President (*Bottom Line*)

" Genius is the ability to reduce the complicated to the simple." C.W. Cerar

" The world is full of educated derelicts." Ray Kroc Founder (McDonalds Corporation)

" Dost thou love life? Then do not squander time, for that is the stuff life is made of." Ben Franklin

" Security is mostly a superstition. It does not exist in nature; nor, do the children of men as a whole experience it. Avoiding danger is no safer in the long run than outright exposure." Helen Keller

" Teach thy tongue to say, I do not know; and, thou shalt progress." Maimonides

" You can't be scared. You do your thing. You hold your grounds. You stand up tall." Donald J. Trump

" The greatest revolution of our generation is the discovery that human beings, by changing the inner attitudes of their minds, can change the outer aspects of their lives." William James

" Ultimately, when it comes to creating wealth, you have to become your own expert." Robert Allen (Author)

INTRODUCTION

Spending and investing habits are deployable among American consumers! According to figures released by the United States Federal Reserve, consumer borrowing topped a historical record high of $1.191 trillion in November, 1996. Impulse spending obligates future earnings. When combined with depreciation, taxes, and inflation; over-extended credit, tends to drive consumers straight to the poorhouse. The saying "pay back is hell" could never be more appropriate when it comes to describing the side effects of excessive consumer debt. 1996, also witnessed a record year for personal bankruptcies! Bankruptcies driven by debt harms society. Future personal earnings obligated to practically worthless merchandise simply can not be used to purchase equity investments at a volume level high enough to enhance the individual, corporate, or government wealth building process.

Without external capital infusion from equity and debt investors, the government and corporate America will seek alternate funding resources. Society will become strained as taxes and inflation push higher after corporate earnings and capital infusion dry up. When providers fail to meet the demand from consumers for new products and services, work force right-sizing (layoffs) will eventually occur. Jobs will be transferred out of the United States in an attempt to boost corporate earnings. The attempt will fail because a majority of consumers will either be unemployed or credit over-extended. Either way, they will not be able to purchase merchandise produced abroad. Displaced workers will become dependent upon a government unable to balance its budget. Stock prices will fall due to low corporate earnings. Individual taxes will rise to replace the taxes lost from corporate revenue. Corporate America and the government at every level; although, not entirely blameless, will falsely become the scapegoat for poor consumer spending and investment habits. We as individuals are the final decision makers controlling our destiny. It does not matter if some bureaucrats are crooked, or if corporate America management salary and benefit perks have exceeded insane heights. What urgently matters is that each responsible person must accept the "challenge of change" not only for themselves but for the generations too follow. Zero debt: the investors choice!

"Wake up America" was the message Presidential candidate Bob Dole preached across America in 1996. Few, if anyone, listened to Senator Dole's important message. To echo the Senators warning, *Don't Die Broke* has been edited to promote the concept of individual wealth building through education, debt reduction, controlled spending, health maintenance, and the inexact science of debt and equity investing. A gross misunderstanding exists within the working middle class, concerning the true net cost associated with income production. The misunderstanding has resulted in the majority of Americans following a lifestyle based upon incorrect assumptions. Some within this group believe they are manipulated for a variety of reasons, from the very moment of birth, into a lifestyle of inadequate education, investments, and over-extended debt only to become an economic slave without any hope for a better tomorrow. Kids graduating from high school may not have the ability to understand the meaning of their diploma; yet, they are bombarded with credit card applications. Young adults serve their country either in the armed forces, or through voting only to be told high education cost places it off limits too them. Accepting this to be true, they settle into a lifestyle based upon false assumptions. The cycle begins anew generation after generation without any real hope of change. Read these words carefully: YOU CAN MAKE CHANGE HAPPEN!

Consumer debt may actually be a controlling tool utilized by corporate America to keep a middle working class buffer between the rich upper class and the lower poor class. Without the middle working class, the rich would not have the tax buffer needed to shield the wealth existing between themselves and the poor. The rich socialite power structure would fail if forced to support the poor. The middle working class is extended unheard of credit by the rich upper class. American workers are trapped into a debt cycle founded upon a superficial appearance of success. Middle class debt obligates trillions of future wage dollars to the coiffeurs of wealthy America. This prevents the working middle class from rising into the rich upper class while guaranteeing they will eventually fall into the lower poor class only to die flat broke. Wealth not robbed away during the productive working years through credit is stolen away by inflation during retirement, or through estate probate after death. It is to no surprise, self made millionaires by the hundreds have surrendered their American citizenship and have left the United States.

President William (Bill) Clinton demonstrated a clear vision of the situation when he invited leaders of corporate America for a White House summit in January, 1997. The President correctly acknowledged the wealthy class business leaders must do more to lift the standard of living among the nations poor. Mr. Clinton indicated the government (middle working class) acting alone could not create jobs for everyone required to find employment as a result of mandatory welfare roll reduction. President Clinton needs to consider creating jobs through expansion of the economy, by having the courage to: revamp social security; establish a national consumer tax, and abolishing capital gains and federal taxes, while eliminating corporate write-off's. Current tax codes unfairly force payment of capital gains tax without considering capital gains purchase slippage due to inflation. Capital gains is akin to gambling, whereas, 100 percent of losses should be credited against an equal inflation adjusted percentage of gains. The middle class complain of high taxes, high education cost, and mediocre salaries; but, think nothing about over-extending their debt to the brink of bankruptcy. As a group, they live in the "me" generation without considering the long term negative effect their actions will have on future generations.

Children are the ones who will eventually suffer the loss of education, health, social, and financial security. Among children of all ages, 20 percent are believed to live in poverty. Reports indicate the fastest growing population among the American homeless community are children. City streets across America receive hundreds of additional homeless children daily. Yet, as a financial disaster begins to emerge on the social security system horizon; consumers continue to sit on their passive duff while displaying poor financial management skills. A 1996 Texas A&M study, as reported by the *Investor's Business Daily*, found spending habits among children tracking parallel to that of adults. Kids are annually dropping an estimated $2 billion on junk food, $1.9 billion on toys, $700 million on clothes, $600 million on movies, and $486 million for video games. Children establish habits through example! As adults, are we setting the correct example? We think not!

Don't Die Broke offers to anyone mature enough to accept the "challenge of change" an opportunity to improve their current lifestyle; thus, possibly benefiting the lifestyle of their children. Nothing in this publication; however, will help anyone improve their financial situation or lifestyle, if they ignore the personal commitment necessary to become motivated enough to make the scarifies associated with change. Readers have access to valuable information. They can plan their financial destiny. Financial security can become a reality. Investors can avoid the poorhouse. They can enjoy peace of mind, during their "golden" retirement years should they become abandoned by their family, friends, employer, government, and perhaps even their religious affiliation.

Chapter 1 gives an overview of how to build a solid financial and investment foundation. Chapter 2 reviews many investment insights, including money saving best deep discount stock brokerage firms, important financial formulas, and additional insights. The insights illustrated can easily eliminate years of searching for the much elusive perfect investment. In some instances, the same insight is repeated several times in a different presentation. The repetition is by design. Review chapter 3 very carefully. Without a working knowledge of the stock market, investors are almost guaranteed to become victims of their own greed. Chapter 4 introduces material designed to aid the serious investor in the development of investment analytical stock selection abilities equal to that of the professionals. We will illustrate how to pick the best investment the market has to offer. Readers will be shown how to determine when to avoid investing. They will also be shown how to determine for themselves when they should be fully invested, or when they should be standing on the sidelines. *Don't Die Broke* readers are encouraged to avoid being ripped off by anyone trying to sell them something they do not need. They are encouraged to review and complete the worksheets provided in the Appendix. Proceed to chapter 1.

CHAPTER 1

BUILDING THE FOUNDATION

It is critical to build wealth upon a solid financial foundation. Concepts recommended in chapter 4 assumes the investor has developed proper investment habits, a knowledge of the subject, a proper financial base; and, skills required to implement a personal investment strategy. Perhaps, knowledge of the subject is the most important. Without being educated on a specific subject matter, no one can derive benefits associated with the subject. Educational material related to wealth building is practically unlimited. Material may be purchased at local book stores, read at the local library, and obtained through mail order. Investment news letter publications are informative; but, they are not necessarily educational. News letters tend to be narrowly biased toward the authors opinion. Investor's with poor reading skills may improve their skills by contacting Active Reading Phonics (1-800-318-5041). The following listing of recommended reading material was selected for their excellent educational, motivational, and inspirational qualities.

Suggested Reading Source

MOTIVATIONAL:

* *Promises To Keep* — Nick Harrison / Author

NOTE: If this book is not on your reading list, you are missing out on perhaps the best devotional and inspirational book ever written.

* *Think and Grow Rich* — Napoleon Hill / Arthur (1937)
(Library or Book Retailer)

NOTE: *Think and Grown Rich* was based upon research into the lives of the world's richest people. It is perhaps the best personal growth book ever published. *Think and Grow Rich* has been in continuous print for 60 years.

EDUCATIONAL:

* *One Upon Wall Street* — Peter Lynch with John Rothchild (1989)
(Library or Book Retailer)

NOTE: Very important book! Mr. Lynch was perhaps the best mutual fund manager of all time. "Stock tips from a master" (source: *USA Today*). "The number one money manager." (Source: *Time)*

* *The Book of Secrets* — Marion Buttagier / Editor
Boardroom Classics
330 West 42nd Street
New York, NY 10036

NOTE: Boardroom offers an excellent variety of motivational books which are easy to read and difficult to put aside.

* *1001 Free Goodies and Cheapies* — Mathew Lesko and Mary Ann Martello

NOTE: Really neat stuff. The book is updated via computer (1-800-524-3388 : representative 168).

* *Make It Last* — Paul Proulx (Yankee Magazine)

* *Free Stuff From America On-Line* — Luanne O'Loughlin
The Coriolis Group; Scottsdale, AZ.

* *The Young Entrepreneur's Guide To Starting and Running a Business*
Steve Mariotti / Author
Times Books Publisher (1996)

NOTE: National Foundation For Teaching Entrepreneurs. Chapters are in New York, Boston, Washington DC, and New Jersey. Check with the Foundation for chapters in your local area. Business instruction for kids.

* *The Burning Match* — Jim Straw / Author
Philander Club
Cleveland, TN
(Direct Mail Order)

* *How to Make Money In Stocks* — William J. O'Neal / Author
Investor's Business Daily
Los Angeles, CA 90066
(Direct Mail Order)

NOTE: Mr. O'Neal takes the reader through a logical sequence stock selection process that is truly "a winning system in good time or bad."

* *Wealth without Risk* — Charles J. Givens / Author

* *Financial Self Defense* — Charles J. Givens / Author

* *Beating The Dow* — Michael O'Higgins

* *The Motley Fool Investment Guide* — David and Tom Gardner

HISTORICAL:

* *Memories of Extraordinary Popular Delusions* — Charles MacKay / Author (1841)

* *Common Stocks as Long Term Investments* — Edgar Lawrence Smith / Author (1924)

* *Security Analysis; Principles and Techniques*	Bengamin Graham / Author (1934)
* *Portfolio Selection*	Harry M. Markowitz / Author (1958)
* *Super Money*	Adam Smith / Author (1972)

NOTE: Consult with your Librarian. Access to these books may be restricted.

Christian, Jewish, and Islamic books offer guidance in areas of debt management and financial growth. The same may be appropriately stated for other major religions.

PUBLICATIONS:

Investor's Business Daily *Wall Street Journal* *Barons*
Money *Forbes* *Value Line* *Standard and Poor's Stock Guide*

Almost any business information publication, or do-it-yourself book can aid investors in the development of a solid financial foundation. Wealth comes from not only preserving what has been earned; but, also though a proper diversification across several investment vehicles. Especially when the diversification is combined with aggressive debt reduction. Debt must be eliminated through controlled spending and debt buy-down. Education, a healthy diet, income shelters, and investments aid in both debt reduction and wealth enhancement. By this point; hopefully, most have read several suggested books, and have began to develop a personal wealth building plan of action.

You have no doubt heard "a penny saved is a penny earned" or "anything worth having is worth fighting for." How about "healthy, wealthy, and wise." These are not idle sayings. Their consideration is essential in the formulation of a successful wealth building plan. If anyone ever expects to succeed, cold hard choices must be made. Habits founded upon social or cultural reinforcement may seem difficult to change. If a person is young enough not to have had the opportunity to establish poor wealth building habits, they are indeed very lucky. On the other hand, if poor debt, spending, and investment habits have been entrenched, they can be quickly changed. Change will generally happen once the individual chooses to dig deep into their self being to search for ways to make the change occur. Everyone must constantly plan today for wealth accumulation tomorrow. Delaying one second longer than necessary could be a drastic mistake. Wealth is only obtained over time, through compounding of growth, and a steady cash infusion. Reliable estimates indicate perhaps upward to 80 percent of all workers approaching retirement have less than $10,000 in a savings account. Couples may work their entire adult lives only to retire with a net worth of less than $50,000. The sad truth is that a majority of retirees will watch their net worth fall below the national poverty level within five years after retirement due to medical cost, improper debt management, wrong investments, taxes, and inflation. Please heed our urgent warning! **You must plan now for financial security tomorrow**. A retirement income source exceeding one million dollars may not ward off the terrible fate of dying flat broke by the year 2025. Forget about social security. It will be broke by 2012, according to the Administration.

"A penny saved is a penny earned" is where to begin. The absolute top priority is to protect what you have worked so hard to earn and save. Very few individuals ever become wealthy through investing; unless, they treat investing as serious business. As with any business, there must always be a revisable plan of action. That is the first goal each investor should strive to achieve. Stock investing, for example, is one business that is rewarding and exciting. It may be operated from practically anywhere; and, may be managed without expensive equipment or employees. A simple stock portfolio requires about one hour annually to manage. Chapter 4 explains how. The story of the Turtle and Hare illustrates the go slow and win philosophy used by so many successful investors. The investors business plan does not need to be complex. In fact, the simpler the plan, the better. The plan begins with a positive attitude toward life, combined with a strong motivation to organize ones affairs through learned skills, education, debt control, and heart healthy habits. Of course, no plan will work without money! However, it is not necessary to win a lottery (would not hurt), change jobs, or panhandle to reach financial independence.

We are convinced that even the potential investor who is stripped for cash, and barely surviving from paycheck to paycheck; can locate investment funds hidden within debt for redirecting into a secure future. To locate the hidden money hidden, turn to the Appendix. Complete the optional pledge, income statement, and balance sheet. Do not be afraid. The process is simple. It is the essence of your investment business plan. Review your expenses very carefully. Hidden within is the cash available for redistribution into investments. Dozens of opportunities may be discovered to reduce taxes, utility bills, transportation cost; plus, a host of additional areas of wasteful spending. It is not uncommon to locate more than $2,000 annually for investing. Money hidden within unnecessary expenses. Mistakes will surely happen. Do not become discouraged. Through persistence, the realization of reaping financial benefits could soon materialize. A key point to remember: 40 percent of all spending is emotionally driven!

HEALTHY DIET: "Healthy, wealthy, and wise" alludes to the basic principle implying wealth may be a benefit rewarding the healthy. **Convenience food consumption is not heart healthy.** Regular long term consumption of "fast food" may actually prove very inconvenient. By some estimates, for each minute a "fast food" consumer patronizes their favorite establishment, they will eventually spend ten minutes with their doctor addressing food related illnesses. We are all aware of the medical cost associated with poor eating and health habits. The majority of adults have been told throughout their life the importance of maintaining an ideal body weight. We have been instructed that weight gain is often correlated with improper eating habits. Most of us have been taught from early childhood the importance of eating a nutritional breakfast. Research supports the important relationship of eating a nutritionally balanced breakfast and weight control. The best time to consume the largest meal of the day may actually be in the early morning. Skipping breakfast is a drastic wealth building mistake!

Doctor Frank Halberg, Ph.D. conducted research using six test subjects at the University of Minnesota. His study cited in *The Health Letter* indicated that when the subjects consumed 2,000 calories for breakfast and none for the remainder of the day, they each lost an average of 2.2 pounds per week. However, when the subjects ate identical portions of food exclusively at dinner time, four subjects gained weight while two lost very little weight. The research strongly suggests a conclusion that when food is consumed early in the morning, it may convert to energy and burn as calories instead of being stored as fat deposits. (*Best Kept Secrets In America* / Boardroom / 1995)

First Place, Inc., a Christian faith health maintenance program; reports that skipping breakfast leads to many health related problems. A healthy body needs to maintain a sufficient energy source of glucose (blood sugar). If after an extended fasting period (such as a 8 hour sleep), the human body does not receive sufficient high levels of carbohydrate glucose energy, the liver will supply the glucose. Frequently stressing the liver can lead to organ damage, or even failure. Low blood sugar will effect our moods, performance, appetite, electrolyte balance, neurotransmitters, and brain functions. The *First Place* program was originated in 1979 by the First Baptist Church of Houston, Texas. It has done a remarkable job helping people of all religious faiths learn how to live a healthier more abundant life. The principles underlying the First Place program are not unlike those necessary for long term wealth building.

First Place reading material references a breakfast eat study of 7,000 men and women conducted by the University of California Center for Health Science located at the University of California in Los Angeles (UCLA). The study discovered that among men who rarely ate breakfast, there was a 40 percent higher heart related death rate than the death rate found among men who ate breakfast regularly. Under identical test conditions, women who skipped breakfast had a 28 percent higher heart disease related death rate than the death rate of their peers who ate breakfast daily.

First Place, also reported the University of Iowa had conducted a breakfast study. Findings of the Iowa study, indicated superior mental and physical performance existed among breakfast eaters when compared to similar qualities found within a non-breakfast eater test group. The test subjects who ate a balanced nutritional breakfast daily were generally more productive throughout the day. They, as a group, had faster reaction times, and fewer job related accidents and injuries. After reviewing the research, one has to wonder how poor student grades, bankruptcy, divorce, and criminal activity stack up among individuals who eat breakfast regularly compared to those who do not. Realizing the importance of breakfast, schools across America serve students breakfast.

Americans tend to be overweight. Estimates indicate approximately 30 percent of all American adults are greater than 10 percent above their ideal body weight. By conservative estimates, millions of barrels of foreign oil imports are consumed annually in both the preparation and transportation of the massive amount of food necessary to support the American fat level. Additionally, millions of nonproductive hours are wasted annually in not only putting the fat on, but also taking it off. The novel concept of achieving higher productivity while becoming independent of foreign oil imports is mind boggling. You read it here first! Consider for a moment the trillions of dollars that could be redirected annually toward wealth building, if every overweight American would commit themselves to a weight reduction of a just 10 pounds. Better yet, consider how profitable business could potentially be, if their work force were encouraged to remain heart healthy by not putting the weight on. Japanese businesses set aside time for mandatory daily exercise tailored to meet individual employee needs. Perhaps they are trying to give American businesses a hint on how to increase work place productivity and corporate earnings.

Without question, remaining healthy reduces expensive medical cost. Everyone should take whatever steps necessary to remain mentally and physically healthy. Maintain a heart healthy diet. Follow a moderate exercise program. Limit alcohol consumption. Smoking is more than harmful to health, it sends millions of investment dollars up in smoke annually. Stick with a low fat, high fiber, and leafy green vegetable diet. Eat fresh fruit daily. Eat soybean by-products at least three weekly. Soybeans contain the very important nutrient lecithin. Lecithin contains lecithin cholesterol acyltransferase (LCAT) which tends to break down fatty body deposits. Apples contain pectin. Pectin tends to inhibit fat absorption. Garlic products tend to reduce body fat when used regularly. Eat garlic with raw vegetables several times weekly. Natural diuretics promote the elimination of retained body fluids. Diuretics include: raw asparagus, beets, cabbage, carrots, celery, cucumber, endive, garlic, horseradish, lettuce, onions, sauerkraut, radishes, and tomatoes (*Wonder Foods and Juices;* 1986: Globe Communications Corp., Boca Raton, Florida). Diuretics accelerate metabolism, which generally slows down during extended periods of fasting. Sleeping automatically creates up to a 12 hour fast. Investors should consider consuming carbohydrates, fiber, and natural diuretics for breakfast daily. Drink a 16 ounce glass of water 15 minutes prior to eating anything.

Individuals failing to break their sleep fasting with a nutritional breakfast will generally maintain a low metabolism rate throughout much of the business day. With a low metabolism, stored fat remains stored. Good health is essential to the logical thinking associated with wealth building. Who can make logical investment decisions when stressed out due to poor health? Always consult with a physician before beginning any diet or exercise program. Health and stress are interrelated. Reduction of stress is of utmost importance. An excellent way to rid stress is to vacation at a spa. Spas promote health, exercise, stress management, and dieting. Spa vacations are generally priced very reasonable. To locate a spa, contact either Spa Finders (1-800-255-7727) or Custom Spa Vacations (1-800-443-7727). A spa vacation is rewarding for most guest long after returning to the daily grind of working.

Dwight C. Byers, author of *Better Health With Foot Reflexology,* writes that more than 2300 years before the birth of Christ, the Egyptians had discovered the ultimate stress relief secret. They had perfected the science of stress relief, and body healing through massage pressure points. By the early sixth dynasty, the physicians tomb of Ankhmahor, Egypt contained paintings illustrating the science of reflexology. Studies conducted within the United States were pioneered by Eunice D. Ingham Stopfel. People familiar with reflexology credit Mrs. Stopfel as the founder of modern reflexology practiced in the United States today. The theory behind reflexology is quite simple. We won't go into detail here; however, interested readers may obtain additional information by contacting the International Institute of Reflexology (1-813-313-4811). Reflexology has reportedly enhanced the quality of life for those who have experienced its pleasure. Speaking from person experience, it has worked well for me.

Osteoporosis the silent killer is not isolated to a specific gender group. However, females over 40, especially those entering menopause, tend to experience bone mass reduction as calcium is extracted from bone to develop blood cells. Women within this suspect group are encouraged to contact the National Osteoporosis Foundation (1-202-223-2226) for information before irreversible damage is experienced. Osteoporosis to bones is akin to termites to wood. The more either material mass is eaten away, the less weight it will support. Eventually, structure failure will occur. Calcium strengthens bone material to support body weight. Loss of calcium combined with obesity is dangerous. Include calcium into your daily diet.

Pork consumption has been taboo throughout most of the world since biblical times. The consumption of pork is specifically prohibited, except under certain circumstances, by at least two major religious groups. Improperly processed pork may carry the trichina parasite. The only safe way to eat pork is to uniformly heat the meat hot enough to kill the parasite. The American Council on Science and Health suggest the proper method to cook pork is to place the meat inside a sealed plastic bag. Cook the meat in a microwave oven according to the microwave manufacturers instructions for minimum of two minutes. The bag reduces areas of uneven surface temperatures. All parts of the meat must be sufficiently heated. After microwave processing, pork my then be cooked or barbecued as desired. If the meat is to be barbecued, microwave processing also reduces the level of cancer causing hydrocarbons by removing fatty residue.

Chicken is quite different from pork! `WARNING:` Under no circumstance microwave that bird. Why? Ruth E. Lindsay, a Nutritionist, at Georgia Southern College (Statesboro) reports that improperly processed chicken may carry harmful salmonella and other bacteria. Microwave technology heats food through water molecular friction. Chicken has rough skin texture in addition to all the crevices around wings and legs. Microwave cooking simply leaves surface temperatures too uneven to effectively kill contaminant bacteria. Nutritionist suggest chicken should be cooked in a conventional heat thermal oven at 350 degrees Fahrenheit until all juices run clear, or until a meat thermometer reads 185 degrees when placed into the breast or thigh. The chicken can now be safely barbecued.

Love that barbecue! `CAUTION:` Unless the meat you plan to barbecue has been microwave processed, parboiled, or baked with all juices drained off; barbecuing could be very harmful. According to a study by James Felton, of the Lawrence Livermore National Laboratory Molecular Biology Section, barbecued meat caused cancer in laboratory test animals. Two problems exist. First, when meat fat drips onto a heat source, polycyclic aromatic hydrocarbons (PAH's) form. The PAH's rise with the smoke and attaches to the meat underside. During the barbecuing process, the meat is flipped from side to side until it is fully contaminated with PAH's. Secondly, as the juice within the meat begins to cook, heterocyclic amines (HA's) are formed. Both HA's and PAH's have reportedly caused cancer in laboratory animals. Be safe!

Cola, a popular soft drink ingredient, according to Doctor Kenneth Weaver of the East Tennessee State University, contains phosphoric acid. When the phosphoric acid is eliminated from the body, it pulls out the vital magnesium. Magnesium depletion can lead to high blood pressure and associated heart diseases. Best bet, is to never consume cola based soft drinks; unless, a precaution is taken to replenish the expended magnesium.

Doctor N. Robert Superko; Director of the Lipid Research Clinic, at Stanford University reported in the *Cardiac Alert* that decaffeinated coffee raises LDL (Bad) cholesterol. His study utilized six healthy middle aged men who normally consumed three to six cups of black caffeinated coffee daily. Prior to the evaluation, each test subjects blood chemistry level was evaluated for LDL cholesterol level. The six test subjects were then divided into three randomly selected groups. One group abstained from drinking coffee. The second group continued to drink regular coffee. The third group consumed only decaffeinated coffee. Groups two and three continued to consume three to six cups of coffee daily. After two months, all subjects were tested again for LDL cholesterol levels. The test subjects who abstained, or who consumed regular coffee, experienced insignificant LDL cholesterol change. However, the test subjects who consumed decaffeinated coffee realized a significantly elevated LDL cholesterol level. Studies have linked elevated LDL cholesterol levels to strokes and congestive heart failure.

Fiber; the often missing nutritional link, reduces the time food "cooks" in the digestive track. A short digestive exposure reduces the likelihood of harmful bacteria accumulation. Grains are the primary source of fiber. The *Lord's Prayer* recognizes the importance of grain when Jesus said, "give us this day our daily bread." Granola is our preferred source of important fiber the human body so critically needs. Not all Granola is equal to the challenge where blend, taste, and freshness is concerned. Consumers can purchase cardboard tasting granola off just about any grocery shelf in America; but, flavor and quality is often inadequate. There is one solution to that problem! We have located a small California Granola producer who offers not one; but, five healthful blends. Their product is available for overnight delivery directly to your home for a modest premium over the big name cardboard aftertaste providers. Valley Native Granola (1-888-965-0148) is all natural with no preservatives added. Give it a try! Leave your order for "Molly" to fill. Valley Native Granola's motto, "a bowl a day" is sound advise difficult to argue against. Native Valley extends a "universal" case discount to repeat mail order customers. Think I'll have a bowl right now!

What does consumption of pork, chicken, cola, coffee, diuretics, fiber, and fruit have to do with wealth building? These products are consumed by the majority of Americans at consumption levels high enough to have a dramatic impact on health and eventually long term wealth building. Investment decisions require a healthy clear thinking mind. A clear thinking mind means eating and exercising right. For healthful eating information, contact your local health department, or the U.S. Department of Health and Humans Service (1-800-575-9355). Their website is http://www.healthfinder.gov. Request information on exercise, low fat, and other food related subjects. Wisdom in "Health, Wealth, and Wise" comes through life experiences and formal education. Young investors are generally life experience limited. If the investor has never traded stocks; for example, they would not be expected to have developed stock investment insights. Life experiences nurtured through education brings about wisdom. Wisdom is the cornerstone to building the foundation of wealth.

EDUCATION: Education is cheap at any cost and within its own right is an outstanding investment. Experts estimate the total return of a single educational investment dollar is somewhere near eight dollars. According to a U.S. Census report, lifetime earnings for a high school dropout caps at approximately $608,810 compared to the capped earnings of approximately $1,420,850 for a person with a Bachelor degree, or $3,013,330 for the Professional degree holder. Who has time for education after working two jobs while raising children? Good question; but, not necessarily valid. A better question would be: With so little time to spare what would be an alternate method of obtaining an education? Perhaps the answer lies in computer based, or audio book learning. It's true! A college degree, or just about any level of education can be obtained at home via a personal computer.

"Distance Learning" is offered at very affordable rates by hundreds of colleges, universities, and corporations throughout the world. Programs range from one hour courses to PHD's. Why not consider keeping the television turned off while meeting with your educational study group through distance learning? Computer based distance learning instruction is akin to the best one-on-one instruction available. Money is saved. First, because courses are priced at reasonable levels well within the cost structure of the majority of American household budgets. Course prices began at about $50 per credit hour plus computer on-line fees. Secondly, money saved on material and books can be substantial. Finally, commuting time and associated travel cost is eliminated. Time is money! Money saved would be available for debt buy down and investments.

How does a person enroll for distance learning computer educational course? Several ways exists. CompuServe offers the "*Electronic Forum.*" American On-line University (1-314-446-0410), and Globewide Network Academy (1-512-473-2579) also offer a wide variety of course subjects. Additionally, many corporations, and government agencies have computer based instruction (CBI) available. As a side note; according to researchers, education reduces crime. Test conducted in the federal prison system indicate a majority of criminals are poor readers and are technically illiterate. As investors, we should insist our educators spend our tax dollars more wisely. Failure, on their part, destroys not only individual wealth building opportunities; but, the opportunities of society as a whole. President Clinton should be publicly praised for his initiative in setting goals to improve the literacy rate among Americans.

Education assistance sources include: co-op programs; grants, scholarships, financial aid, and employer, or union education assistance programs. Reports indicate approximately 50 percent of all full time undergraduate college students receive educational financial aid. One investor with a family of four sent each family member to college through public assistance. Three obtained a Bachelor degree with one receiving an Associate degree. Total direct cost to the investor for all four degrees was less than $7,000. Benefits to society for its sponsorship of the education could reasonable be estimated into the millions of dollars. That's what education is all about. It is a tool used to provide a service to society through the enhancement of individual lifestyles. Eventually the tax base broadens as salary requirements rise to meet the education experience. Traditional sources of educational financial aid can supplement educational cost even for upper income families. Federal aid programs include: Peel grants, Supplemental Educational Opportunity grants, College Work Study programs, National Direct Student loans, Guaranteed Student loans, Parental loans for undergraduate students, Corporate assistance; and, the Reserve Officer Training Corps (ROTC). Private student loans may be located by contacting the United Student Aid Fund (1-800-428-9250). **CAUTION: Never pay someone to search for college funding.**

State government financial aid programs vary between states. Georgia offers free tuition to students who maintain a "B" average throughout their education careers. Governor Zell Miller of Georgia funds the *Hope Scholarship* program with lottery money to the betterment of all Georgia citizens. Thank you Governor Miller! Many states offer financial aid through various critical career work-study programs. Contact your local college Financial Advisor or State Board of Education for details. Students may consider taking a GED test in their high school sophomore year along with a college entrance examination. If college entrance eligibility is met, apply for college entrance. A degree at age 20 is worth a lot more than one at age 23 when considering the career head start advantage.

Scholarships; unlike loans and grants, are awarded for specific academic achievement. Grants are usually awarded in the form of gifts; whereas, loans must be repaid. Academic performance is an on-going process throughout the scholarship term. For example, a scholarship based on athletic performance may require the scholarship recipient to maintain a "B" average while receiving scholarship funding. Scholarship sources are extensive and are worth checking out.

College Fund Source Guide

* College or university; especially with students having a music or sport program interest.

* National College Services LTD. (Gaithersburg, Maryland)

* National Scholarship Research Service. (San Rafael, California)

* National Society of Internships and Experimental Education
  (Work study programs) (Raleigh, North Carolina)

* Octomeron Associates. (Alexandria, Virginia)

* Federal Office of Student Financial Assistance
  U.S. Department of Education (1-800-433-3243)

* Citizens Scholarship Foundation of America. (1-800-248-8080)

* New York State Financial Aid Association (http://www.new paltz.edu/faam)
  The website also links to the U.S. Department of Education and an interactive scholarship search service.

* Reserve Office Training Corps. (ROTC): Check with the local college, university, military recruiter.

* National Center for Educational Brokering (NCEB)
  405 Oak Street; Syracuse, New York 13203

* Catalyst: Career counseling for women.
  14 East 60th Street; New York, NY 10022

* American Council Education
  One DuPont Circle; Washington, DC 20036

* Association for Intercollegiate Athletics for Women (AIAW)
  1202 16th Street NW; Washington, DC 20036

* *The Princeton Review:* "The student guide to paying for college"
  Chany/ Villiard Books (1-800-793-2665)

* *Fund Your Way Through College:*
  Debra M. Kirby (1-800-776-6265)

Colleges and Universities across America offer limited residency degree programs based upon a combination of traditional college credits and life experiences. The Regents College, a division of the University of State of New York (Albany) (1-518-464-8500), and Edison State College (1-609-984-1100) offer Bachelor External Degree programs without residency requirements.

Limited residency Master degree programs are offered through Empire State College (1-518-587-2100), California State University (1-310-516-3743), and Syracuse University (1-315-443-3284). Ph.D. programs are offered by NOVA University (1-305-475-7300) and Union Graduate School (1-513-861-6400). GS Graduate School, USDA (1-888-744-4723); website http://grad.usda.gov, is "the government's trainer" since inception in 1921. USDA has six regional training centers plus distance learning and independent study programs. Students have access to over 1500 course titles annually taught by 1200 instructors. Excellent training for a promising career.

Hundreds of universities and colleges offer correspondence or video based courses. Each course extends to students full course credit after the student passes a final examination. Check with your preferred educational institution for similar programs. Do not forget to use the College Level Examination Program (CLEP) to test-out for college level credit without taking the associated course. The average adult with several years of work experience can pass many level one and two college courses through the CLEP process. Additionally, many colleges and universities offer "pass-fail" examinations on practically every course they provide. Seek out ways to improve skills. Pass up no opportunity to enhance your education. To seek guidance order: *Paying for your Education: A Guide for Adult Learners* from College Board Publications : Box 2815; Princeton, New Jersey 08541.

AUDIO EDUCATION: The easy way for the commuter to learn as they drive. Workers waste valuable time and money commuting down that boring highway to and from work each day. That need not be the case! A five hour weekly commute equates to 250 hours annually of totally nonproductive time. Missed opportunities! How about "listening" to a book while you drive? Learn a new language? Perhaps, plan a business. Thousands of spoken word book titles are in circulation on audio cassette tape. Record Books (1-800-638-1304) ships unabridged titles. Books On Tape (1-800-626-3333), Sounds True (1-800-333-9185), Dove Entertainment (1-800-328-3683), and Time Warner Audiobooks (1-800-759-0190) are excellent starting points to end nonproductive commuting forever. Taking a driving vacation, stop by Cracker Barrel restaurant or most major truck stops (Flying J, Pilot, Texaco) to rent book tapes by the day. Forty five work days from today, maybe German, French, or Russian could be a second language. Or perhaps, you could be putting your investment plan into action.

CUTTING COST: Opportunities to cut cost exists on practically every transaction we conduct. The majority of us, in the heat of the moment, give away - yes - give away thousands of dollars throughout our lifetime. The problem with this great give-a-way program, is that for the most part, our families, friends, or favorite charity benefits very little monetarily. We give our money to people we do not know and who could care less about our financial well being. Why should they? We gave the money away! The people who willing take your money are the ones you see everyday living in the big houses, driving the fancy car, or playing golf, while you strive to make it from paycheck to paycheck. They are the folks most of us only dream of being. Perhaps, they would not be so rich; if it were not for the consumer suckers who complain of always being broke; yet, still manage to squander away thousands of dollars throughout their lifetime. Before spending your next dime, consider the consequences.

No consumer can really be ripped off unless they allow it to happen. We, as a group, insist businesses take our hard earned money. The merchant may price a product; but, it's the buyer who ultimately sets the price. If the sucker consumer would limit spending; or better yet, refuse to pay prices inflated hundreds of percentage points, supply and demand economics would naturally trend prices toward true values. If you cannot control spending, or walk-a-way, at least consider establishing a set of personalized consumer rules. The following pages contain ideas presenting opportunities to pick-up great deals, after economics have driven the price to a true supply and demand value. Being a smart consumer is not being cheap (do not believe your friends). It's being wise. Someday in the not to distant future it could be you driving that fancy car. The big difference; however, you've paid cash for it!

Cutting cost on small profit margin items is difficult at best. However, on big tickets items there is usually plenty of room to negotiate for a fair price. It's not that you should cheat the business out of profits. The opposite is true. They should be prevented from cheating you. Better yet; you should not let the business trick you into cheating yourself. Cost cutting is not isolated to coupon clipping scams, which usually drives total consumer cost up. It is not a light hearted project either! Instead, cost cutting should be a way of life. I know what you are thinking. In the eyes of consumers who waste money, those who practice cost cutting techniques are considered cheap. Not to worry! As the character in the movie *Forest Grump* said, "stupid is as stupid does." We all have been told by society, to a certain degree, that *Forest Gump* exist within each of us. Based upon incorrect social class casting, bad economic habits transfer from generation to generation. If you have completed the Appendix financial forms: have read the suggested reading material, or have enrolled into an educational course, then society created habits have already begun to change. Let's continue the change by exploring methods to kept more of the money we earn without reducing our long term quality of life.

TAX SHELTERS: The easiest and smartest wealth building techniques include deferred or exempt federal and state tax shelters. Hundreds of tax shelters exist. Shelters range from real estate ownership to bonds, stocks, stock options, limited partnerships, insurance annuities, low income housing and various tax deferred retirement accounts. Chapter 4 covers low income housing investing in detail. Regardless of which program you choose, one fact remains clear. When investors authorize someone else to manage the investment underlying assets, the investor must insist on maintaining control of all account transactions. Avoid any account which assigns an "Account Executive." Do not waste time and money paying someone for something you can do equally as well.

Initially, investments should be limited to employer sponsored 401(K), 403(B), individual retirement accounts (IRA), employee stock ownership plan (ESOP), Keogh account, or a simplified employee pension plan (SEP). Account applications may be obtained from employers, bank trust departments, brokerage firms, and mutual fund sponsors. Insurance companies also offer annuity tax sheltered programs. It may be advisable to avoid annuity programs; except when they have employer matching funding, because of high commission loads and administrative fees. Began investing into your preferred tax shelter without delay the moment of eligibility. Pay yourself first, at least the minimum dollar amount necessary to receive the full employer matching contribution every paycheck. Strive to invest the maximum allowed by law. The IRS raised the employee contribution limit to 20 of gross pay with a $10,000 cap in 1997. Your current tax base will be deferred by the amount deposited. Taxes are deferred on both the employee core and employer matching contribution to provide for equity growth until the funds are received. Earnings accumulated through a qualified tax deferred plan, with a few exceptions, are taxed when distributed during retirement.

CAUTION: Exercise extreme caution when investing into a retirement plan dominated by the employers stock. Limit employer stock dominated investments to 20 percent of individual net worth. You only work for your employer; not married to it. Think about the phrase: **"Under-funded pension account."** Request your employer to provide to you, an accounting copy of their pension fund. After discovering exactly how much of an under-funding short fall exist, make a strong commitment to protect your retirement. Skimming retirement fund interest earnings is rampant among corporations across America. The employees contribution is the only money protected. Accumulated interest, capital gains, and employer matching funds can be, and are often raided by the company. Nobody can manage your money better than yourself, once you have been taught how. Does your employer have a training program to teach its employees how to manage individual assets? No! Why not? I'll tell you why not! People who manage assets well are a threat to corporate America. The ideology being that a hungry worker financially dependent upon the company works at a cheaper pay rate. That philosophy has changed little over the past one hundred years, and was a major contributor to the creation of organized labor. "Unions" for lack of a better word! Never "owe your sole to the company store" as Tennessee Ernie Ford sung in *16 Ton*. As personal wealth increases, the need for labor protection and corporate dependency decreases while the necessity for tax shelters increase. Home ownership is incorrectly considered an investment by most Americans.

Home ownership is not an investment in the truest sense. It is simply, a place to live. Personally owned real estate may not even be a tax shelter. True tax shelters appreciate in value greater than the inflation rate while eliminating tax obligations from current income. Tax shelter value should never depreciate. Investments which depreciate simply reduces the original cost base. The larger the depreciation credit, the wider the gap between the cost base and true market value. Upon liquidating the position, capital gains tax is levied against the difference between the net selling price and the adjusted cost base price. Back-end tax obligations can wipe the investor out. Where is the shelter? Professional investors identifies the investment profit before entering into the deal. With real estate, that is nearly impossible! The main attraction to home ownership, from most owners point of view, is the ability to write down the mortgage interest and property taxes against current income, and not the deferred capital gains that may never materialize. The problem with that ideology; however, is that for interest to be credited against current tax obligations, the property must have a debt lien. Debt is not good! The subject of tax shelters is very complex and apply totally differently for each investor situation. Investors wishing to shelter income should seek advice from a competent Tax Attorney. One alternative is government sponsored housing tax credit programs.

HOUSING TAX CREDIT PROGRAMS: The Congress of the United States of America invites every investor to join with them in providing affordable housing to low and moderate income Americans. Review chapter 4 for additional details. Low income housing investing offers the astute long term investor many advantages.

HOME OWNERSHIP: It is not home ownership which provides interest tax write down. Interest write down is only associated with the debt associated with the property. Home ownership does; however, provide for the opportunity to cut total living cost. That is positive for wealth building. Residential operating cost is an area which can make or break any financial business plan. Lights left on, the television unattended, water faucets dripping, clogged heat recycle filters, vacuum cleaner bags filled; and, the improper heat or cooling temperature setting do waste money. Make a monthly log of your residential habit pattern. It will identify areas of waste. Additional cost cutting can be accomplished by plugging up the leaks around vents, doors, and windows. Set heating at 68F degrees and cooling at 78F degrees. Use a blanket to wrap up with in the winter. Consider using a small electric fan to supplement air conditioning during the summer months. To improve efficiency, clear bushes away from the air condition unit. Vacuum cleaner bags, as well as, refrigeration units are practically useless once they reach approximately 80 percent of their full capacity. The same holds true for environmental system return fan filters. Request a utility audit of your residence. Follow the audit recommendations. Leaking water faucets not only rob investors of water; but, also of fees associated with sewage treatment and water heater heat energy. Energy cost dramatically increases when water leakage in a hot water line creates a constant heating demand. Water faucet leaks are generally considered a minor repair problem and are often fixed with simple hand tools and a rubber seal kit. Kits may be purchased at local hardware or plumbing supply retailers. Genova Products (1-800-521-7488), a plumbing supply manufacturer, reportedly provides homeowners with telephone assistance to resolve minor plumbing problems. Water heaters located in unheated areas should be wrapped with a thermal blanket, to reduce radiation heat loss. Consult with you plumbing company before wrapping the heater. Blocking gas vents is deadly.

Keep window shades and curtains closed. Airspace between windows and curtains form an insulation barrier. Improper use of a fireplace steals valuable heat. Fireplace heat radiates into the immediate area; however, most of the heat rises with smoke up the chimney. As the heat rises, it thermally drafts air from the house. Rooms furthest from the fireplace begins to drop in temperature as cold air is drafted into those areas from the outside through vent, window, and door gaps. Eighty percent of fireplace heat exits up the chimney along with those investment dollars. Except in an emergency, a fireplace should not be used as a primary heat source. Cheaper alternative fuels (wood stove, gas furnace, heat pump, etc.) are available. When using fireplace heat to cut the chill, the most efficient temperature for fireplace utilization is when the outside air temperature is between 45F and 65F degrees. Lower temperatures may be acceptable once all air draft leaks are plugged. Contact your local utility company for an energy audit. Do not wait until all the faucets are fixed, or the window and door leaks are plugged before beginning a total mortgage cost buy-down. Eliminating costly interest will save most home owners literally thousands of dollars over the term of their mortgage. Dollars which are generally more productive invested elsewhere.

Ask yourself two questions. Do I have an emergency cash reserve equal to three months of my gross income? Are my credit card revolving charges paid in full monthly? If <u>both</u> questions are answered with a "<u>yes</u>" then you should consider cutting total housing cost on the next mortgage payment. Here's how:

First: Obtain a current mortgage amortization schedule from the mortgage lien holder. An amortization schedule is normally available on all fixed term mortgage loans; but, may not be available on a variable rate loan. The payment terms should be identified at the top of the schedule accompanied by a full description of the mortgage terms. The loan account number must be clearly identified. The schedule should also have columns with header subtitles that include: payment number, principle, interest, and outstanding balance. Investors having a variable rate mortgage usually receive a monthly statement. The statement lists the outstanding loan balance, as well as providing space to add additional principle payments.

NOTE: As the payment number increases, both the monthly interest amount and the loan outstanding balance decline while the principle increases. Debt is being bought down as equity is being increased. Both actions enhance personal wealth. Accelerating debt buy down is important. Obtain a mortgage contract with the authority to prepay the mortgage without penalty. If you fail to obtain satisfactory prepayment terms, not to worry. Prepayment penalties are usually limited to 5 percent of the extra principle payment. Never enclose a penalty add-on with the payment. It is highly unlikely, the payment will be rejected. Review the following 30 year fixed term amortization schedule illustration.

Loan Amortization Schedule

Wizbang Banking Outfitters
Residential Mortgage Group

7417 Ripple Way
Americana, USA

Account: 641943-YOURS
Starting Balance: $85,000.

PAYMENT	AMOUNT	INTEREST	PRINCIPLE	BALANCE
originate				$ 85,000.00
# 1	$698.29	566.66	61.63	84,938.37
# 2	$698.29	566.25	62.04	84,876.33
# 3	$698.29	565.84	62.44	84,813.89
# 4	$698.29	565.42	62.86	84,751.03
# 5	$698.29	565.00	63.28	$84,687.75

INTEREST 8.000 Percent
TERM 30 YEARS (360 PAYMENTS)

PAYMENT INCLUDES PRINCIPLE, INTEREST, INSURANCE AND PROPERTY TAX. WILL CHANGE ANNUALLY.

Second: Make the first payment (#1) with two checks. Write one check for the $698.29 monthly note plus a second check for the payment #2 principle amount of $62.04. Strike a line through both horizontal columns of payment #1 and payment #2, stopping before reaching the outstanding balance block in the payment #2 column. The balance of $84,876.33 will be owed after the payment is posted by the lien holder. On the second check, write the words "Principle only #2." Always write the account number on every correspondence and check sent to the lien holder.

Third: Repeat the procedure whenever you have enough spare cash to make a full extra principle payment. Do not forget to always list the payment number covered by the extra principle payment. Prepayment of the principle eliminates a whole lot of interest debt. The prepayment of payment #2 principle eliminated $566.25 in interest. Twenty years later, that $566.25 may come in handy, even after adjusting for inflation.

WARNING: Although payment #2 principle may have been prepaid, it is very important to pay a full mortgage note each month. In this illustration, the second month payment will be for payment #3,and so on. Always include the account number on all payment checks and correspondence. Additional principle payments should be made by writing a second check to be enclosed with the primary mortgage payment. If the additional principle payment and primary payment are combined into a single payment, the mortgage company will be left to choose where to credit the additional payment. They could post the additional payment as the last payment on the amortization schedule. Incorrect posting of additional payments can cheat the payee out of hundreds of interest dollars. Always designate the additional payment to a specific month.

Fourth: On payment #3, draw a line through the balance of line #2 and line #3 up to the balance. If the principle for payment #4 is made, the line will stop short of the payment #4 balance.

Fifth: Twice annually confirm with the mortgage holder your account outstanding balance. It should be the same as on your schedule.

Sixth: To avoid very costly late charge penalties, never mail your monthly payment later than ten days prior to the due date. Payments received by the mortgage holder; but, not posted within 15 days of the due date will trigger late fees. Never give them an excuse to rip you off because their employees were late posting the payment. Mortgages due on the first day of the month should be mailed no later than the 20th day of the previous month.

Finally, Never authorize electronic automatic draft authority against a bank checking account, if you plan to buy down your debt. The mortgage company will not draft extra principle payments. Extra funds you pay through checks may not be properly posted, since the transaction will most likely be processed by different personnel.

Mortgage buy-down promotes positive wealth building habits. Early mortgage pay-out eliminates thousands of wasted interest dollars. Investors pay more than 300 percent for a mortgaged home over the original price if minimum monthly payments are made. The habit of investing can continue after the mortgage has been terminated. Positive investment and asset management habits provide long term financial benefits. The earlier in life a house can be purchased; the earlier wealth building can began. Eventually, at age 55, the possibility exists, to sell the property without paying capitol gains tax.

<u>Logical Wealth Building Sequence</u>

* Birth.
* Youth.
* Education.
* Job
* Retirement plan.
* Love.
* Marriage at 28 for males and 23 for females.
* House ownership.
* Children.
* Diversified investment program.

* Retirement.
* Death.

If the purchase of a house is so important, why do so many people rent their entire lives? Reasons for life long renting could be many. Perhaps, the renter works on Wall Street. Renting an apartment nearby eliminates transportation cost plus hundreds of hours wasted annually waiting in traffic backed up interstate 95 all the way to the Connecticut state line.

Another reason someone may rent their entire life is perhaps they have no idea how to set aside a proper mortgage down payment. Lot's of renters have lost the opportunity of home ownership by "over saving" for a mortgage down payment. It would be drastic mistake to attempt to save for a 20 percent down payment toward a $100,000 house. House market values will usually increase through inflation and local market corrections faster than savings would increase. The purchase down payment should only be high enough to get the monthly mortgage note to within your current rental budget. Limit the initial maximum home purchase price to two times your current gross annual income; plus, the down payment less 4 percent of twice your gross annual income. For example, a person earning $26,000 gross income annually with $5,000 saved for a down payment should limit their initial home purchase price to: ($26,000 x 2 = $52,000 + $5,000 - $2080 = $54,920). The $2,080 represents 4 percent of twice the annual gross income, and should be held in reserve to cover administrative fees, plus utility and escrow deposits.

Humans are creatures of emotion. They tend to overextend themselves in just about every endeavor they attempt. Renting is usually no different. People will tend to rent at the maximum affordable payment rate. They want three bedrooms when they only need two. They want a swimming pool, even if they hardly ever swim. Rental management companies are aware of these human traits; and, that's why they conduct a salary history check. The rental application will be denied if their rental fee exceeds a certain percentage of the applicant's gross income adjusted for outstanding debts. Put another way, the current annual rent an individual is obligated to pay is very close to the mortgage amount a bank would approve for a home mortgage loan.

DOWN PAYMENT RULE-OF THUMB: Purchase your house, condo, ship, etc. as soon as you can accumulate a down payment high enough to secure an outstanding loan balance low enough to provide a monthly mortgage note, including insurance and taxes, equal to your current rent payment excluding utilities. For example, assume your current rent is $650 monthly, excluding utilities. A house should be purchased the moment it can be acquired with a down payment large enough to bring the loan balance low enough for the monthly mortgage to equal $650 including insurance and taxes. Rental payments indirectly include the landlords tax and insurance obligation. The monthly mortgage payment should not exceed current rental cost! If the current rental agreement include the utilities, contact all utility providers serving your address and request a utility usage history. Subtract utility cost from your monthly rent to determine the mortgage bottom line.

Approximately 15 percent of both mortgage and rental payments is allocated toward payment of taxes and insurance, while 85 percent is allocated toward principle buy-down and interest. Based upon the percentage assumptions, the maximum monthly mortgage note, excluding taxes and insurance, would be $552.50 ($650-15%). Based on a an 8 percent 30 year mortgage, the original mortgage loan balance for our illustration is limited to approximately $75,000. The limit assumes the property was purchased today! Why today? Because there is economic slippage biased against anyone saving for a future home. The only way to beat the slippage is to invest in superior investments in order to reach maximum funding in the shortest possible time frame.

For example, assume the decision has been made to purchase a $75,000 house. A goal has been set to accumulate the down payment of $7,000 over a three year time span. Market forces plus inflation, assuming the interest rate remains constant, could push the property market value up by 4 percent annually. After three years, the house value may exceed $84,000. Your banking interest rate, plus capitol infusion when adjusted for by taxes and inflation will simply not appreciate fast enough to offset the property appreciation. Therefore, the account growth is totally dependent upon the net amount of funds deposited above the tax and inflation slippage rate. Another consideration when saving for a down payment, is that your plan will need to be adjusted periodically to accommodate for changes in personal income, rental fees, insurance, taxes, and utilities. Each, are sure to increase over the three year saving period.

Sounds like obtaining a mortgage down payment is almost impossible. It is possible to obtain, once you know how. Check with your Realtor and government housing authority for up-to-date details on special first time buyer programs. They can provide information, or offer suggestions that could help in reaching a very important goal. To locate government distressed properties selling at a substantial discount to true market value; plus, thousands of local real estate listings across America, surf along website *Homeseekers. com and Reo. com.* Mortgage rates are adjusted daily and not only vary between lenders; but, also throughout the regional economic zones. When qualifying for a mortgage, do not overstate your earnings beyond what you reported on the previous year Internal Revenue Service (IRS) tax form. Your lender is required by federal law to report all claimed income indicated on the loan application. The IRS has discovered that folks trying to qualify for a mortgage tend to be more truthful than when filing income tax forms Income information will be audited. Being untruthful when qualifying for a mortgage will put you on a fast track for a fully paid extended residence at the "big house."

Important Mortgage Sources

* Fannie Mae Foundation.
* Federal Land Bank.
* Friends.
* Federal Housing Administration.
* Retirement account.
* Banks.
* Veterans Administration.
* Family.
* Mortgage company.

IMPULSE SPENDING: Studies conducted by the Point of Purchase Advertising Institute implies that impulse purchases make up about 40 percent of all in-store sells. If the studies are correct, every $100 in spending represents $40 of impulse waste. Worse yet! Products are routinely marked up 300 percent or more at the retail level. This means that for every $1.00 spent on a product, the real worth at time of purchase is only thirty cents. Ask yourself. Who could every reach financial security, by wasting hundreds of dollars annually on products they don't need? No one! Studies also indicate that impulse spending is not partial to a specific gender. Women tend to impulse buy highest percentage of small ticket items. However, men are guilty of impulse buying large ticket items such as cars, boats, planes, and other toys. Double damage occurs when any item is purchased through credit. Gentlemen, before you make your next purchase, review *Large Purchases* of this chapter. Do not accuse someone who loves you of spending all your money when the opposite is most likely true. For those of us who shop regularly, a set of simple consumer rules could practically eliminate the ever present temptation to impulse spend. The temptation will always exist; but, it can and must be controlled. Develop a check list of "what not to do" during shopping and stick to the list. Your financial security is at risk if you don't.

Impulse Spending Control List

* When shopping for family provisions: Never take children.
* Never grocery shop while hungry.
* Never shop without a purchase list.
* Never buy from end of aisle displays.
* Always purchase products by the "unit" price.

* Always buy products placed at the back of the display.
* Shop early mornings before the crowd picks over the supply.
* Use coupons only to purchase your shopping list items.
* Stay away from aisles where list items are not located.
* Buy discounted slightly damaged merchandise.
* Shop to win! Manage both time and money.

Shopping is serious business not to be interrupted by children running throughout the store; or, distracting the shopper by wanting "mom" or "dad" to buy them everything they see. Don't let little junior destroy his or her future inheritance by causing you to impulse spend. Leave the child with a friend while not only shopping for yourself; but, also for items your friend may need. Barter child care of one or two hours for the time spent shopping for the friend. A shopping list will eliminate impulse spending. End-of-aisle displays are not normally good deals. The location triggers impulse buying and demand. Demand (greed) always pushes prices higher as long as supply last. When the supply runs out, the price will collapse to zero. "Take a walk save a lot."

Almost without exception, end-of-aisle display items can be found cheaper along the aisle center span. Many products are similar in design, quality, and content; but, vary greatly in unit price. The unit price is indicated in very small print normally at the top of the price label: I.E: 15 cents per oz., $1.25 pound etc. During the inventory rotation of bread, milk, eggs, and vegetables, the newest (freshest) products are rotated to the rear of the display. First-in-First out (FIFO) is a universal inventory control. Shop early and beat the crowd. Utilize coupons for cost cutting only for those items on your purchase list. Product coupons may be obtained from the merchant, local papers, and through the Internet. Discounted products, due to damage, is usually safe; or, it would be removed from sale. A dent in a can could shave 50 percent off the original price. Read the label! Keep the fat gram content as low as possible. Use your imagination and additional ideas should come to mind.

Impulse spending temptations will never be eliminated; but, they can be controlled by simply staying out of stores. To that objective, mail order and computer shopping has become the shopping choice of millions of Americans. Clothing, shoes, tools, books, vacations, etc. may be purchased and delivered directly to your address. Computer and mail order shopping has been around for years. Sears , Montgomery Ward, Service Merchandise; plus, hundreds of other merchants have offered home shopping for half a century. Home shopping not only helps control impulse spending, it conveniently saves time while reducing total shopping cost. Ask your favorite merchant for a catalog. Should they not have one, request they mail you their weekly price sheet. Place your orders via telephone. When merchant sees your order coming in, they will happily be making money while you save a bundle. Computer shopping is convenient; but, caution must be used to keep credit card information private. Never give credit card or bank information over the Internet; unless, the company accepting your order provides to you their established security procedures. The safest bet is to shop with companies you trust!

<u>Computer Shopping Merchandisers Sample List</u>

CD Now	1-215-283-4926
Halloo Marketing	1-708-647-4814
Harbor Freight (Tools)	1-800-423-2567
Lands End (Clothing)	1-800-356-4444
Liquor by Wire	1-800-774-7483
L L Bean (6 Departments)	1-800-221-4221
Mason (Shoes)	1-800-826-7030
Pottery Barn	1-800-922-5507

Present Perfect	1-801-563-0708
The Computer Jewelry Exchange	1-800-347-3544

Never send cash through the mail. Many merchants refuse to send C.O.D. (cash on delivery). Use a credit card, should the product need returning. Inspect the product shipping packaging for damage. If the shipping package has been damaged, notify the local postmaster. Inspect the product for damage, quantity, color, and package content. If you are not satisfied with the product, contact the company for return or exchange instructions. If they won't stand behind their damaged product, their insurance carrier should. Refuse any damaged product. Ship it back to the merchant within three days with an explanation letter as to why the merchandise was rejected. Forward a copy of the letter, along with a copy of the bill, to your credit card company requesting a full credit. Consumers are entitled to a full refund, if the product is shipped back to the merchant in the original shipping package within three business days of receipt.

CAUTION: One negative aspect of computer shopping, or shopping by mail, is the placement of customer names on the mailing list of other merchants. If you do not want a flood of junk mail, instruct the merchant you are dealing with, in writing at the time of your order, not to release your name to anyone. Additionally, express your wishes to: Mail Preference Service, PO Box 9008, Framingham, NY 11735. Junk mail does burn well in Winter months. If that is a primary source of heat, then by all means get on every mailing list available. I do!

LARGE PURCHASES: Before spending more than $100 on anything; ask yourself: Do I really need the product? Can I really afford it? Will it increase my net worth? Is it worth going into debt? If you answer any of these questions with "no", then pass it up. If you answer all the questions "yes", wait 72 hours and ask yourself the questions once again. There is an excellent possibility you'll pass it by. If you don't, it may be something you really need. Before plunking down cash or using a credit card; ask yourself one additional question. Do I need it today? Should the situation be that ownership a month or so later would be acceptable, consider the merchants "lay-a-way" program. Put down a deposit, pay off the purchase over a month or two, and bring the product home.

In recent times, merchant lay-a-way programs have given way to checking, cash, and credit card payment methods. However, programs still flourish. The lay-a-way concept allows customers to lock in a fixed price by making an up front restocking deposit of about 10 percent of the merchandise retail cost. Once the product is in lay-a-way storage, the customer can purchase the item through interest free installment payments. Lay-a-way payment schedules are generally flexible. Be aware that if payments are not made in a timely manner, the merchant will restock the product. Restocking causes the customer to forfeit both the deposit and subsequent payments. Merchants who do not offer lay-a-way plans, often will hold the merchandise in storage for a reasonable length of time at the customers request. A "*Lay-a-way Purchase Plan*" brochure may be obtained from The Federal Trade Commission; Public Reference Office, Washington, DC 20580.

CREDIT CARDS: Thirty thousand credit card providers are bad news; unless, they offer their product to financially responsible individuals interest free! According to *The Atlanta Journal-Constitution* (2-3-97), there are more than 500 million credit cards in use today. "As credit card debt increases to record levels, more consumers are falling behind in payments. Banks are charging off billions of dollars of bad debt," reports staff writer, Gene Tarp. Are consumers irresponsible? Not necessarily! With corporate right-sizing on the rise, jobs are being transferred out of the United States. Consumers have been forced into a more nontraditional use of plastic cash. It's very easy to grab for the plastic when trying to survive until the next job comes along. After all, when jobs were lost in 1994, 1995, and 1996; banks didn't terminated card holder credit authority as workers hit the street searching for employment. The opposite occurred! As unemployment increased, so did the low interest credit card advertisements. If consumers were not hounded by mail, they were bombarded via telephone. As parents struggled to meet financial obligations , the banking industry targeted their college bound children by issuing to the 18 year old group at least 5 million credit cards. Under the disguise of "helping the young adults" establish credit, the banking industry hooked people at a very young age on a credit card lifestyle. The majority of consumers will get stuck covering the bad debts as interest rates rise. Rising interest rates will force retailers, to eventually increase prices. Corporations will be forced to reduce or suspend dividends as future earnings erode. Money earmarked to pay credit debt will not be available to fuel the stock market engine. Eventually an economic collapse will develop. The Dow Jones Industrial Average (DJIA) may have already started the dividend adjustment.

Dividend yields for the DJIA hit a five year low in May, 1997. DJIA corporations are not increasing dividend yields fast enough to maintain the historical annual yield of 3 percent. With yields dropping to a low 1.68 percent, who would invest into something paying less than the net inflation rate, especially if the investment would need to retrace previous gains by 50 percent in order to raise the yield back to historical range. Credit debt increased by 90 billion dollars between 1992 and 1997. The runaway credit epidemic has been accompanied by record setting stock prices and personal bankruptcy filings. Looking long term; that is bad for businesses, bad for the economy, and bad for financial security. Credit card users could at least make an attempt to find a card provider fitting their credit pattern. Credit addicts, who normally carry forward a month end charge balance, should consider a low interest rate, no annual fee card, with a 25 day grace period. Avoid minimum payment traps by paying off the entire charge account balance upon receipt of the monthly statement. Consumers making minimum payments could easily pay up to 90 percent of the original product purchase price in excess interest. Not a good deal with any stretch of ones imagination. Remember: retail merchandise is marked up 300 to 400 percent over actual production cost. Making a minimum monthly payment could boost the final cost up to 800 percent above true production value. A $100 purchase worth $30.00 could easily cost $190.00 if paid off through a minimum payment schedule.

Grace periods give a false security. The majority of card holders truly do not understand the grace period concept. In a nut shell! When a charge transaction is not paid in full within the designated grace period, there will be an interest charge back dated to the original purchase date. The grace period never extends past the next monthly statement payment due date. It is void, if a partial payment is made. For example, a charge transaction occurred on the 20th of the month having a 25 day grace period. The statement closing date is on the 27th of the month; and, the payment is due on the 5th of the following month. The grace period has been reduced to about 15 days. Why? The grace period begins at the moment of purchase; and, never extends past the payment due date. Credit transactions are payable due-on-demand loans. Loans not settled by the payment due date, will trigger interest back to the transaction date. The grace period is canceled for that particular charge transaction.

RECOMMENDATION: First, avoid using charge cards whose interest charge cycle begins on the transaction date instead of the billing date. Second, never use credit; unless, funds have been set aside to cover the purchase cost. Third, do not use credit within the ten days immediately prior to the statement billing date. The interest free loan float is not long enough to be beneficial. Finally, use charge only to float a short term interest free loan.

As previously suggested, the majority of consumers experiencing credit management problems, actually had sufficient funds available to pay for the merchandise at the time of purchase. For a variety of reasons, they charge the purchase and then usually impulse spend the money on something else. Wealth building demands positive credit management. Avoiding the use of credit; however, is perhaps worse than poor credit management. Positive use of credit can enhance wealth just as negative use of credit will destroy it. An excellent example of negative credit, is the minimum payment concept (creates debt). An example of positive credit usage, is the use of credit to float short term interest free loan (creates wealth). Interest free loans allow the cash on hand to increase through interest accumulation and compounding.

A checkbook ledger is an excellent credit management tool everyone should consider utilizing. Positive credit management only begins after the consumer acquires enough funds to pay for the merchandise at the time of purchase. Once adequate funding has been obtained, the checkbook ledger can be used to reduce debt load, while cutting check writing banking cost. We suggest limiting checking account balances to 150 percent of your monthly cash flow requirements and savings account balances to 200 percent of gross income. Checking balances will tend to be higher using this concept. Why pay banks for both the use of credit and banking activity? At first, the concept will seem strange; but, with a little practice, long term benefits emerge. One early benefit, is a reduction in the number of checks written monthly. A single check can cover dozens of purchase transactions. At ten cents a check, over almost any time span that amounts to a lot of money. Another early benefit, is the avoidance of credit related interest while accumulating compound interest on the checking account. Finally, consider the postage savings.

Work through the following checkbook ledger credit management and wealth building exercise. It is most urgent to keep an open mind. Seek long term benefits. The process is simple and will be rewarding. Again, the primary benefit is the writing of a single check to cover several credit card transactions.

Checkbook Credit Use Concept

* With each credit card purchase, place the card symbol in the check number location.

* Log the charge transaction date as if a check was written.

* In the description column, describe the crediting merchant.

* Subtract the charge amount from your previous check balance. Rebalance the ledger.

* Place the charge receipts with the bank slips.

* Credit payroll checks, rebates, and other deposits.

CHECK BOOK LEDGER

CHECK #	DATE	DESCRIPTION	DEBIT	DATE	CREDIT	BALANCE
101	3/12/97	Wal*Mart	$ 10.00			$ 250.00
M	3/12/97	Texaco	$ 50.00 (/)			$ 200.00
102	4/05/97	Master Card	$ 50.00	4/05/97	$ 50.00(/)	$ 200.00
S	4/06/97	Sears	$ 100.00(/)			$ 100.00
103	5/05/97	Sears	$ 100.00	5/05/97	$ 100.00(/)	$ 100.00
		Payroll Dep.		6/01/97	$ 345.00	$ 445.00

(M) Master Card : (S) Sears Charge Card

As illustrated, two charge transactions occurred between March 12 and April 6th. The check ledger balance was adjusted to absorb the transactions. Money used to pay off the charge loan was hidden within the account balance while collecting interest. As a side note, the use of a credit card offering a cash back provision, or airline mileage works excellent with this concept. It is possible to receive substantial cash rebates on every transaction.

When the credit card statement arrives, take the following steps:

* Compare the card statement amount to both the corresponding charge slip and check book ledger.

* Place a check-off mark (/) adjacent to all charges reflected on the statement and ledger.

* Credit the check book ledger with the dollar amount specified on the statement.

* Credit back all charge entries listed on the statement. Re-balance the check book.

* Write one check to pay the total statement sum.

* Place an (/) adjacent to the credit back amount when the credit card statement is paid.

In this illustration, two different charge card providers were used to float short term interest free loans. Both statement were paid in full upon receipt. The total number of checks written were reduced. The concept benefits are magnified when a single check is used to pay off 30 to 40 charge transactions. Be sure to make a separate ledger entry for each charge transaction. Treat all open ledger entries as an outstanding check when balancing the check book ledger monthly. Do not delay seeking professional advice once debt run-a-way occurs. Run-a-way debt is not normally identified until the card user has problems meeting minimum monthly payments. Professional help may be obtained from the Consumer Credit Counseling Service (1-800-251-2227). Serious credit trouble exists when a revolving credit balance exceeds 20 percent of gross income. Credit mismanagement tends to occur frequently among individuals having substantial income. They usually have no personalized long term investment business plan. Regardless of personal income, do not consider utilizing a credit card until after reading the *Consumer Credit Handbook* published by the Consumer Information Center; Dept. 450W, Pueblo, CO 81009. All credit card statements should be settled in full each month. First USA Bank (1-800-347-7887); Oak Brook Bank (1-800-536-3000); USA Federal Savings Bank (1-800-922-9092), and the AFT Industrial Bank (1-800-776-2265) are representative of banks offering low competitive rates. You tell your card provider your interest limit. If they will not negotiate a fair rate, cut their card in half and return it to them at once. What is a fair credit usage rate? We suggest it should never exceed a 50 percent premium above the current 30 year treasury yield.

BANKING CONCEPT: The business of banking affects the financial worth of millions of Americans. Banking can be very expensive. Shopping for a bank best suited to customer needs can be a complicated task. Banks are very competitive; and, are often dependent upon customer ignorance to generate profits. Large banks may offer free checking, if account balances remain above $2,500. Sounds like a good deal. Don't be fooled! Why? Bank accounts are in reality a cheap loan from the depositor (you) to the bank. As with any loan, the lender (you) should receive a fair market valve for the use of their equity (money) to compensate them for higher returns lost elsewhere. "Free" is really never free especially when alternative investments offer yields far superior to bank yields. Equity investments, unlike debt investments (loans), generally offer superior total returns. Anyone insisting on loaning out their money should consider a quality money market fund managed by someone (anyone) other than a bank. Other options include, credit unions, brokerage certificate of deposits, and treasuries. Generally, the best checking account is with small town banks. They are generally more responsive to depositors needs. The bank chosen could be out of state or across the street. Either case, consider banking by mail. Request your employer make "electronic direct deposits" instead of writing you a paycheck. They'll save money on checks and you'll save money by not having to waste time makeing the deposit trip. Direct deposited funds are generally electronically transferred several days prior to the actual pay day; therefore, the account actually begins to accrue interest earlier. Considering offshore banking? Be safe! Research the bank before making a deposit. Review

Polk's Directory of International Banks found at most public libraries. Bank customers should always keep their funds in the highest yielding account. Interest should be credited daily; or, at least weekly on the highest outstanding balance. Avoid accounts where interest is posted monthly on the lowest account balance for the previous month. A wise policy would be to keep approximately 150 percent times normal monthly cash flow in a checking account. Savings account balances should be limited to 200 percent times monthly net income. Transfer money to keep a checking balance level low enough to meet monthly cash flow requirements. Always seek accounts offering free automatic checking overdraft protection and free unlimited automatic teller machine (ATM) transactions. Banks don't charge customers for using the services of a "real person" teller! Fact of matter, the ATM allows the bank to reduce "real person" cost. Operational savings should flow through to the customer. What a deal! Banks charge the lender (you) for helping it reduce operating cost. Where else but America!

Ask your banker questions related to the type of account you wish to open. Pay close attention to the interest calculation method, Federal Deposit Insurance Corporation (FDIC) insurance, and checking account policies. FDIC insurance is indirectly charged back to banking clients through lower interest yields. Considering the infrequent number bank failures, since the 1980-1990 banking crisis; investors, perhaps would do better financially, if they forgot about FDIC protection and sought higher yields outside the banking industry. If bank failure is a concern, consider diversification over two or three banks. Regardless of the type account, always seek accounts where the interest begins on the date of deposit; and, is compounded daily until the withdrawal date. Depositors, with funds exceeding $25,000 should negotiate for a more advantage rate. After all, anyone loaning money should have high expectations of receiving a good rate of investment return. Rest assured, banks will pay the lowest rate they can get away with while charging depositors the maximum rate allowed by law. Before loaning money to any financial institution, it is important to understand, the loan is not supported by collateral. They will not pledge acceptable property as security for the loan. Therefore, it would be foolish to carry a balance in any debit account greater than that absolutely necessary to meet monthly cash flow demands. To balance the scale of economics on this one sided deal, it is extremely important to seek answers to the following questions:

Bank Questions To Ask

* What is the primary account: checking or savings? Credit unions use the savings account as the primary account whereas banks use the checking account. Banks are cheating their lender (you) out of interest.

* How does the bank calculate account balance interest? Watch out for lowest balance in monthly calculations. Interest compounded and posted daily on the highest balance is most desired.

* Is there automatic overdraft protection? The bank should float a short term loan to cover overdraft accounts. There should never be a "bounce check" charge.

* Does the account carry credit life or disability insurance? Avoid such accounts unless the insurance is free. The bank is usually the beneficiary and not the customers estate.

* What is the bank deposit clearing policy? Expect seven business days for out of state checks to clear.

* Is a debit card available? Debit cards eliminate the need to make purchases by check. Never use a debit card to pay a liquor tab. The bar could placed a "funds hold" on the card until the tab is cleared. A "funds hold" prevents writing checks on the account until the "hold" is lifted.

* Free automatic teller machine (ATM) transactions?

* Direct or mail deposit procedures in place?

Check supply is a major banking cost. However, it need not be. Checking cost can be reduced by up to 50 percent by taking advantage of introductory mail offers from check providers. When ordering checks via mail, order the maximum quality authorized. Order checks from companies who are members of the American Mail Order Check Association. Representative membership of the association include: (1-800)

<u>Discount Check Ordering</u>

Checks-in-the-Mail	733-4443	Current, Inc.	426-0822
Designer Checks, Inc.	239-9222	Image Checks	562-8768

NOTE: Checks are usually imprinted with the customers name, address, and telephone number on the face. If your personal information changes, do not discard the checks. Order address labels to stick over the old information.

Want to locate the best advantaged CD, money market; or, mortgage rate? Surf the *Bank Rate Monitor* website at *http:// www bankrate.com.* Research the best deal. Long distance banking often provides excellent wealth building opportunities that should not be taken lightly.

LIFE INSURANCE: Perhaps billions of dollars are wasted annually on incorrect life insurance by intelligent people who were sold policies they simply do not need. Life insurance should never be considered a "nest egg" for loved ones as the benefactor of the insurer's death. Life insurance is a financial instrument used to prevent estate devaluation. It should be used to eliminate all outstanding debts of the insurer's estate at the time of death. Individuals who perhaps should consider avoiding life insurance are: children under the age sixteen, wealthy individuals owing no outstanding debt, and anyone else who having a cash reserve substantial enough to cover debts. Who should be insured? Everyone carrying over-extended debt; or, having the potential to create debt obligations for someone else through actions resulting in death. Teenagers could easily create unexpected liability for their parents at a time when they would not normally have a need for insurance. Children are perhaps the most over-insured group prior to their vehicle operation years; and, the most under-insured after they begin to drive. Prior to reaching driving age, they usually never carry over extended debt. After beginning to drive, they put their parents assets at risk. The death of a passenger while "little darling" or "junior" is in lack-of-control operating their wheels will wipe out years of parent wealth building. The child's debt indirectly becomes an extension of the parents debt. Therefore, it is the parents assets which need protection. Parents with children under age 21 who operate a motor vehicle of any kind should always carry liability and life insurance covering the child with the parents as the beneficiary.

Parents assume debt obligations created as a result of the minors privileges. Although, insurance rarely covers debt associated with the wrongful death of an occupant killed while your child operated the vehicle; life insurance on the driver, should they be fatally injured, can offset legal expenses. Parents with children who drive; or, of children with a parent cosigned credit card should carry life insurance on the child equal to at least three times the family gross annual income. The insurance cost will be very cheap when compared to the potential benefits. As the child moves into adulthood, the majority of insurance providers will authorize transferring the policy to the young adult. Additionally, every child should have a social security account assigned at birth. Social security provides limited disability and burial benefits.

Asset protection may be secured without actually purchasing an insurance policy. If debt doesn't threaten the estate, funeral and burial expenses should be financed through estate liquidation, loans, or through a credit card. For example, a low annual fee $10,000 limit credit card carrying a 15 percent annual interest rate may be used to pay final expenses instead of paying years insurance premiums. In the absence of a credit card, select an insurance policy with adequate coverage considering the current estate financial circumstances. Adjust the policy annually to maintain the lowest premium. Avoid policies advertising "cash value" build-up. Insurance is not an investment but asset protection. It's the insurance and not the "cash value" which provides estate protection. Cash value policies are normally termed "whole life" or "universal life". They are poor insurance choices at best when compared to "term insurance" specially when the premium difference properly invested. Cash value policies return poor yields while removing investor management control and flexibility. Level term insurance policies offer the best investment choice and insurance protection.

Level term insurance is available from over three hundred providers. It offers enhanced benefits, through low guaranteed level price monthly premiums spread over a specific time span. The insurance can be bought for 10, 20, or 30 years and is automatically canceled if the monthly premiums are not paid. Premium differences between "whole life" and "level term" can be diversified across meaningful wealth building investments. Regardless of the length of term selected, always purchase a policy based upon the lowest per $1000 unit cost. Most employees, almost without exception, will purchase insurance recommended by their employer. That could be a drastic mistake, since the objective is to obtain the maximum insurance for minimum cost. Shop around for the best policy. It is not unreasonable to locate a level term one million dollar policy for about $1,000 annually.

Sounds tempting; but, what average person has a million dollar debt liability? Don't over insure! Locating the best insurance deal is simple. Suggestion! Hire, at no cost, an insurance comparison service to search for a policy ideally matched to current personal circumstances. Shop for the best deal annually. Switch insurance carriers as necessary to reach your asset protection objective. Insurance search companies include: (1-800)

<u>Insurance Search Companies</u>

Quote Smith	431-1147
Matrix Direct	728-3101
Life Insurance Wholesalers	860-9230
Insurance Quote	972-1104
Insurance Information	472-5800

TRANSPORTATION COST: Transportation cost includes a whole lot more than just fuel. To figure total transportation cost, everything from tires, fuel, vehicle maintenance, depreciation, insurance, parking fees, and monthly finance charges must be given serious consideration. 1997 mileage cost estimates are staggering. For every mile a typical automobile is operated, sooner or later, someone will cough up to an estimated 52 cents per operational mile. As previously stressed, wealth building requires holding on to what has been earned through controlled spending. American's rarely ever consider the real cost of transportation; nor, its drastic destructive effect on wealth building. We think nothing of hopping in the old family car to drive ten miles in order to purchase a single item, not realizing the item cost just increased by $5.20 above the product retail price. Do you know anyone who has paid $7.00 for a pack of cigarettes? Most of us do!

Commuting transportation cost is often unwisely disregarded when job hunting. Perhaps that explains why a majority of workers actually work their entire life only to eventually die broke. Using pretax income estimates for food (10%), housing (35%); and, Payroll adjustments of (45%), it is easy to conclude why workers ignore transportation cost. Let's illustrate the dramatic impact transportation cost can have on wealth building. Assume for a moment, a person holding a job paying $10 per hour located 25 miles from their residence. Based on a standard 40 hour work week, their monthly gross income is $1,733. The commute to work is 1042 miles monthly after adjusting for a typical two week annual vacation. Based upon transportation cost estimates, the commute robs the worker of $541.84 monthly (.52 x 1042 miles = $541.84). Food each month cost approximately $173.30 (.10 x gross income). Housing $606.55 (.35 x gross income). Monthly payroll adjustments $779.83 (.45 x gross income). Entertainment is excluded. How well is the worker doing financially? Not good! After reviewing the illustration, we encourage everyone to review their unique situation. Should your review prove disappointing, please relax. *Don't Die Broke* will provide the guiding light necessary for you to succeed.

<u>Real Income Breakout</u>

$10.00 Per hour (x) 2080 annually		(=)	$20,800.00	Gross annual income.
Monthly Gross Income		(=)	1,733.00	
Expenses Are:	Transportation	(-)	541.84	
	Food	(-)	173.33	
	Housing	(-)	606.55	
	Taxes/Insurance	(-)	779.83	
Monthly Expenses (fixed)		(-)	$2,101.55	
Monthly Profit / <u>Loss</u>			< $368.55 >	

The worker is loosing approximately $369 each and every month; excluding costs for entertainment, clothing, medical, education, union dues, and, current monthly finance payments for the vehicle. Chances are, the worker will also be experiencing credit card debt over-extension. Clearly, the worker is in financial trouble. Sadly, they may not realize it. Rest assured they soon will. Home ownership in this situation would not resolve the workers situation. Home ownership would at least have a potential of helping the worker build net worth equity. The only real hope for the worker is to either seek a 50 percent pay raise, take a second job, force family members into the work place, car pool, use public transportation, seek employment closer home paying an adjusted equivalent rate of pay; or, any combination of the above.

Transportation cost must be controlled through careful planning. Plan shopping and social stops on the way to and from church, school, or work in order to combine all transportation related functions. Keep the transportation operational cost to a minimum through the use of multiple enroute stops and alternate modes of transportation such as: car pooling, public transportation, bicycling or walking. Transportation cost cutting should be a top priority beginning long before employment is secured.

Selection techniques for a pre-owned and new vehicles are quite different; yet, the end result is always the same. The consumer will become the owner of a product that will cost up to 52 cents per mile to operate. To offset future transportation cost, vehicle utilization must be given serious consideration. Additionally, every avenue available to purchase the vehicle at the lowest possible cost must be explored. Consider the following:

<u>Pre-Owned Vehicle Search</u>

Pre-owned automobiles present excellent bargain opportunities. However; use of extreme caution in the selection process, will reduce the risk of experiencing problems later. Considerations for selecting a pre-owned vehicle should include questions like:

* Is the car located on a used car lot, dealer lot, or is it advertised in the classified ads?

* What's the vehicle operational and maintenance history?

* Is the current registered owner, the owner of record one year ago?

* What's the cars age?

* Does the mileage actually represent true mileage, etc.?

Begin your pre-owned vehicle search only after you have decided on the vehicle make, model, and year desired. Automobiles four years old with mid-mileage (40 to 60 thousand miles) are generally marketed at 40 percent below their original Manufacturer Suggested Retail Price (MSRP). After the decision has been made regarding the desired vehicle, began searching with the classified ads. Cars marketed through the classified ads, by a current owners of at least a year, will tend to be in better shape mechanically than pre-owned units sold through dealer outlets. Once a candidate for purchase is located, it's time to begin a serious selection screening process.

Pre-owned Vehicle Selection Screening

* It is utmost important to acquire the Vehicle Identification Number (VIN).

Why? The VIN is the automobile tracking number. Through the VIN, information pertaining to prior ownership and insurance claim damage can be retrieved. CARFAX (1-800-444-0145): a title search company, can provide a vehicle ownership history for a modest research fee. Also, check within your local area for motor vehicle title search companies. The VIN is located on the forward left side glare panel. It may be viewed from outside the vehicle through the windshield. If the vehicle is offered for sale through the classifieds, request the VIN from the owner. A sample VIN might be similar to JK2VFS148LO777477.

* Check with previous owner for vehicle insurance claim, operational, and maintenance history.

A very important; yet, often overlooked step in the selection process. After the background check with previous owners, what next?

* Do an on site inspection of the machine.

Jot down the option package; i.e., power door locks, automatic transmission, air, anti-locking power brakes, anti-thief device, tented windows, electric seats, etc. Check tire wear. Tire edge wear could be an indication of serious front-end alignment problems. Worn tires on the back were probably rotated from the front. New tires, especially on the front, red flag potential serious trouble. Do not believe for one minute the owner installed new tires out of the goodness of their heart. Take photographs (at least 36 exposure); or, video tape of the entire vehicle. Photograph the vehicles inside from both front door angles; and, also from the center of the back seat looking forward. Photograph the tire tread of each tire including the spare. Exterior photos should include shots with the trunk and hood open. Photograph the vehicle underside. While underneath the vehicle, inspect for evidence of tampering and leaks. Examine the bolt heads around the transmission for dirt and grime. A clean bolt head should be suspicious. Record the mileage. Do not test drive the vehicle during the initial inspection phase. Allow time to absorb what has been observed. Request the seller to give you their asking price in writing. The hand writing sample should be compared to the sellers signature on the title information provided by the title search company. Wait two days before carefully reviewing the photographs or video, for items easily overlooked during the Inspection. Shoppers miss seeing a lot when under the stress of vehicle shopping. After carefully considering the additional information revealed by the photographic documentation, a decision can be made as to continue the selection process or to terminate the candidate from further consideration. Be careful not to talk too much during the initial inspection. Rest assured the seller will be sizing you up for a plucking. The least they know about you personally, the better your advantage will be during the final price negotiations. Never give your telephone number! The car is what you want. The price is right. A review of the documentation reveals no problems. You will buy.

* Now for the money! Visit your loan officer requesting their assistance in preparing the *True Value Offer.*

Lending institutions have a current copy of the National Automobile Dealers Association (NADA) (1-800-544-6232) "Blue Book"; or, the "Red Book" published by MacLean Hunter Market Report, Inc. (1-800-621-9907). Never obtain pricing information from a dealer reference source.

Your *True Value Offer Sheet* purchase price should never, never, never exceed the NADA "Auction Price" minus adjustments for high mileage, vehicle condition, and inoperable options. Using the "Blue or Red Book" to work-up an offer, use the four numbers, or letters beginning with the fourth character from the left to locate information about the vehicle. Using the VIN illustrated, these figures should be VFS1. Next, review the "Red or Blue Book" for the manufacturer of your vehicle. Locate the year of production. Adjacent to the production year; locate the VFSI vehicle model number. You are now on the correct line to determine important pricing information. Options and mileage adjustments will be footnoted. Next, scan across the top of the page for the column headings: *Avg.Trd-In, Body Type, Model Number, M.S.R.P., WGT, Avg. Loan;* and, *Avg. Retail.* In the block where the horizontal column starting with VFS1, and the vertical *M.S.R.P.* column intersect, is the retail price suggested by the manufacturer. The *Avg. Retail* column lists the price most sellers will ask. Your financial officer sets the maximum loan at between 70 and 90 percent of the *Avg. Retail* price. The price from which the buyer should negotiate from is the *Avg. Trd-In.* The *Avg. Trd-in* represents the dealer wholesale auction price. It is also the price a dealer would pay if the vehicle was used for a trade-in. Buyers should never pay a premium above the dealers price.

* Your *True Value Offer Sheet* price should never exceed the *Avg. Trd-In* wholesale price.

Conduct a second inspection. Request a test drive. Operate all equipment. Make a record listing inoperative equipment. Ask for the owners permission in writing to have the vehicle inspected by a dealer technician, at your expense. Prepare an *Inspection Permission Agreement* before the test drive to be signed by both parties only if the drive meets your satisfaction. **Never take the vehicle for an inspection to anyone recommended by the seller!** Be sure to test the engine cylinder compression and for compliance with the Environmental Protection Agency (EPA) emission standards. Problems identified during the test drive should be reported to your technician prior to their inspection. The technician inspection report must detail the estimated repair cost and out-of-service time it would take to repair all inoperative items noted during the text drive and their inspection.

* Car acceptable to you! Do not reveal your offer price to the seller when returning the vehicle. Request the sellers mailing address and fax number. Leave the property without the vehicle. Now you can deal!

Mail or fax your *True Value Offer Sheet* to the seller, including a copy of the technicians report (only if the car has problems). Give the seller a time and date deadline to either accept or reject your offer. Request the seller to respond to your offer either by mail or fax before the deadline. Indicate in your bid, the offer price will not be extended past the dead line; but, a counter offer may be reviewed for consideration. The waiting game usually works to the benefit of the buyer. If the offer is refused, present it again one week later. Still refused, forget it!

* Seller takes offer!

Make arrangements to pay via certified bank check or money order upon vehicle delivery. Should the seller insist on cash, for personal security, do not under any circumstances finalize the deal alone. You could lose more than money! Before handing over the payment, do an acceptance walk around inspection of the vehicle. Double check everything, to insure the vehicle is still representative of what you originally inspected.

WARNING: Pre-owned vehicles can be an excellent bargain; or, they can be your worse nightmare. You can reduce risk by conducting an investigation to determine what your pre-owned candidate actually represents. Money spent checking out your dream machine could cost upward to $500. All inspections, inoperative equipment; and, abnormally high mileage should discount the purchase price. Consider the Advantages and disadvantages.

Disadvantages include: (1) vehicle lacks seat belts, (2) gas guzzler, and (3) worn parts; i.e., brakes, ball joints, shocks, engine cam shaft, piston rings, exhaust system seals, C.V. joints; and, other non-visible parts. What you can't inspect is where the real hidden cost is located. Lack of available parts for a specific vehicle is another big disadvantage. The impact of the disadvantages; however, may be reduced by bidding a price low enough to offset future repair cost associated with worn out components found in every dream (nightmare) machine.

Advantages include: (1) usually a free auto wash, wax, and interior cleaning, (2) less costly to insure, (3) lower taxes and tag cost, where applicable, (4) cheap parts may be located through after-market parts distributors, auto clubs, junk yards, and swap meets, (5) thieves are smarter than buyers; they usually avoid stealing junkers, (6) construction superiority, and (7) well maintained pre-owned vehicles begin to rise in antique value after twenty-five years, as supply diminishes and demand increases.

Test driving a pre-owned vehicle is a very important step in the selection process. The technician report is another important step. Neither, should be done until information has been provided to your financial loan officer; and, they have made the a determination a loan is appropriate. Loans should be limited to 24 months because interest rates will be at a premium. Interest rates charged on used car loans often exceed the best advantage credit card rate. Do not finance a used vehicle from anyone except a reputable financial institution. **Repeat!** Do not finance through the dealer! Pre-owned (used) car dealers ask for a down-payment which almost always exceed their cost for the vehicle. Additionally, when they finance the sale, finance charges exceeding 15 percent annually with prepayment penalties of up to 10 percent of the car original finance loan is not unusual. Do not forget to take the owner along for the test drive. It makes it more difficult for them to lie to you when they witness the same problems you experience. Operate every system and optional package on the vehicle. Before getting inside the vehicle, raise the hood and check all fluids; i.e., brakes, power steering, anti-freeze coolant (overflow tank only); and, the engine oil level. When checking the engine oil, smell it. The oil should not have a burnt smell. Listen for squeaks and grinds when applying brakes, making turns, and shifting gears. Any noise should be further investigated by your technician. Wring the vehicle out. Sellers who decline to accompany the customer on the test drive may request the test driver leave their personal vehicle keys with the seller as (hostage)insurance the driver will actually return the vehicle. Refuse the request! Never surrender your personal vehicle keys to anyone. If they insist, leave at once. It only takes a good thief a few minutes to make a duplicate key; or, swap out your transmission for a junker. Purchasing a pre-owned vehicle is serious business. It can be a pleasant experience, or your worse nightmare.

A Pre-Owned Nightmare

A real life nightmare occurred in 1992. A young couple bought and financed a 1985 Challenger from a used car dealer in Texas for about $9,500. The three year note carried a 17 percent finance charge. At the insistence of the dealer, the car was taken to a mechanic for a complete check out. Three days later, the mechanic telephoned the young couple with good news. "That's the best darn car I've seen around here for some time!" he exclaimed.

Based upon the mechanics statement (no written report), the young couple bought the car. Two months later, they drove the car to Georgia. While in Georgia, the vehicle broke down. A mechanic in Georgia did a tune-up, replaced the control computer, a clogged air filter, and a clogged fuel filter. Cost $900. Upon their return to Texas, the car quit yet another time. Another $600 shot out the window; plus, hotel expenses. Less than eight months later, the transmission would not accept fifth gear. A local transmission company inspected the transmission only to discover the transmission had been water damaged, parts installed improperly, transmission filter missing; and, the serial number had been scratched out indicating the unit was either scrip or stolen. Replacement transmission: $1,865. Less than four months later, the engine timing belt broke.

During the timing belt replacement, it was discovered the engine head, valves, and camshaft were damaged due to lack of top-end oil supply lubrication. Lack of proper oil lubrication had caused extensive wear damage. Another $916. Further investigation discovered the turbocharger had seized. The oil supply line was clogged. A rebuilt turbocharger priced at $1,200. Next, came $500 for Shelby special shocks. Finally new brakes for $340.

A 1985 vehicle having a "blue book" *Avg. Trd-in* value of $4,000 eventually cost the couple over $15,000 before they dumped it in 1995 for scrap. They got paid $300. They were ripped off by the seller and his buddy mechanic.

Sad to say, stories of this kind is repeated across America every day! The young couple needed transportation. They trusted the dealer. Because of trust, they were defrauded! Perhaps they were defrauded, because our society condones such actions as normal business practice. Name one student graduating from high school, who has been taught by our expensive education system, how not to be ripped off when purchasing anything! Didn't think you could! Education expenses should not be used to fund teacher retirement plans, to fund sport programs fostered by egomaniac coaches; or, to bus students out of their chosen neighborhood. Education dollars should be spent for the sole purpose of teaching our children the survival skills they need to be consumer and investor functional in a society of educated derelicts. Education failed to teach this young couple consumer skills. **Wake Up America!** Adults must become more active in the educational process. Insist on children be taught survival skills necessary to insure they are fully prepared to deal with the real world before they graduate from high school.

The cost of doing business with the dealer drove the young couple into financial distress, bankruptcy, and eventually divorce. Their experience could have been prevented had they been trained to spot a con-job. The couple held to a standard of high morals which practically dictated everyone should be trusted. Blind trust is foolish. Society looses yet again, as another broken family is driven by a crooked businessman into the need and demand support cycle of the tax economy. Perhaps this is not the correct place to mention the primary cause of divorce in America is over financial stress; but, I will anyway. We firmly believe the techniques illustrated throughout *Don't Die Broke,* when taught at a very early time in the educational cycle, would help any young adult build a solid financial base providing for a long and prosperous stable marriage relationship. Just a thought! Rip-offs do not always occur with pre-owned vehicles. The buyer must stand firm by insisting on quality. New vehicle purchases can be just as devastating to wealth building as a poorly selected pre-owned vehicle.

New Vehicles

Purchasing a new dream machine could be more stressful than buying a thoroughly screened pre-owned vehicle. For example, a new car will surely depreciate in value. However, the pre-owned vehicle may have already stabilized at scrap material value; and, has begun to rise in price due to antique value, or construction material price up-trends. As plastic, rubber, steel, and chrome prices increase so does pre-owned car values once they have reached residual value. No one really gets a good deal when purchasing a new vehicle, except the dealer. The moment a title changes hands, the now used vehicle resale value begins to fall like an avalanche. The new owner is trapped. They are abandoned to smoother under a debt load often taking years to dig out. Low interest rates, rebates, red tag sales, "will pay off your credit card debts," or "well take anything on trade" are schemes bias against the purchaser. Rebates, for example, are often returned to the dealer. Should the buyer receive the rebate, it is only a return of money already financed during the initial purchasing process. Rebates should flow back into the account for debt buy-down; however, the mass majority of consumers will consider the money (theirs) as gift or reward to be spent elsewhere. Always reapply rebates to the car loan

Avoid the trade-in syndrome. You will loose every time. Usually, the need for a another car arise because repair bills are mounting. A new car appears to be the answer. There's no spare cash for a down payment, so the buyer will use their currently owned vehicle as a trade-in in lieu of a cash down payment. A alternate choice would be to use an advance against a low annual fee, 12 to 15 percent credit card rather than to trade the vehicle. Why? The interest required to pay off the advance will generally never exceed the losses associated with the trade-in process.

Auto dealers rarely ever pay more than the "*Avg. Trd-In*" for trade-in's minus any outstanding loan balances or liens. The dealer is limiting their downside risk, until the trade-in can be resold at retail. If you trade-in a junker, you'll get a low trade-in offer. It is important to remember, that buying one car and selling (trade-in) another car are distinct and totally separate transactions. Do not commingle the two. You will lose money! As previously mentioned, the use of a credit card cash advance to cover the down payment could be a better deal than giving up your present car to a low ball dealer trade-in offer. After you've completed researching for your new car, take a credit card cash advance to cover 10 percent of the maximum price listed on the window sticker. For example, if the highest price listed is $20,000, try to secure an advance for $2,000. Limit the loan to six months. During the six months, sell the old vehicle and repay the advance. Pay the balance on the new car loan. Why use a credit card advance instead of doing a trade-in? Assume, if you will, the trade-in vehicle was purchased four years earlier for a MSRP of $16,000. The current *Avg. Trd-In* value is about $4,800. Now consider the purchase of a new $20,000 vehicle. On the typical trade-in, the dealer would credit a maximum of $4,800 toward the new vehicle purchase price (assuming no outstanding loans or liens existed against the trade-in). The loan balance would be $15,200. Without the trade-in; and, assuming a $2,000 cash down payment, the financed outstanding balance would be $18,000. At first instance, the trade-in appears to be the best deal. It's not! Here, why.

After taking delivery of your new car, it's time to market your spare. Advertise the car at *Retail* "blue book" value through classified ads, Auto Trader, and word-of-mouth. When the car sells, you would receive approximately 40 percent of the four year earlier MSRP ($6,400). Assuming it took six months to sell the trade-in, a 15 percent annualized interest rate against your $2,000 credit card advance would cost $150. Subtract the $150 from $6,400 for a net balance of $6,250. If insurance was kept on the vehicle during the six months, estimate another $350 charge against the sell. $5,900 would available to buy down the new vehicle loan. Subtract the dealers offer of $4,800 from $5,900; and, you've made a cool profit of $1,000. Pay off the $2,000 advance and put the $3900 balance against the $18,000 auto loan. The outstanding loan balance is now drops to $14,100 and that sure beats $15,200. There are usually no pre-payment penalties for auto loan buy downs. The point is not to muddy the deal by rushing blindly into a trade-in situation. Seek alternatives to meet the down payment obligation. Precautions must be considered when selling the trade-in car. Do not accept personal checks. They tend to bounce or get canceled. Do not take cash, or close the deal on weekends unless a witness is present. Once the title has changed hands; and, the *Bill of Sale* is signed, you are subject to being robbed. Never allow anyone to drive your vehicle alone. Keep the gas tank near empty.

Motor cycle sellers, are advised to keep less than one-half pint of fuel in the gas tank. Always arrange for someone to accompany the test driver. Never let anyone drive a vehicle for sale until after the test driver has been interviewed. Check and record information from at least one photo identification source and two supporting documents with their signature affixed. Compare the document signatures with each other. Write down the driver's address, name, age, sex, race, and social security number. It may be prudent, to take a thumb print! Remember that "nothing is better for you than something you don't like." If you are not happy with what you've seen during the identification phase, even if the driver was to be accompanied, refuse to let them drive the vehicle. It is far better to lose the deal than to lose the vehicle. Thieves love do-it-yourself vehicle sellers. The thief is invited to drive the vehicle, given the keys, and then allowed to drive away without preset test drive conditions. Often, the gas tank is full. It takes less than fifteen minutes, for thieves to totally strip most automobiles. It would be as the character *Forest Gump* stated "stupid is as stupid does," if anyone allowed themselves to be ripped-off. To avoid dirty tricks played on consumers by new car dealers everyone should learn the following *Auto Buyers Rules of Engagement.*

<u>Auto Buyers Rules of Engagement</u>

* Gather information on your future vehicle during non-business hours.
* Establish your "afford price" before shopping.
* Never reveal your "afford price" to a salesperson.
* Never allow a salesperson to intimidate you.
* When approached, simply tell them you are looking and wish to be left alone.
* You'll contact them.
* Never price shop by telephone, salespersons tend to be less than truthful.
* Never chit-chat with a salesperson. He or she is not your pal.
* Obtain financial backing before shopping.
* Refuse to pay administrative fees, locator cost, and dealer preparation charges.
* Fax a price offer to the dealer with an deal dead line.
* Avoid special sales.
* Shop the last day of the month.
* Shop on the three Mondays before Christmas, especially if it's raining.
* Retain a buyers agent to purchase the vehicle for you.

If the salesperson you are dealing with can't strike a deal, allow them to consult with their management only once. If they leave the negotiations a second time, tell them to forget the sale. Get up and walkout! Deal with only one person. If anyone else joins the party, run-run-run-from the area for your financial wealth sake. A third person joining the discussion is a clear signal you are about to become a victim of something you really may not want to own. When the salesperson can't make the deal, they will bring in the "enforcers."

A majority of problems can be avoided by looking at the window sticker information beforehand. After obtaining important sticker information, leave the dealership property so serious thought about the car can be meaningful. Finally, year end sales really don't save true dollars, because as new models roll in, last year models will loose 20-30 percent in value simply because they are past history. Year end sales are not true sales. They are designed to get the dealership off the oversupply inventory hook at the customers expense. The deal the customer thinks they are getting is usually not a deal at all after considering true value.

Window sticker price listings are generally located on the drivers side rear window. They are installed by the manufacturer prior to shipment. The sticker includes the Vehicle Identification Number (VIN). The sticker VIN can be cross-checked with the VIN data plate. The VIN data plate is easily viewed through the left lower windshield. It contains information about the vehicle's year, make, model, and color. The typical window sticker begins with the manufacturers suggested retail price (MSRP) and concludes with a "total price" after applying the dealer add-on's. Dealer add-on's are subjective at best and leave a lot of bargaining price flexibility.

Sales personnel receive a commission based on the "total price" which they often proudly referred to as the "listed price." The "listed price" is where the sales person works from during negotiations; but, it is the wrong price from where the buyer should negotiate. Consider several important facts. First, the MSRP has a built-in profit for the dealer. Secondly, dealer installed options are typically marked up by 400 to 1,000 percent. Third, if the vehicle is financed through the dealer, the dealer often receives from 1/2 to 1 percent commission for functioning as a loan broker for the lender. Finally, the dealer receives volume incentives, bonuses, and rebates from the manufacturer. They could sell practically any vehicle the MRSP still make money after the option package addition.

To negotiate a true bargain, the buyer needs an ideal starting point. First, add up all the options. Then cut the sum by 50 percent. That should still cover installation labor cost. Next, cross-check the VIN to the latest edition of *Edmunds* for "new car prices"; or, the "MSRP" to determine the base price the dealer paid the manufacturer for the specific vehicle. Information may also be accessed through the manufacturers website. It is conceivable to estimate the dealers actual cost to within a few percentage points. The "MSRP" gives the dealer a profit allowance of between 2 and 25 percent; excluding rebates. Now you can deal. Illustration:

Best Offer Price

STICKER PRICE		BEST OFFER PRICE	
MSRP	$20,000	MSRP	$24,390
(+) Dealer Adj.	1,000	(-) 5% MSRP	1,000
(+) Dealer Options	3,000	(-) 50% option	1,500
(+) Administrative	90	(-) Admin Fee	90
Prep. Charge	300	(-) Prep. Charge	300
LIST PRICE	$24390	OFFER PRICE	21,500

Never bid above the best offer price. Always insist on receiving the rebates. Recently, a customer in Georgia walked out of three hours of negotiations, after the salesperson refused to cut another dollar off the dealers last offer. The customer purchased a new vehicle three days later for $50 over the dealers true cost and $4,000 below the MSRP. Anyone paying $24,390 for the illustrated vehicle car would loose up to $8,300 the moment the sale transaction was completed. Almost anyone would agree, wealth is not built doing business that way.

The best approach to the purchase of any vehicle, is to formulate a plan of action aimed at getting the lowest possible price. Once the make, model, color; and, option package has been determined, it may be best to shop across America. The price is determined by which economic zone in which the car is located. A vehicle shipped to Oklahoma, for example, is often priced much cheaper that an identical vehicle destined for Georgia, Florida, or New York. Began the purchase process, by obtaining information on the VIN through CompuServe, or America on-line. If the car is out-of-state, request the dealer fax a copy of the window sticker, or dealer pricing sheet. It is important to know what items make up the list price structure.

After obtaining VIN information from the dealers lot; or, through the Internet, it's time to get your loan officer involved. Request they provide you with: (1) a computer print-out of the factory invoice for your specific VIN including available dealer option cost, and (2) a list of all dealers within your economic zone who offers the best "final sale over invoice" deal. The manufacturer may be contacted directly to obtain the information. Information can also be obtained from the latest edition of *Edmund's New Car Prices*. If your loan officer is unable to obtain the invoice information, then use the window sticker information. Work up a "best offer price." Remember, dealers often exchange inventory. Therefore, send the initial price request message directly to the dealer business manager of every dealer within a two hundred mile radius of where the car you want is located.

The message should read:

"Please fax to me your best price over factory invoice, on VIN (list number), with a (color/style) exterior, a (color/style) interior, having the following option package. Options include: (listing). The vehicle is located at (name) dealership, in (city, state). Your response by no later than 2:30 p.m. today is appreciated."

After receiving the dealers response, review it carefully. Prepare to submit your first counter offer. **The counter offer should never exceed your pre-determined best offer price less 10 percent.** In the first counter offer, request the dealer make the sale a personal transaction without involving his salesman. Request a response to your counter offer within thirty minutes. If the first counter offer is rejected, lay your best offer price on the table. If it is rejected, walk away. If it is accepted, telephone the business manager indicating you'll accept the deal at the last offer and that you will pay for the taxes, tags, and registration. Inquire about rebates! Make it clear rebated come to you. Arrange to take delivery of the vehicle at a location other than at the dealers lot. Prior to the appointment, pickup a bank check from your loan officer for the total closing price (i.e., car, taxes, tags, and title). To seal the deal, send the business manager a certified check payment via private courier. Notify your insurance company of the purchase.

Every dollar saved should be applied directly toward wealth building investments. Don't be confused by phrases like "list price," "final offer price," or "invoice price". The terms are used by sales persons to close the deal. "$50 over invoice" may seem like a good deal. In reality, the dealer still earns thousands of dollars from the sale through various manufacturer promotional deals and rebates.

Traditional new vehicle purchasing methods no longer apply. Dealers tend not to dicker over prices except at year end close-outs where either the dealer or customer will take the depreciation hit. Additionally, the best deals may be found during final days of the month, especially when quotas have not been met. The three Mondays prior to Christmas are especially attractive. Consider traveling outside the local area to save thousands of dollars. Afraid to deal! Consider hiring a consumer buying service. Independent services are provided by: (1-800)

Auto Buying Services

American Car Buying Service	223-4882
AutoVantage	999-4227
Consumers Car Club	227-2582
Nationwide Auto Brokers	521 7257

Vehicles depreciate very fast. To aid consumers in their selection process, there are many websites assigned to vehicles. Manufacturer websites include photos, option packages, VIN information, pricing, and consumer tips. Additional sites include after market venders and survey companies. Important sites include: http://www.

* Alldata.TSG.com * Edmunds.com * Intellichoice.com * jd power.com

BUYERS AGENT: Before purchasing any high price merchandise, consider hiring a buyers agent to purchase the product on your behalf. Hire, for example, an experienced auto trader to represent your interest at a dealers auction. Pay the agent $200 plus 5 percent of the amount they shave off the list price. If the agent purchases a vehicle $2,000 below retail, they should be compensated $300. The agent will need to purchase the vehicle and upon resale to you, you'll pay normal tax, tag, and title fees in addition to the agents fee. Never advance the agent money. Always sign a *Letter of Agreement* detailing the service requested, before they perform a service.

AUTO INSURANCE: The forced alternative of most drivers. Most states require auto insurance. Although no national law exist requiring automotive insurance, local law enforcement, find it more convenient to spend tax money acting as agents for insurance compliance than to use tax dollars in pursuit of more important crime prevention programs. Law enforcement across America check auto insurance cards of motorist daily; yet, the police vehicles they operate may carry no insurance at all. Governments are exempt from insurance coverage. Speaking of one sided legislation. States, acting on behalf of insurance companies, legislate auto insurance requirements down consumer's throats. Therefore, since they are generally left without the freedom of choice, it is wise for consumers to select the best insurance coverage available. In states not legislating auto insurance coverage, it is wise to carry coverage. To cover deductible cost, consider a companion no annual fee $10,000 limited credit card. Decline medical coverage for the driver, if they have coverage through their employer.

Insurance premiums are generally computed based upon local claim data. Factors used to determine rates include: (1) automobile risk category, (2) drivers age and gender, (3) rate zone, (4) marital status, (5) insurer's accident and moving traffic conviction rate, (6) vehicle utilization, (7) projected annual mileage, and (8) the vehicles location.

Premiums are usually discounted for: (1) driver training programs, (2) a low driver conviction and accident record, (3) multiple vehicle coverage, (4) auto anti-thief devices, (5) senior citizen status, (6) radar detectors (except GEICO. They consider a radar detector implies speeding), (7) level of coverage, and (8) whether the vehicle will be garaged or left outdoors. Each insurance company offers different discount programs. Checkout several prior to signing up. Avoid companies who send salespersons to your home. Personal sales service will cost the consumer plenty without enhanced benefits.

One excellent insurance company, and there are many, is the Government Employee Insurance Company (GEICO) (1-800-841-3000). GEICO; a non-government insurance company, is a very popular insurance firm offering excellent coverage at a liberal discount rate. Compare current policies with GEICO coverage; and, the odds are favorable in the probability of switching carriers.

Drivers education is an excellent parent asset protection investment. Encourage your child to get as much training as possible before they assume the privileges associated with motor vehicle operation. Not only will they tend to have less accidents, they will generally accept a higher level of operator responsibility. Nothing is more nerve racking than to spot junior speeding down main street with a car load of buddies. Insurance cost are directly correlated to risk. Parents must first teach and then insist young drivers accept motor vehicle risk management.

AUTO ACCOUNT: A concept formulated to eliminate debt while freeing critical funds for wealth building. It works best with pre-marketed vehicles bought for cash. 'Power-by-the-mile" forces the auto user to establish a life long savings habit that provides lifelong benefits. It's a simple concept overlooked by practically every automobile owner. Parents should never give their child an automobile without first setting up an auto account. The concept has a strong potential of producing wealth building benefits beyond anyone's wildest imagination. To establish an account, review the following recommendations.

* First, its okay to give high school students their starter car, if an auto account is opened prior to giving junior the vehicle. The account should be opened with the "best yield" brokerage money market fund.

* Secondly, instruct the child that with the privilege to operate a vehicle comes equal responsibility. Responsibility involves financial obligations well beyond fuel; small maintenance items such as tires, brakes, oil changes, and insurance. Responsibilities include planning for vehicle depreciation and eventual replacement.

* Next, set up a "power-by-the-mile" fee equal to 80 percent of the most recent American Automobile Association mileage estimates. Keep a mileage log. Require the child to pay weekly for each mile driven. There is no such thing as a free ride. The child should be taught the importance of financial responsibility from the earliest age.

* Finally, deposit the funds directly into the child's auto account within two business days of receipt. Repeat the procedure week after week. It will pay off really big, when the time arrives for the vehicle to be replaced.

Do not tap into the account for daily operating expenses. Equity in the present vehicle combined with the account equity should be applied toward the purchase of a replacement vehicle. It is senseless, to waste investment dollars financing any product that depreciates in value. We all know, that is exactly what vehicles do!

Illustrating 31 cents per mile; at 60,000 miles of vehicle usage, the auto account will have appreciated to over $18,600, excluding interest. Most children drive 60,000 miles in less than four years. Many young people practically live in their cars. They should build wealth faster. The auto account forces the child to save money based on real time vehicle usage. The real payoff is the elimination of monthly payments and finance charges on subsequent purchases.

"Power-by-the-mile" can put anyone on the right track to wealth building. Assume the purchase a new vehicle, for $20,000. After 4 years, or 60,000 miles which ever occurs first, the vehicle should retail at approximately 40 percent of the original MRSP. Combine 40 percent "x" $20,000 ($8,000) with 80 percent "x" ($.52) the current AAA mileage factor "x" 60,000 miles for this illustration, and the auto account value could easily exceed $33,000. Pay cash for the replacement vehicle. However, there is now a major difference. Continue to "power-by-the-mile; but, add to the account all monthly vehicle finance payments that would have been due if the vehicle had been financed. This concept is so powerful, it alone can lead to extreme wealth and financial security. Implement now!

THE EXECUTIVE WOMEN'S TRAVEL NETWORK: The network offers to women great travel bargains, airline seat upgrades, discount companion fares, travel and safety tips; plus, a whole lot more. Contact The Executive Women's Travel Network (1-800-657-8305). The website is http://www.deltaair.com/womenexecs.

HOTEL SAVVY: During hotel stays, security should be first order of business. First floor rooms can be entered from the outside by prowlers. Rooms located higher than the second floor could have exits blocked during fires. Rooms at the back of hotels may not be accessible to emergency equipment. For these reasons, rooms located on the second floor street side are the choice experienced travelers. Be specific about the room location choice when making reservations. Before entering a room, request hotel security check the room. After entering the room, lock the door. Do not open in response to a knock, or for complimentary gifts from the manager. Request room service to telephone before delivering any item. Contact the front desk anytime someone knocks on the door. Once a stranger is inside the room, it's difficult for anyone outside the room to hear cries for help.

Hotel telephone systems should be avoided when making long distance telephone direct dial or collect calls. Hotels often charge a steep surcharge fee (up to 100%) if the call will be on their monthly telephone statement. Guest insisting on charging several long distance calls to their room can reduce the hotel surcharge by utilizing the # button on the phone. Instead of hanging up after each call, press the # button then make any additional calls. The hotel will generally charge only for the first connection. Make direct and collect calls from a pay phone.

TELEPHONE EQUAL ACCESS: The cheapest way to place a call being paid for at time of placement is through a [1 +] carrier. Calls placed within the same state should also be accomplish through a [1 +] carrier instead of through the regional telephone system. Local telephone companies charge up to $.50 per minute for intrastate calls; whereas, a [1 +] carrier may charge below 10 cents per minute. Review the local telephone directory "Equal Access" page for available [1 +] carriers servicing your local area. Three long distance carriers are MCI (10222), AT&T(10288) and Sprint (10333). Procedure: Dial [1 +] the equal access code (+) area code (+) the telephone number of the party you wish to contact. Pre-paid phone cards also carry a low per minute rate structure.

On the subject of equal access, always try to reduce cost by using the lowest [1 +] carrier. As with any competitive industry, telephone companies do offer sales. Shop for the best provider suitable to your specific calling habits. For instance, if most long distance calls cross different local area network (LAN) systems are between 6 a.m. and 8 p.m. daily, the calls should be made through the lowest cost [1 +] carrier available during that time of day. Although every telephone is assigned a primary carrier, a [1+] customer may utilize the [1+] carrier of their choice at any time without changing their primary carrier status. It would be wise, prior to making any long distance call, to contact each "equal access" carrier and request a quote price for the specific connecting telephones. Deregulation of the telephone system was one of the best consumer deals in recent history. Review your local telephone directory subtitle *Equal Access for Long Distance Carriers* and start reducing long distance cost today. Customers who have problems keeping telephone cost low, should request a free audit. Abide by the audit recommendations.

AUCTIONS and SALES: Consumers can save or earn money through advantage buying. Cash is king at both auctions and sales. Buyers always set the price; therefore, there are few excuses to pay the retail asking price for anything. The manufacturer recommends a retail price. Retailers generally stick with the recommendation; but, only as long as the product sells. Walk away from retailers not willing to deal.

Sales do not include red-dot specials offered by retailers True sales cut up to 75 percent off the manufacturer's recommended retail price. The best deals are found with: (1) manufacturer close outs, (2) floor samples, (3) damaged freight goods, (4) seconds (irregular) merchandise, (5) liquidation's, (6) retail open or closing of business sales, (7) inventory adjustments, (8) excess inventory, (9) out-dated products, and (10) slow moving merchandise. A true sale, offers products cheap enough for buyers to re-market at a profit. A sale is never really a sale if you can't use or re-market the product at a profit. Never pay for something you can get for free!

Auctions are perhaps as close to the "pot-o-gold" at the end of the rainbow as it can get. Auctions occur by the thousands across America annually. A majority of auctions are never publicly advertised.

Government agencies appear to be the leading source of auctions. Agencies are constantly discarding outdated products, once the product no longer meets current project mandates. An excellent source of auction information is through direct contact with every government agency within your area. Request information on their procedures for disposing of excess products. Regional US Postal Centers conduct monthly "lot buy" auctions where whole bins of lost mail merchandise is placed on auction. The U. S. Department of Housing and Urban Development (HUD) hold auctions monthly selling excess real estate inventory. Check with the local reality board for information on Realtors who specialize in HUD auctions. Local colleges and universities auction surplus property periodically. Auto auctions usually require a dealer's license. At any auction, do not be surprised to find the inventory has already been picked over. Employees usually get first shot at the merchandise. Local auction firms, as well as, the National Auction Bulletin (1-800-327-2049) are excellent sources of information regarding upcoming events.

CAUTION: The wisest approach to any auction is the use of extreme caution. Auctions can be a clearing house for bogus merchandise. It is important to know the marketability of the product being auctioned. Auctions can destroy wealth quickly, if the bidder doesn't understand basic; yet, almost secret bidding rules. Make no doubt about it, every auction is worked by professionals who know how to play the game very well. Basic auction rules:

Basic Auction Rules

* Never bid at an auction until after attending several auctions as an observer.
* Inspect the merchandise before bidding.
* Never bid on merchandise without first establishing a resale value.
* Never bid on products with a short shelf life.
* Set your maximum price and write it down before the auction begins.
* Stick to your price. Never emotionally bid up.
* Never get carried away.
* If you don't understand the marketability of a product, consult with an expert before bidding.
* Cash is not king! Take a cashiers check valued at 20% over a predetermined bidding limit.
* Best auctions occur on bad weather days. Rarely are auctions canceled.
* All sales are final. Inspect the product before paying.
* Stick to your game plan.
* Rock the boat! Yell out your offer the instant the item number is called and before the auctioneer begins the bidding process.
* Don't sit up front. Sit as far to the rear as possible. Rest assured, when you yell out your offer, most potential bidders will not bid at all.
* Don't get shilled! A Shill (decoy) could be in the crowd to bid against everyone in order to drive the price as high as possible. Shills never have an intention of buying. Shilling is illegal; but, it's very difficult to prove and more difficult to take legal action.
* Photograph every item you plan to bid for during the public inspection. Review the photos for negative points. It is important to correct the bid price for anticipated repair costs.

SELLABLE MERCHANDISE: Locating and selling merchandise can be profitable, fun; and, as easy as child's play when the rules are followed. There should always be a potential buyer before purchasing the product. Aside from auctions, research classified ads to determine potential customers. Classified ads targeted for weekend release are usually posted on the newspaper website on Thursday preceding the weekend. Finding a buyer is not really difficult. For example, a typical want ad might read "want to buy a canoe, call Joe at ." The ad tells us several things about Joe. First, he wants to buy a canoe. Secondly, he has a contact phone number. And finally, Joe may not really know much about canoes since he was non-specific as too what type canoe he was wanting to buy. Idea! Telephone Joe and inquire about his price range, canoe style, material; and, what the canoe will be used for. Inform Joe there may be a canoe similar to what he seeks available in about three weeks and ask if it would be okay if you contacted him later. If he agrees, its time to get to work locating his canoe. This is where the Internet earns money!

Joe's canoe may be advertised outside the local area. Scan newspaper websites for Joe's canoe. Once the canoe is located, request the seller forward to you a photograph of the canoe. After reviewing the photographs looking for damage and general condition, make a low ball purchase price offer. If the offer is accepted, contact Joe. Give him a price (don't forget to include shipping from the seller to you) with instructions indicating where he may pick up the canoe. Issue to Joe a *Bill-of-Sale* fully describing the canoe with a statement that all sales are final. $50 per hour is a reasonable return for matching Joe up with his canoe.

Sources of merchandise include items personally owned, consigned by a friend, found in classified ads, or at auctions. It could be an item manufactured for a specific target consumer group. Children's toys and clothing are excellent resale items. Hand tools are another. Idea! Do you live near a large apartment complex or university? If so, chances are favorable there is available a steady supply of top quality, cheap to purchase merchandise. The investors edge lies in the knowledge of two basic facts. First, residents of these types of neighborhoods move frequently. Secondly, novice movers are notorious for improperly packing moving trucks. Almost without exception, they will either need to repack, attach a trailer, or abandon the property. Do yourself an them a favor. Help out your neighbor. Examine the excess items. Make a low ball offer to purchase the item before they have the opportunity to consider repackaging. Never suggest you are buying for resale and don't overextend. Purchase only items which can be stored in a spare room. Limit the purchase offer to not more than 40 cents on the dollar. Market your inventory through yard sales and flea markets.

CO-OP BARGAINS: Want to purchase just about anything cheap? Form a co-op. Combine your consumer needs with fellow church members, students, and coworkers to purchase insurance, medical coverage, or special consumer products at deep group discount. A group of 20 to 30 people can usually obtain substantial discounts. Groups do have buying power. Locate group members through advertisement. A typical ad might read: " Insurance cooperative is now accepting members." or "Need ten people to travel to Hawaii." Opportunities are endless!

BARTERING: Instead of using cash, consider bartering. Bartering goods and products between individuals is very acceptable. Need a birthday cake? Ask someone you know who has excellent baking skills to bake it for you. In return, you perform an odd job for them. Practically everyone who owns a car needs it washed. You've got the idea, so let's move along.

YOUR BUSINESS: Life experience and education are the two basic ingredients which create resale value; yet, Americans tend to give away the store where information is concerned. Proof that Information has value lies within copyright and patent laws. The moment a patent or copyright expires, copycats flock in to scoop up the idea. Giving away information is a serious American cultural flaw which has cheated millions of idealist out of personal fortunes. "Lose lips sink ships" has pulled the plug on many of business plans. The Coke Cola Company has been aware of the information trap for over 100 years. Coke realized that if they patented their safe drink formula, once the patent protection expired, copycats would steal the highly profitable concept. The Coke Cola formula is a closely guard secret hidden within a vault. Copycats are forever attempting to capture the taste of "the real thing."

Wise individuals blend life experience into their business plan. Business is the sharing with others a product or service in return for a fair compensation. Compensation comes in the form of either experience, money, or bartering. Lets examine a barter business in it's simplest and purest form. **In exchange for six non-canceled United States Postage stamps; plus, one self addressed stamped envelope (SASE),** the business will provide a delicious fruit drink recipe. The recipe uses ingredients found in most kitchens. With the texture of a smooth milkshake, it is a healthy substitute for both ice cream and frozen yogurt; and, takes the average person less than five minutes to make. Parents can treat themselves and their children while saving time and money. Adults and children alike have expressed enjoyment of this cool refreshing treat. The excellent recipe may be obtained by contacting: *Jean's Recipe at Swan Lake;* 370 Lakeshore Drive, Stockbridge, Georgia 30281-1709.

As a **free gift**, *Jean* will share a recipe she uses to convert outdated whole milk into delicious cheese. The process also takes about five minutes. The cheese may be eaten as a snack or as a noodle stuffier. *Jean* request that customers allow 4 weeks for her to fill their order.

Beneficial information can offer profit margins exceeding 1,000 percent. **Every idea, no matter how seemly foolish should be jotted down.** Formulate a plan of action to find a market for the idea. Market the information. Never conclude the idea is bad, if it doesn't sale. It may just need repackaging. One classified advertisement, returning 100 percent per week over the cost of the ad, when multiplied across several media providers can make anyone very rich. Thomas Edison tested hundreds of light bulb ideas before he struck success. Light bulbs are a big hit, no doubt about it. The donut is another simple idea generating fortunes. A single donut cost around five cents to produce in volume; yet, sells easily for 35 cents. Millions are sold annually by dozens of very popular donut companies. Everyone, at sometime or another, has an idea for making money pop into their thought process.

Every idea should be considered very important and jotted down. A single idea could lead to extreme wealth.

BROWN BAGGING: A personalized micro age alternative to the hot meal choice, at a fraction of cost. Hot breakfast and lunch meals away from the worksite typically cost around $6.50 excluding transportation and lost productivity associated with off-site meals. Productivity is impacted by late returning employees from lunch. Lost productivity lowers corporate profit margins while indirectly affecting stock prices. Employee compensation eventually suffers. Every employer should provide a facility for employees to enjoy a hot meal during their work day. Corporations without hot meal facilities should consider installing a smoke free eating area with plenty of micro-wave and refrigeration technology available. Brown-baggers really do become wealthy. James Stowers Jr., investor and money manager, in his book: *Yes you can....Achieve Financial Independence,* admits to brown-bagging peanut butter sandwiches to work. He is not alone. Mr. Sam Walton of Wal*Mart and Sam's Club fame became the richest person in America before his death. Mr. Walton was reported to be a brown-bagger. The author of this publication has been a brown bagger for the most part of forty working years.

Microwave technology easily converts a brown bag meal into a hot meal within minutes. A cost savings of up to around $3 per meal when compared to off-site hot meals is realistic. An annual savings of $750 can be leveraged into thousands of dollars through debt buy down or equity investing. Another important benefit to brown bagging is the social contact it often provides. New friendships are often found at the brown-bagger table. Friendships can lead to romance or group investment ideas. My wife and I met at the brown bagger table more than thirty years ago.

Avoid sitting at your work station during lunch. Consider meeting with fellow brown-baggers to exchange social and wealth building investment ideas. Perhaps, the group can chat about how they'll pay off their mortgages before the hot lunch crowd does. Perhaps, they will form an investment club. For club organizational guidance contact:

Club Assistance

* American Association of Individual Investors	(1-312-280-0170)
* Investors Alliance	(1-800-848-8900)
* Netcomplete - wed site information	(1-800-638-2661)

GET-A-JOB: What a novel idea; but, often easier said than done. Job applicants can reasonably expect to receive one interview offer for each 200 resumes' they submit. They could expect to receive one offer of employment for each six interviews. Employment opportunities are found through job fairs, union sponsored training programs, management councils, State labor departments, friends, family; and, the Internet super highway. Web based job search services connect employers with highly qualified job seekers. Resumes' are submitted electronically to prospective employers within a selected specialty and geographic area. The web service may charge a modest fee; however, the benefits associated with quick employment with a quality company generally far outweighs the cost.

Internet Job Centers

America's Job Bank:	http:// www. ajb.us
Career Mosaic:	http:// www. careermosaic.com
Career Path:	http:// www.careerpath.com
The Monster Board:	http://www. monster.com

The truth of "the wider the base, the taller the tower" directly correlates with wealth building. Next chapter please!

CHAPTER 2

WEALTH BUILDING INSIGHTS

WEALTH BUILDING: The stuff which creates a new millionaire in American several times throughout every day of the year. Solid motivation, developed through common sense, education, gut-feeling; and, street wise insights are the corner stones necessary for building a solid wealth foundation. Stocks are the long term winner, where investments are concerned; but, it's also an area where losers are generated, if the investor doesn't understand the game rules. "Investors are not as sophisticated as they should be. Widespread financial illiteracy exist among investors," according to Arthur Levitt, Chairman of the Securities and Exchange Commission (*Mutual Funds Magazine 8/96*). *Don't Die Broke*; can help investors correct practically any individual financial or investment illiteracy situation!

Investments offer no guarantees. No investment is good, unless it makes the investor money through well managed; yet, acceptable risk! A modest level of risk produces the fruits of success. As Chairperson Levitt suggested, "Investors are not as sophisticated as they should be." Risk associated with stock investing, for example, is not limited to the stock selection process. Risks must also include the investors ability to understand the total market process. Bank account holders and bond investors, are often exposed to a greater principle inflation adjusted risk, than stock investors. Lets make one thing clear. Anyone responsible for managing money, is exposed to a certain level of risk. Therefore, it is most critical to learn how to manage money within an acceptable risk level. Assuming acceptable risk often requires learning new skills; and, always requires enhanced motivation. Motivation leads to success and success is wealth rewarding. Review the following wealth building investment insights to gain a better understanding of asset management.

* Do not procrastinate. Procrastinating will dramatically alter investment objectives. Investment strategies must begin at the earliest possible age. Parents should encourage children to learn asset management, spending, saving; and, investment concepts at the earliest age. Children should be included in family asset management discussions.

* HALT any consumption binge! Avoid the temptation to destroy future wealth. Set aside big ticket items until investment returns can purchase them for you. Living for today leads to dying broke tomorrow.

* Do not shun risk associated with stocks, bonds; or, real estate. The risk of loss in purchasing power associated with taxes, inflation; and, depreciation are much greater than the long term risk associated with equity or debt investments. CD's, banking accounts; and, bank money market accounts offer the poorest long term investment total return of practically any other type investment. Avoid whenever possible!

* Reserve cash (rainy day stuff) should be parked in a Broker CD; or, money market account. Limit checking account balances to 150 percent of the required monthly cash flow; and, savings account balances to 200 percent of monthly gross income.

* Invest enough money into an employer sponsored retirement account necessary to trigger 100 percent of the employer contribution matching.

* Stock investing is not a get rich quick program; nor, is it started with no money down. Risk of losses are inversely proportional to the available investment principle. Low dollar investment sums, except through DRIP, DPP; and, retirement programs, will usually create loses. $10,000 is the school of thought of some professional stock traders.

* Stock and mutual fund trading is controlled through predetermined rules supported with a strong financial base. Stock trading mandates the investor make trading decisions without emotion. Ever heard the term "poker face?"

* Knowledge is gained through the pain of losing as well as through the pleasure of winning. Past results never guarantee future results; however, history tends to repeat itself. Jump start your portfolio, based upon years of proven investment strategies outlined in chapter 4. It is not necessary to recreate the investment wheel, just roll what exist.

* Seek investments with a Return on Equity (ROE) yielding a minimum of twice the 30 year treasury bond yield.

* The Price to Earnings Ratio (P/E) reflects the number of years it will take the investor to recoup the initial investment through the current level of generated company earnings.

* Holdings within Bond a portfolio should be limited to 80 percent of the investor's age times the investors net worth. Social Security account value must be considered bond holdings when computing any net worth to bond holdings ratio. Social security account value is approximately 15.7 percent of reported earnings.

* Retiree's generally make a drastic mistake by investing 100 percent of their retirement funds into a bond mutual fund seeking income. Growth of equity, is far more important than dividend yields, if yields are not absolutely essential, to meet basic life support needs.

* Strive to seek net returns exceeding taxes, commissions; and, inflation. Anything less looses wealth.

* Every category of investment has a cycle. Every investment will develop into a cycle hitting new low and high price points.

* Stocks may provide wealth opportunities regardless of the stock price direction.

* Stocks with a sustained price momentum up trend should be bought "long" against the market; and, sold when down-trending.

* Stocks experiencing a sustained price momentum down trend should be sold "short" against the market. They should be repurchased when cycling into a new up trend off a price low point accompanied by volume trading activity above the stocks historical moving average.

CAUTION: Short sellers can get burned, if the shorted stock price continues to rise above the short sell price; or, if the owner, from who's account the short sell stock was borrowed ,decides to sell during a downtrend.

* Each stock is a market unto itself. Stay out of the market; and, hold cash; unless, a specific stock, bond; or, mutual fund can be identified as a potential profit performer.

* The cost of a single cup of coffee, when diverted daily into an 8 percent yielding account; compounding monthly for 30 years, can realize a total return exceeding $45,000, excluding taxes. Not a bad deal! Get the idea! A small amount of money when deposited regularly can make a big difference if yields are compounded over a long time.

* "Rule 72" illustrates the compounding principle. The rule is; however, over simplified. It doesn't adjust total returns for taxes, commissions; or, the creeping decease of inflation. "Rule 72" illustrates how to determine the specific number of years it should take an investment to double by dividing 72 by the yield rate.

EXAMPLE: A typical bank savings account yielding four percent will take, in theory, 29 years to double the original bank deposit. A $1,000 initial deposit into a bank savings account yielding 4 percent, after being adjusted returns for taxes, commissions; or, the creeping decease of inflation. "Rule 72" illustrates how to determine the specific number of years it should take an investment to double by dividing 72 by the total rate of return.

EXAMPLE: A typical bank savings account yielding four percent will take, in theory, 29 years to double the original bank deposit. A $1,000 initial deposit into a bank savings account yielding 4 percent, after being adjusted for a 28 percent federal income tax, 6 percent state tax, 2 percent inflation; and ½ percent bank administration fees annually, is at best the poorest total return investment available. The exception, of course, would be a lower yielding account or no account at all. Not a good deal for wealth building!

* Unexpected reported earnings exceeding analyst projections will tend to push stock prices. Be alert for earnings exceeding analyst projections by 3 to 5 percent; or, higher especially if management is holding a large block of un-exercised options and the company leadership has announced retirement plans. Liars exist throughout every economic sector. Misrepresenting earnings to boost personal insider gains can not be discounted by investors. Do not be surprised if insider selling accompanied by an amended earnings report occurs shortly after a report exceeding analyst projections is released. Amended reports are often released after the market closes. IT SHOULD BE A VIOLATION OF FEDERAL LAW TO DELAY THE MARKET OPENING OF ANY STOCK, FOR ANY REASON; OR, TO RELEASE CORPORATE REPORTS OF ANY NATURE AFTER THE MARKET HAS CLOSED. AFTER ALL, SHOULDN'T INVESTORS HAVE A SAY IN THE RELEASE OF ANYTHING THAT EFFECTS THE STOCK OF THEIR COMPANY. Mail your opinion regarding this matter to the CHAIRMAN of the SECURITIES and EXCHANGE COMMISSION. DO IT!

* The stock market has historically yielded a gross total return of approximately 10 percent annually since its inception 200 years ago.

* A reasonable target investment rate of net total return from the stock market is twice the 30 year Treasury bond yield, after adjusting for taxes, commissions, spreads; and, inflation.

* Inflation, appreciation, depreciation, fees, commissions, liquidity, yields, taxes; and, the investors time horizon must be considered when selecting an investment sector.

* Inflation, depreciation, bank fees, commissions, taxes; and, impulse spending are wealth destroyers eating away assets.

* Depreciation is loss of value due to usage (automobiles wear out). Inflation is the cost of replacement at some point in the future. Inflation is illustrated by a $100 purchase in 1996 costing $320 at 30 years hence. Remember when good old Coke Cola cost a nickel. In 1997, the price could easily exceed a dollar. That's inflation!

* Automobiles depreciate at a replacement cost of between 35 and 50 cents per mile (1997 dollars), until the vehicle reaches raw material value, at which time, the value will rise as raw material cost increase.

* Social Security: A hidden tax never intended to be a retirement plan. A bad idea gotten worse. Contrary to popular belief, Social Security distributes checks to the disabled, dependent children of deceased tax payers, non-citizens; and, to mentally insane life term criminals. Social Security is anything but secure. Since inception, it has been a dumping ground for low yielding treasury bills, bonds; and, notes the investment community has considered valueless. Investments held within social security rarely keep up with inflation. The system exist through ever increasing contributions from the current workforce accompanied by ever-changing age and qualification benefit rules. Social Security was a bad idea made worse through outdated technology. In countries without a government managed social security system, members of society needing charity generally receive

better attention from their families and religious leaders.

The federal government must cease dumping treasury junk into the program; and, began to seek returns from common stocks; or, similar investments offering equity growth. For example; Mexico, in 1994, approached default and was bailed out through substantial loans from the United States. By February 1997, Mexico had repaid the loan, creating a handsome 500 million dollar profit for the International Monetary Fund, according to President Bill Clinton, during a television interview. The Social Security Administration could have loaned Mexico the money with little risk. After all, doesn't Mexico have an abundant supply of natural resources they could have used as collateral.

Top quality corporate bonds, international mutual funds; or, the *Standard and Poor's 500 Index* beats the investment total return on Social Security investments hands down. Social Security, perhaps should be reorganized to eliminate the bureaucrats who apparently missed the boat when it comes to understanding true investment concepts. Investors (practically every tax payer) should seriously consider insisting the system be privatized and managed by a board of governors consisting of world class investors, such as Warren Buffet, Boon T. Pickens, Ed Johnson, Peter Lynch, and John Templeton. There are many top managers with a track record of investment success. The Social Security folks are not even close to being ranked among the true investment winners. It's ironic that the same federal government who insist Americans are inept in managing their investments actually exempts Congress and thousands of government workers from paying the hidden tax of Social Security. Waste and fraud allegations are widely reported within the system, clearly illustrates that no one will ever care about your money as much as you do. A true; yet, simple concept promoted by the Investors Alliance (1-800-848-8900). "Social Security Computer glitch shorted recipients by $850 million" (*Investor's Business Daily* Oct. 7, 1996). For over 22 years, Social Security cheated 426,000 elderly recipients out of proper accreditation for retirement compensation. The shorting of retirement checks began in 1971 and went undetected until 1994. Two years after identifying the problem; 295,000 retirees were still not paid. Sadly to report, more than 57,500 retirees died never knowing they were cheated.

Don't be passive! Workers putting money into the social security system work hard for their money. They have the right to speak out regarding social security, flat tax; or, any of the numerous taxes used by the hill gang to destroy individual wealth. Register concerns with your congressional representative via telephoning their district office; or, the Capitol switchboard at (202-224-3121). Remind them about the county governments near the Houston, Texas area, who opted out of Social Security prior to Congress changing the law, only to pay their retirees 500 percent more retirement benefits than their Social Security counter parts employed by neighboring counties. An employee of the opt-out counties, retiring after 30 years of service, can receive retirement benefits of up to $3500 monthly, compared to about $600 monthly, a worker employed by a social security backed county would receive after working under identical conditions for the same 30 years. Is there a conspiracy to keep workers poor? Remind the elected officials, they are removing from you a basic right to acquire property guaranteed by the *Constitution and Bill of Rights* of the United States of America. They remove investor property rights by: first, collecting social security; and, secondly, by not insisting the administration of the system seek a maximum investment total return through a well balanced diversification of investment assets.

If Japan, China, Mexico; and, other countries around the globe are allowed to purchase U.S. Treasury investment instruments tax free, at American tax payer expense, why shouldn't our social security system invest in their real estate, utility companies; and, food suppliers. Communist and democratic countries around the earth have unrestricted free access to invest their money into American debt. Why don't we smart Americans return the courtesy by investing into their various economic sectors. Instead, the federal government will excessively over tax the American worker and use the money to pay foreign governments interest on their treasury debt holdings. Many foreign governments are presently allowing our government to pay them tax payer money so they can build war machines capable of attacking our homeland

* Every investor should obtain a benefit statement from the Social Security Administration (1-800-772-1213) semi-annually. The statement is an important document necessary to compute net worth. All investment considerations are based upon net worth allocation percentages.

* Speaking of addressing concerns to elected government officials, don't forget the importance of attending every local town hall, Board of Education; and, County Commissioner meeting. Your wealth may depend upon you knowing what is happening within your local area. Public meetings are an excellent source of investment information.

* Earnings Growth Rate (EGR) is the percentage of change in earnings measured over a specific time. EGR is usually measured over the most recent quarter when compared to the same quarter one year earlier. An EGR of 25 percent annually; or, twice the Price Earnings Ratio (PE) is very positive (bullish).

* A (PE/EGR) ratio of less than one is bullish.

* As previously discussed, a key element in the investment game is to keep "spreads" and commissions as low as possible. "A penny saved is a penny earned," should never be forgotten. Investors having developed investment skills well enough to conduct their own stock analytic research, should utilize the services of deep discount brokerage firm. Limiting commissions to less than one percent, of the trade transaction value is a very realistic goal. Try 1-800:

Deep Discount Brokerage Firms

Accutrade	858-9771
Ceres Securities	628-6100
Freedom Investments	424-1014
Investex	822-2050
J.B. Oxford	656-1776
Kennedy, Cabot Company	252-0090
Midwood	643-9663
Mid America	320-1214
R.J. Forbes	754-7687
Regal Securities	786-9000
Wall Street Equities	796-3456

* Due to trade settlement time limitations, the majority of deep discount brokerage firms recommend investors: (1) open equity accounts initially through the brokerage money market account, (2) stocks be held by the firm in a "street name," and (3) the account number be included with all correspondence and deposits. We endorse the recommendation for many reasons. First, the real possibility of valuable stock certificates being lost in the mail is eliminated. Secondly, the funds keep working for the investor.

* A majority of discount brokers require their brokerage money market account be established through a margin account. "Margin" is a fancy word for " payment on demand " loan; whereas, investors put up a percentage of the investment money necessary buy a particular amount of stock while borrowing funds from the brokerage firm to purchase additional shares of the same stock. Don't let this frighten you. Investors are never obligated to borrow

money for stock investing. In fact, for the majority of investors, it shouldn't even be a consideration. Go ahead and open the margin account. Simply don't use it to leverage a position unless the position is purchased and sold according to the *Winning Strategies* outlined in chapter 4. Keep the margin position low and always track the stocks 15 week *Exponential Moving Average.*

Margin enables the investor to increase potential profits through leverage. Let's illustrate. An investor purchases $10,000 of stock while borrowing $10,000 from the broker to purchase additional stock. Each puts up 50 percent of the investment money. The brokerage collects interest, usually at the brokerage call rate plus two percent. Some brokerage firms may charge margin interest based upon a "prime plus" fee schedule. Leverage works only if the stock value rises. Should the stock price rise by 10 percent, the investor's equity moves by $2,000 ($20,000 times 10%). A brokerage annual interest rate of 8 percent would reduce the $2,000 by $800 ($10,000 times 8 percent). Should the margin be held a full year before the position is liquidated, the brokerage would be paid $10,800 while the investor would receive $11,200. The investor would have a slight $200 advantage. The advantage increases with stock hitting higher prices over a short time span.

WARNING! As tempting as margin may be, it can destroy investor wealth very quickly in a stock price down-trend. Brokerage firms will generally call their loan when the stock price drops 20 percent below the price set at the time the margin was granted. Avoid using margin: (1) until trading skills are developed, (2) if the stock or general market is in a down-trend; or, (3) the investor does not have cash available to pay the brokerage firm should a margin call occur. Never be forced into selling an investment to cover a debt.

* Social Security, retirement accounts; and, debt investments, such as money market funds, are the three vehicles providing income to a major portion of the retirement community. Money during retirement must be actively managed in order for the investor not to die broke. Yield distribution and time are the elements factored into the maximum investment draw down allowed annually. One question asked by a lot of retirees is: How long will my retirement money last? The answer to their question may be computed from the following matrix.

Rate of Yield to Year Percentage Draw-down

					(A)				
		3	4	5	6	7	8	9	10
	6	23	28	36					
	7	19	21	25	33				
	8	16	17	20	23	30		**(D)**	
	9	14	14	16	18	22	28		
	10	12	13	14	15	17	20	26	
	11	11	11	12	13	14	16	19	25
(B)	12	10	10	11	11	12	14	16	18
	13	8	9	9	10	11	12	13	15
	14	8	8	9	9	10	11	11	13
	15	7	7	8	8	9	9	10	11
					(C)				

(A) After tax rate of return yield percentage.

(B) Pre-Tax rate of spending percentage of total principle.

(C) Years to zero principle balance (broke).

(D) Funds will never diminish in the blank matrix.

EXAMPLE #1: Account of $10,000
Yield 7%
Rate/Spending 7%
Balance never diminish

EXAMPLE #2: Account of $10,000
Yield 7%
Rate/Spending 10%
Balance zero in 17 years

NOTE: The matrix does not factor for inflation. Additionally, life after retirement could exceed 20 years. Therefore, the draw down should be calculated annually.

* Investor Protection Trust, Inc., of Arlington, Virginia estimates that less than 20 percent of investors are truly knowledgeable about financial matters.

* Ibbotson Associates of Chicago reports their research indicates the growth of one dollar between 1929 and 1994 produced a total return of:

1929-1994 Dollar Equity Growth

Inflation	$ 8.35
T. Bills	$ 12.19
T. Bonds	$ 25.85
Common Stock	$ 810.54
Small Cap Stock	$2,842.77

* Raw farm land has also performed very well as a long term investment. Farm land located throughout the Midwestern states sold for about $1.50 per acre in the late 1800's. However, by 1996 the same farm land had appreciated to an average of $3,500 per acre. Farm land value has doubled about every 8.3 years as the land becomes scarce due to over population across the grain belt of America. On a side note: Over population of the American heartland will eventually shift away from the United States the honor of being the worlds top grain producer. A few forecasters are so bold as to predict either China and Russia will hold that title within the next 100 years for several reasons. Both nations have millions of non-polluted mineral rich farm land lying unspoiled by agricultural chemicals and gas powered farm equipment pollution. Secondly, both countries restrict immigration into their land. Finally, their population expansion is under control. What does this all mean? Inflation will run rampant as future food prices escalate when Americans become dependent upon foreign grain as we have oil. Grain will become a weapon of war more powerful than all the nuclear weapons and smart bombs combined. The United States military may protect the interest of oil producing allies; but, it can't force foreign governments to plant crops. Food prices will rise faster at the market place than at the supplier. Food merchandisers will report enhanced earnings and their reports will boost stock prices. Looking long term, watch the food sector stock very close.

* A $10 per share investment in the early 1960's into Warren Buffet's Berkshire Hathaway Corporation (BRKA) appreciated to $48,600 per share by July 9,1997. That's the stuff millionaires are made from! Mr. Buffet has perhaps created more millionaires than any single person alive today, yesterday; and forever more.

* How about 300 shares of the Minnesota Mining, and Manufacturing Company (MMM), purchased in 1913 for one dollar apiece; splitting 1 share into 460,800 shares by December 1995, worth approximately $27 million with an annual dividend of $800,000.

* Every stock has a price cycle based upon investor greed.

* No stock trader is a 100 percent winner. The game is to win on a majority of trades.

* Loses will occur if the wrong stock is bought; or, the right stock is sold at the wrong time.

* No single stock theory will guarantee profits in all market conditions.

* No investment is good; unless, it increases in value. That includes stocks!

* Professional investors and financial managers, as a group, are correct on their investment choices only about 60 to 70 percent of the time. Independent investors can easily beat the pro's for a variety of reasons.

* The Standard and Poor 500 is an unmanaged index.

* Few professionals can beat the S/P 500 Index growth year after year.

* We dare say, anyone can develop critical stock selection and selling skills through motivation and practice. In fact, 9 year old children have reportedly done very well in the stock market.

* The years between 20 and 70 are very short. Begin an investment plan at the earliest age.

* Successful investment plans are easily understood, offers simplicity, provides steady growth; and, is liquid.

* Get an education, obtain employment, establish finances, keep charge debt low then purchase a house. Reach a reserve cash position of at least three month reserve cash plus $10,000 before purchasing a single issue stock.

* Under-capitalization creates losers. To illustrate: consider the purchase of 100 shares of a stock priced at $10 per share. A $1,000 stock purchase could cost the investor a minimum of $100 in commissions (round-trip) through a full service brokerage firm. The stock "bid" price would need to increase 11.3 percent just for the investor to break-even on the "bad" deal. Purchasing the same stock through a deep discount broker; DPP; or, through a DRIP program. Assuming the commission cost is set at a flat fee of $96 (round-trip), the $10,000 investment would need to increase a mere .0098 of one percent for the investor to break-even on the "good" deal. Should the stock rise by 11.3 percent, the $10,000 investor, who mistakenly purchased their shares from a full service firm will lose money after adjusting their gain for inflation and capitol gains tax. Guess what? The $10,000 investor, who purchased identical shares through a deep discount broker, walks away with a substantial net trading profit of up to 9 percent! Invest through a mutual fund, DRIP; or DPP until a positive net worth allows individual stock selection.

* The seller sets the bid price; whereas, the buyer sets the offer; or, acceptance price. The buyer sets the price the moment the seller agrees to accept the buyer's money; and, the product exchange occurs. Every buyer, automatically becomes a future seller.

* Every item purchased, should be bought, at the best auction price. America consumers are in the minority where wise shopping for the best deal is concerned. Around the Earth, most consumers "price haggle" for the best price.

* Americans tend to accept at face value, prices as they are marked on products. Negotiating for an advantage price is not customary in the American economic culture controlled by big business. Consumers rarely deal

directly with the business owner (stockholder);or, management for an advantaged price. Management generally won't price deal because they are either bonus; or, option motivated to show profits at any cost.

* Stock traders who win, do so with a strong defense against losses. Stocks should never be purchased during a down trend; unless, the down trend is off an historical high price with the current price not more than seven percent off the high point.

* Don't buy a single share of stock in the months of May through October; unless, the *Dow, Standard and Poor's 500 Index*; plus the *NASDAQ Composite* are each tracking in an up trend to their 200 day arithmetic moving average. Investors may view the market direction daily within the *Investor's Business Daily* publication.

* Any investor expecting to double their money within a year will usually fail. Net equity growth of 10 to 15 percent annually is reasonably obtainable. It is critical for every investor to know their net worth value throughout their investing career.

* Thousands of stock fluctuate from 1 to 5 percent daily; or, 10 to 20 percent annually. However, perhaps less than 100 companies realize a 100 percent stock price growth annually.

* A stock experiencing a 50 percent down trend requires a 100 percent rise off the bottom to get back to a break-even point. Think about those odds!

* Every stock price hitting a new high level obtained new high points along the way. A stock entering the IPO market at $10 per share reaches new high points all the way to $100 per share and beyond.

* "Greed" is a two edge sword of destruction; but, when used with caution can make investors rich.

* Stocks in the $20 range, according to *The Wall Street Digest* (1-941-954-5500), tend to double in price more than any other stock price range.

* Stock traders tend to "hold-em and fold-em" during the wrong price performance cycle. They tend to sell stocks moving up in price, while buying or holding stocks going down in price. Both actions are wrong! Why sell a stock making money; or, buy one loosing money?

* Never buy a stock which has developed a performance down trend that has extended beyond seven percent off the historical high price point. Why? As a stock trends downward, current investors will tend to buy more instead facing the cold realization they've made a mistake. They actually believe, although incorrectly, that by averaging down they'll make more money as the stock price rebounds. What they fail to realized, is that they are harming themselves by helping the stock develop "overhead supply" pressure while the short sellers are creating the potential of a "short squeeze." Both situations can be disastrous for the shareholder. Overhead supply and short squeezing will depress future price upward momentum price acceleration.

* "Overhead Supply" hinders the stock price rebound. Investors who purchased the stock during a price decline have a tendency to liquidate as the price rebounds back to their initial purchase price. They generally will not sell as the price drops for fear of losing money. What they don't realize is they have already lost their equity. Holding on for a rebound only aggravates the loss as inflation eats away at future purchase power.

* "Short Squeeze" develops as short sellers begin to sell short on small up tick corrections during a sustained price down trend. Then without warning, the: (1) price begins to rise above the short sell price; or, (2) the

shareholders who's account the short seller borrowed the position against, decides to sell. Either case, the short seller has to purchase the stock off the auction open market to cover their short position. Initially, the short covering will push prices up The upward price movement will trigger an overhead supply stock sell off. The stock will develop a price downward trend almost without exception, enter into a base line; and, rise after the overhead pressure has been removed. Overhead pressure is only removed by current holders either selling at a break-even or loss point. That's assuming, of course, the company doesn't eliminate the pressure through bankruptcy.

* Repeat once again! "Overhead Supply" and "Short Squeeze" are two excellent excuses to always dump (sell) a stock down-trending. Their absents, is an excellent reason to buy stocks up-trending past a previous historical high. Investors purchasing a stock at an historical high point is well ahead of the game because overhead pressure and short squeezing does not exist. Often or not, the investor will actually be buying low and selling higher! The selling point materializes at the moment overhead pressure increases the risk against future substantial gains.

* A stock moving down one penny below the initial purchase price is a loser. Investors generally will not sell stocks going down in price due to human emotions associated with failure. The sad truth is that a loss has already occurred; and, will usually continue to occur, until the investor shifts the equity into a winning investment.

* Every stock has a "bid/ask" ratio commonly termed as a "spread."

* The "bid" price is what the market maker will pay for a stock purchased from the investor.

* The "ask" price is what the investor will pay the market maker for the stock.

* Spreads are hidden commissions; and, as with the cost of any commission must be reduced when possible.

* Stocks trading above $10 per share tend to be traded by several market makers; have good supply and demand volume, have the least price manipulation, and lower spreads.

* Stocks hit historical high price points when demand is outrunning supply. The price will usually trend higher until the supply/demand equation balances. Stocks closing at the top of their daily price trading range with a strong volume well above the stocks historical 50 day arithmetic moving average are potential profit makers.

* Stock charts help investors identify winners.

* Momentum trend performance monitored through a moving average curve has the potential to produce substantial wealth with limited downside risk.

* There are no single stock selection strategy; rule-of-thumb, formula; or, theory, which will produce consistent profits 100 percent of the time.

* Stocks develop price movements for a variety of reasons. Eventually every stock will weaken and develop a price failure.

* Do not allow emotions to control investment decisions. If the numbers aren't right, stay out of the market!

* Once a stock price trends above the purchase price, never let a profit convert into a loss. Sell losers!

* Never average down. Always average up. Should a stock price double; buy more, if the stock still meets the buy characteristic discussed in chapter 4.

* Tracking a stock price moving average reduces downside risk.

* Take-over tender offers are excellent opportunities to sell. Why? The reason you bought the stock has changed.

* Stock "float" is the number of authorized shares less shares held by management. It represents true market supply.

  CAUTION: Companies reporting, "the Board of Directors have authorized stock repurchasing" could be a trap. Why? Repurchasing stock from the open market eludes to removing supply (float) from the market place. Investors perceive the supply will be restricted allowing demand to push prices upward. As prices move up; however, corporate insiders holding substantial blocks of stock could sell out. Supply is flooded and prices fall. When prices bottom out, the company now utilizes stockholder's equity (cash on hand) to repurchase the stock (demand) which will reduce the "float"(supply) while forcing the stock price to rise. Management gets rich at stockholder's expense. Money is used to purchase stock instead of corporate expansion, research; or, dividend payout. A high percentage of announced repurchase programs fail to materialize. After all, why should management follow though with their program, after they have accomplish their objective of making themselves richer at shareholder expense. Wait until a stock repurchase program begins, before buying into this game. Corporate debt often accelerates after a stock repurchase program is announced, especially should management sweep away the company cash reserve ; or, borrow funds to implement the buyback.

* After purchasing a stock, watch the stock price daily to determine if the stock is forming a price base, down-trending; or, up-trending. If the stock is trading within a narrow daily price range, even if it is experiencing a slight down trend (losing), hold the position until the price falls to 7 percent below the purchase price. A potential breakout into an up trend is extremely possible before the price down trend will trigger a sell signal. Should the stock price fail to up trend within 15 weeks after purchasing, consider liquidating.

* Stock price down-trending is often very positive for future appreciation, if the down trend is off a historical high price point; and, the stock price has developed into a base within seven percent of the high point. Hold the current position; but, be mentally prepared to sell should the down trend exceed seven percent off the high point. Allow the stock to fluctuate during inter-day trading. It's the final tick that really counts.

* Stock price up-trending, when confirmed by two consecutive Wednesday closing price ticks, is very positive. Once the price up trend is confirmed, investors can generally relax while monitoring the price weekly. Don't be a Chicken Hawk! There is no reason to watch a stock price each minute, hour; or, day once an up trend has been confirmed through a moving average computation. Review chapter 4 moving average strategy of investing.

* Taxes and commissions are deferred while holding on to an up-trending stock.

* Investments should make the investor money. Pure and simple! Hire a stock to create wealth. Fire it, if it doesn't!

* Retired folks usually make three mistakes. First, they invest into income producing investments that generally always fail to beat tax adjusted inflation. Secondly, they tend to avoid stocks. Finally, retirees are usually weighted too heavily into bonds; or, real estate, based upon their investment allocation to net worth. Review chapter 4 for our suggested asset investment diversification schedule.

* Net worth = Assets - Liability.

* Assets are the total market value of everything owned.

* Liability is the credit lien against assets.

* Never put all investment eggs into a common basket.

* Diversification requires the adjustment to an investment portfolio with age, economic and political events, plus net worth change.

* Net worth growth is mandatory for wealth building. It's very important!

* Stock "float" price correlation to the company it represents is a myth. After an IPO is completed, stocks trading in the float auction benefits the company very little. The company received their cash from the stock sell to their underwriter often years earlier.

* Stocks with an annual revenue growth rate exceeding 25 percent; or, twice the (P/E) ratio are very attractive.

* Bonds fall way short on total return performance when compared to stock investment performance. Bonds purchased through annual employer sponsored bond drives should be purchased only after very careful consideration of how the purchase will fit into a well laid net worth growth oriented investment plan.

* Direct bond purchases prior to retirement should be limited to mutual funds and money market accounts.

* Investment liquidity is the key term to remember.

* Learning stock analytical concepts is easy.

* Nothing a stockbroker sells, is guaranteed to enhance your wealth. They do not have enough faith in their recommendations to issue a written contract offering investor protection against losses. Why not?

* Hang up the phone fast when contacted by cold caller selling anything. If you listen for 30 seconds, you are subject to becoming a victim. You won't insult the blood thirsty idiots, who think nothing of invading the privacy of your home time. They don't respect your rights. No one should have their quality of life interrupted by outside intruders. Telephone solicitors will make you a victim no differently then a thief burglarizing your home.

* Hot tips burn! Many excellent reasons exist illustrating logic as to why one should never purchase a stock based upon hot tips. First, the tipster could be distributing illegal insider information. Secondly, stocks purchased based upon hot tips lack investor self evaluated analytical advantages. Third, hot tip purchases are strictly emotion driven. Finally, the person offering the tip could be a seller. Beware of any market maker of a stock trying to sell! If the numbers are not favorable, avoid wealth divesting!

* Investing is a serious business. Keep records. Pay taxes. Learn from mistakes, as well as from success. Hone analytical skills through a "play portfolio" before putting real money at risk. Learn the game. Establish a solid financial base. Complete the income and balance worksheets in the Appendix. Develop the mind set required to prevent emotional knee jerk reaction to market tricksters. Investors ignoring these rules will eventually fail.

* *Investor's Business Daily, Wards Business Directory, Standard and Poor's Stock Guide, Value Line;* and, the

Security and Exchange Commission: website (http://www.sec.gov.cgibn/srch-edgar), offers critical subjective information on public corporations.

* Pay yourself first, at least 10 percent of each pay check, before paying or giving charity to anyone. The "golden years" are mighty lonely when you are abandoned by those you've supported throughout your working life.

* Never forget! Allocate funds to pay for transportation as they occur. The shop visit to your favorite mechanic or dealer may exceed $500 just for routine maintenance. "Power by the mile" is not a new concept to business; yet, it is drastically ignored by practically every American worker. Deposit into a brokerage money market count, each and every paycheck, funds equal to 80 percent of the American Automobile Association mileage cost estimates for your location to cover transportation cost for each mile you've operated your vehicle since the last pay check. THIS IS CRITICAL FOR WEALTH BUILDING!

* Charity is not always a situation where it is "better to give than receive." Before getting carried away with giving away your future security, ask yourself how many charities or religious organizations offer retirement security, medical insurance, asset management training, legal assistance; or, free elderly care. Bet, most investors can't count the charities they know who provides these services on one hand! People who have not achieved personal financial security should revisit their charity beliefs. They should first strive to obtain a level of wealth that will eliminate the need for charity during their golden years, before even thinking of giving equity valued gifts to charity; or, anyone else for that matter. Do not be offended by taking on the responsibility of caring for yourself in the "golden years" before giving away equity gifts. Charity can be in the form of volunteering time. Time is very valuable. Giving to charity during wealth building years may be the ideal ticket into the poorhouse for you!

* Peace of mind is essential.

* Debt is a wealth killer and should be limited to 20 percent of gross earnings, excluding mortgage payments. Debt loads exceeding 20 percent, could be an early warning alert of the financial storm on the horizon. Never be ashamed to seek professional credit help. Most states have approved credit counselors.

* Why are stocks the number one preferred investment choice of many? They are easy to manage, have liquidity; and, low start-up cost. It is truly a transportable business that can be operated from any where on the earth where telephone service; or, computer on-line service is available.

* A stock investment plan must be easy to manage, offer liquidity, have low commissions, low spreads, low downside risk; and, a potential steady growth up trend.

* Eliminate the investment over-choice syndrome. Stick with one or two proven investment strategies. Remain focused on a well defined investment plan. Avoid trying to beat the market through switching between the hundreds of alleged winning stock picking schemes in existence on any given day. NO ONE CAN BEAT THE MARKET BECAUSE THEY ARE THE MARKET!

* Learn to say "NO" with a click.

* Cold callers push junk to the investors disadvantage. They know that one out of ten people will impulse buy just about anything. They also are aware that most investors actually work for a living; and, are either tired or hungry after a full days work. In short, they know you are disadvantaged. Level the playing field. Hang-up!

* Flexibility, time, compounding, remaining focused, learning from mistakes and success, being properly financed,

knowing the game rules; and, eliminating emotional responses to market corrections will reduce stock market associated risk.

* Equity investing (stocks, real estate, precious metals, antiques, etc.) offer superior investment returns over debt (bonds, CD's, money market, bank accounts, etc.) investing.

* The average person can beat the Wall Street pro's simply through: (1) flexibility, (2) dollar-cost-averaging to the upside, (3) DRIP and DIP investing, (4) conducting their own analytic studies; or, (5) investing into indexed mutual funds during sustained market and sector up trends, especially during the good Dow months of November through April. During bad Dow months invest into a high yielding money market account. The "Lazy-Hazy Days of Summer" can wipe out wealth very fast. Take a vacation while keeping your money liquid between May 1st and October 31st annually. In all fairness, the month of May has for several years produced some of the *Dow*'s best single month returns; however, May has also seen it's share of market corrections.

* Want to locate stocks selling at wholesale to book value? Consider market capitalization (MC) and private value (PV). MC = shares authorized (x) current price. PV = total assets less total liabilities. MC/PV Ratios of less than "one" are usually a good long term bet toward future equity growth, as market forces push the floating stock evaluation toward book value.

$\frac{MC}{PV} = 1$, represents book value. $\frac{MC}{PV} =< 1$ represents under value. $\frac{MC}{PV} => 1$ represents over value.

* A stock selling 10 percent below book will yield 11.1 percent as the stock price fights negative "overhead pressure" forces to regain book value evaluation. On the other hand, a stock selling at 34 percent discount will yield the investor a hefty 50 percent return as the stock rebounds, if the stock ever rebounds. Ironically, the 50 percent does not mean much if the price rebound takes 10 years. In fact, the stock could rebound 50 percent and still be an inflation adjusted looser.

* Value Line (1-800-535-9648), is an excellent investment tool covering over 1,700 companies. The survey includes data on stocks which Value Line has determined to be selling at wholesale to book value. Value line services are available through CD-ROM, mail order; or, the library system. We suggest investors use library resources until a financial base has been developed. As wealth increases, expand into other methods of reviewing the excellent services offered by Value Line.

* All the money does not matter, if the importance of good health maintenance is ignored. It is quite possible to exhaust life long savings on medical cost, during the last two years of life. Enter into an exercise program without delay regardless of age. Do not smoke, avoid drugs, limit alcohol consumption; and, eat nutritional foods. A healthy body promotes a healthy mind. Logical thinking is essential for successful wealth building.

* Slavery is; was, and has always been a violation of natural law; yet, American workers insist on laboring their entire lives only to die flat broke. Why? First, they discount the importance of education. A majority of kids graduating from high school want no more of a system that took away 12 years of their life without so much as providing an opportunity for finical independence. Kids spend years running around the playground, learning how Columbus discovered America (which he did not); or, fancy mathematics totally useless in the real world. Secondly, workers tend to ignore the actual cost associated with income production. They fail to consider themselves a production cost center where income producing expenses are a major factor of income production. One critically overlooked income production expense is transportation cost.

Finally, workers make a gross mistake by entrusting management of their retirement money to their union, employer; or, the government. Few retirement funds prohibit corporate America from dipping into the fund to sweep profits away. Your investment contribution may belong to you; but, the profits from those contributions often belong to the corporation managing the account. The Federal government retirement system is no different. It is in worse financial condition than most private pension funds because under-funding shortfalls are not insured. The Federal Government Retirement System shortfall could easily exceed an estimated $14 trillion. Perhaps, to reduce the short fall disparity, the government went on a firing binge in early 1995. The "reinvented government" concept backfired, as services to the consumer taxpaying public were curtailed. Like it's sister plan, Social Security, so much for security. Every worker should follow the example set during the 1997 strike against the United Parcel Service (UPS) by the Teamster represented workforce, by insisting their employer provide an independently managed diversified retirement portfolio. After all, why should anyone have their finger in the retirement fund except the worker. It's your money. Watch it closely!

* Do not become an economic slave! Keep track of your cost to produce income. Be efficient and productive each moment you work. Be interested and involved in your employer objectives. Develop good work ethics while demanding acknowledgment of achievement. A big salary will never signal success, if the cost associated with producing the salary does not remain under control.

* Teach children early in life asset management skills. Establish a "home bank" with Mom or Dad playing bank teller. Issue the child a checkbook including deposit slips. Pay the child an allowance for small household chores while encouraging them to open their bank account. Issue monthly bank statements. Insist the child balances their bank ledger monthly. Treat the system as a real bank. Have lots of fun and enjoyment teaching your child asset management skills. If you do not take the time as a parent, to teach these important skills, rest assured no one else will. Drug addiction across America is not a natural state of affairs. It is a by-product of failure within our society because we have failed to teach our children asset and financial survival skills. Without skills, children turn to the easy way of coping with today's problems.

* Play "Stock Pick" games utilizing strategies found in Chapter 4. Teach children early in life how to analyze, buy; and, sell stocks. Portfolio management skills often take years to develop, except when utilizing proven strategies outlined throughout *Don't Die Broke.* As the child develops expertise at their stock investing skills, parents should consider opening a deep discount brokerage account in their name but allowing the child to actually trade the account. By age 18, any child in America should have reached an expertise of stock selection and trading skills rival to any acclaimed professional trader. Developed skills could reward the child throughout life and their parents during retirement years.

* Cease forever impulse spending. Wasteful spending for second homes, luxury cars, boats, exotic vacations; and, living the "good life" through debt over-extension harms society to the betterment of a few. The public eventually pays the bill as the over-extenders' wimp into poverty, eventually entering into the social service circle only to die broke.

* The path to success follows: (1) learning childhood management skills, (2) obtaining higher education, (3) getting a job, (4) starting an investment portfolio; and, (5) marriage somewhere around age 28. A deviation to the sequence guarantees a financial disadvantage often taking years to recover losses..

* Expenses will always increase to eat away income; unless, the cancer is stopped by a good dose of motivation call prevention.

* Living standards accelerate to a higher levels only when accomplished through debt free growth based upon

investment yields exceeding taxes, inflation, spreads; and, commissions.

* Start a 401K contribution the first day of work. Next establish emergency funds. Then pay off revolving charge debt. Purchase a house; then, purchase stocks, bonds; or, mutual funds to within percentage limits based upon net worth. Investors without a net worth should never purchase equities subsequent to purchasing their first residence. Of course, bond ownership is unavoidable with the current Social Security system. Workers having a negative net worth enter into investing when more important goals should be their objective. Folks who can hardly afford to pay their rent are forced into investing by a government who cannot balance its own budget. To the opinion of some, that is a national disgrace.

* Stocks trading within a narrow daily price range over an extended time frame while remaining within 7 percent of a median price, tend to break out of the price base into an up trend. Since stock prices rise a majority of the time, those with an extended base line have a strong probability to up trend out of the base. A price breakout accompanied by a volume above a 50 day moving average could easily push the stock price up by 10 to 25 percent within a few weeks. Review the *IBD* stock charts. Take notice of the percentage of price gain, once a stock price breaks above its moving average line.

* Stock prices rise due to an investor belief that future benefits are forthcoming (greed). Prices fall when the crowd looses faith in the stocks' ability to return their investment.

* Stock supply is usually fixed while the demand fluctuates moment by moment. A weak demand will force the market to realign the supply and demand equation through supply restrictions. Restricting supply will eventually create a bidding war among traders. As prices move up, the market maker will begin to release their house inventory to capture profits.

* Cost associated with income production include: local, state or federal taxes, meals, health insurance, life insurance, social security, association or union fees, transportation cost, clothing; and, education.

* Transportation cost is perhaps the greatest charge against earned income; yet, it's the least understood. The "power by the mile" automobile concept discussed in chapter 1, suggests the best way to keep control of this misunderstood expense, is to pay-as-you go. Transportation cost is not cheap! For example, the U.S. government, in April, 1996 estimated workers within the Atlanta, Georgia commuting area spent 52 cents per mile to operate a standard mid-size automobile. Their estimate is not far off target according to mileage cost computed by the American Automobile Association (AAA). As a result of the estimate, the government has encouraged ride sharing and public transportation utilization. Most, if not all, government agencies set aside privileged parking areas exclusively for car pool vehicles. Many agencies allocate funding to assist employees in offsetting the cost of public transportation. Additionally, many large cities have designated high occupancy vehicle (HOV) traffic lanes along main highway routes to encourage car pooling. How many times have you heard someone say: "I get good gas mileage, it only takes a tank a week to drive to work." Similar comments occur daily across the United States. Gas expense is only a small factor of total transportation cost. Depreciation is the culprit in need of addressing.

* Americans, unlike most workers throughout other countries, tend to commute great distances to work. Personal economical hardships are self inflected only to become more intense, as fuel supply and transportation replacement cost escalate. Considering the government and AAA transportation cost factors, a 60 mile round trip commute to work daily, chops off $31.20 from post-tax income. The worker looses about $7,800 annually. The cost will escalate year after year until the worker either quits the job, moves closer to work; or, cuts the cost through either walking, bicycling, car pooling, or utilizing public transportation.

* Maintain a balance between earnings and the cost associated with the earnings' production. Keep the cost of income production low. Income production expenses include; housing, union fees, transportation, food, clothing, tools, supplies, taxes, social security, retirement contributions, health insurance, life insurance, and education maintenance cost.

* Lock-out Rate is the gross compensation required to satisfy a current standard of living. If earnings are not sufficient to satisfy a specific lockout rate, then consider a lifestyle change. The lockout rate is adjusted periodically. It is based upon the federal minimum wage standard.. Consider the following lock-out rate examples:

Lock-out Rate

A high school graduate is residing with their parents while holding employment requiring a 10 mile daily transportation charge. The parents are assisting the worker through providing meals, housing, education; and, insurance coverage. The student could accept a lock-out rate of $5.68 per hour after factoring the earnings for transportation expense. Federal minimum wage standards rose to $5.15 per hour in September, 1997.

$5.15	Federal Minimum wage -- 1997
+ .53	(10 miles x .42 mileage cost = $4.20 divided by 8 hours = .53)
$5.68	Hourly lock-out rate.

NOTE: Twenty percent of the AAA transportation mileage estimates include gas and general auto repairs. I.E. Oil changes, brake repairs, etc..

"Distance" workers assigned to work at their residence must carefully consider all factors associated with income production in order not to accept substandard compensation; or, lose the position due to excessive compensation demands. All costs of income production still exist. However, transportation cost is now exchanged for utility, computer maintenance; and, on-line service charges, etc. Additionally, costs associated with office space and benefits are added. Home based workers should earn a minimum of $1,000 for each year of age. Although it may seem difficult to accomplish, that figure should be a minimum objective. Computation into an hourly compensation package, the employee expense necessary to offset home operating cost must be carefully evaluated. An alternative, would be to factor a "phantom" daily transportation charge into the lock-out equation equal to the distance the worker would have driven, if they worked outside the home. Additionally, adjust the Federal minimum wage upward by 85 percent for a college degree, or for trained specialized skills; plus, 2 percent for each year of the workers' age. Let's illustrate a 25 year old homemaker or college student working at home, located 30 miles from their employers primary business location.

Illustration

$5.15	Federal Minimum wage -- 1997
+3.90	(60 miles x .42 = $31.20 divided by 8 hours = $3.90); or, actual cost.
$9.05	
+2.58	($5.15 x.50 {25 years x 2 percent} = $2.58)
$11.63	
+ 4.38	($5.15 x .85 {education / skill adjustment} = $4.38)
$16.01	Hourly lock-out rate at residence or, at employer site.

The lock-out rate presentation is to motivate investors into thinking about the total cost associated with income production. Everyone is encourage to give consideration of income production cost when accepting an employment position. The basic minimum wage takes into consideration only essential human needs to survive. Workers must adjust the minimum rate to accomplish a lifestyle they desire.

High salaries are not enough, if debt rules the roost. Work up a cost sheet and set your personal lock-out-rate. Knowing the income to support your lifestyle will eliminate wasted time seeking employment with firms who cannot afford your services. On the other hand, you may soon discover to your surprise a lifestyle set way too high.

<u>What to do: NOW!</u>

* Make the maximum contribution allowable into an employer matching retirement program.

* Car pool.

* Take public transportation. Ask your employer to pay the cost.

* Live as near to work as possible.

* Total time allocated for working outside the home includes commuting time. Figure your total work allocated time divided into total compensation. One hundred dollars per hour does not mean a damn, if it equals minimum wage across the street.

* Cut debt. DO IT NOW!

* Brown bag work meals whenever possible.

* Consider short term part-time employment. Target the income first toward debt buy down, followed by education; and, finally life enhancing old fashion fun.

* Pay cash for anything that depreciates in value. Finance items that appreciate in value; if the product cost can be covered within one year. This does not include the purchase of a residence. Purchase your first residence the moment a down payment is high enough to bring the monthly note down to 85 percent of your current monthly rent; less utilities.

* Return all credit cards, except for the one with the highest limit having the lowest interest; and, longest grace period. Instruct the card provider to close the account. Request they notify their credit bureau associates of the account closure; and, forward a copy of their notification to you.

* Establish a personal investment financial plan.

* Know your salary (lock-out-rate) requirements before applying for employment. Should the application, or interviewer inquires of your salary requirements, be honest. Do not waste your time; nor, theirs, interviewing if you know the potential employer can not afford your salary rate.

* Children should understand current family financial situations. Keep children informed, in a loving way, of the current family financial situation. Their understanding is critical, if better times are to come later.

* Never be ashamed to move to a different neighborhood. It is better to swallow pride and move to a lower rent district than face the disgrace of bankruptcy created by trying to keep up with the "Joneses." Accept responsibility for not dying broke!

* Learn to increase income without increasing associated expense. Checkout adult education classes. Remain focused while increasing investment awareness.

* Parents must insist children graduating from high school be financial literate. Reports indicate 20 percent of graduating students cannot read their diplomas. Congress should review their own ability. "The blind shall lead the blind" has never been truer. Congress has demonstrated its monitory management skill. Members of the Senate credit union bounced so many checks in the early 1990's; it, triggered an investigation. How can politicians balance the federal budget, if they cannot control their personal checkbook?

* Studies released by the U.S. Department of Health and Human Services indicate 96 percent of Americans never reach financial independence.

* The U.S. Internal Revenue Service reports 85 percent of Americans reaching age 65 have less than $200 in a bank account. Most retirees have a net worth of less than $50,000.

* Another report by the U.S. Census Bureau indicates that 87 percent of Americans retire on an income of less than $10,000 annually.

* To enhance wealth, get politically involved. Do not sit at home sadly mistaken your vote does not count. Hold politicians accountable. You pay them to work for you. Elected officials who have become self-serving, deserve a certified letter of complaint. Nothing can prevent those letters from being published during an election year.

* Let's review the big picture! You're broke, kids can't read, congresspersons can't balance their personal checkbook, politicians can't use their Harvard brain to balance a simple budget, 96 percent of Americans die broke, and the government pays billions of dollars annually to citizens of foreign governments due to debt liens against our great nation. Worse yet, politicians at all levels of government are aware these problems exist. Why? Every American should demand a resolve! Wealth building will never occur if congress does not attempt to improve individual growth through better education, health maintenance; and, a lower personal income tax base. Voice your opinion via certified mail! Many advocates recommend collecting a National sales tax on every item sold. We agree the current personal income tax system should be simplified, if for no reason other than eliminate the billions of totally wasted hours used to fill out the paperwork. It is amazing how an advanced Nation could be so archaic on such a simple matter. Let the consumer share in paying for the government expense they incur while conducting business transactions within American airspace, waterways, and borders. Millions of foreign nationals flock to the good OLE USA to benefit off the sweat of hard working Americans. Stand on the Florida state line where interstate I-75 cross into Florida and notice the car tags from the border north of the United States. It will shock the average person! Why should Americans support the world population simply because we are smart enough to gain wealth? A national sales tax of 15 percent would place the burden of government service cost where is should be: on the consumer!

* What do the studies conducted by the Census Bureau, Health and Human Services; and, the IRS truly indicate? Americans are a society of economic slaves receiving a mere penance of their total gross national product contribution. The current situation is not a fluke. No indeed, it is by design. Big money controls the government through thousands of lobbyist manipulating the "hill" like puppets on a string. Big money over shadows the American worker, because most workers fail to take the political elective vote process serious, only to become

passive lambs, led to their own economic slaughter. Big money rewards the government for controlling society through legislation, taxes; and, bias education objectives. The objective of the super rich is clear. They want to become richer! Their objective is unobtainable without an ignorant middle class workforce. To the rich, the middle class must remain stupid and in debt. Congress appears to foster that viewpoint. Has there ever been a Bum elected to congress? Not likely! Only the rich make it to the hill. When your elected official reaches the hill, voters outside the politicians' interest group can forget representation. That is unless they raise enough hell to get attention. You got a gripe? Send it to the hill via certified mail. Demand a resolve. If it does not happen, publish the letters subsequent to the next election.

Big money talks a good line when they utilize college credentials to weed out employee candidates. The majority of newly hired employees assigned to management positions cannot balance their checkbook let alone control finances. Yet, most of them have "pre-approved" lines of credit increasing with earnings. Being aware the present education system is an asset management failure, how many companies offer their employees training in debt management; or, wealth building concepts, as an employee benefit? Does not management realize a financially secured workforce enhances long term productivity followed by corporate profits and stock prices up trending. The cycle will never end unless individuals make it stop. Meanwhile middle class worker after worker continues to die flat broke. Congress should break loose of the big money. The government should stop funding free education for foreign nationals, at the education expense of our American born children. Redirect foreign aid funds to provide free education to every American citizen. Stop supporting foreign nationals who attend our military or university system while forcing middle Americans to pay the bill. NOT ONE SINGLE TAXPAYER PENNY SHOULD BE PAID TO ANYONE FOR EDUCATION SUPPORT WHO IS NOT AN AMERICAN CITIZEN. Does anyone know the tax costs necessary to train a foreign national a specialized skill only too have them booted out of the service, to return to their homeland? Wake up America! Now is the time to demand fairness and sharing of the wealth. Stay on top of your elected officials like stink on a cow chip.

* *Investor's Business Daily* reported in April 1996, that Fidelity Investments replaced 15 fund managers who had reportedly under-performed the S&P 500 Index. Under-performance, by about 60 percent of all mutual fund managers, when compared to the S&P 500 Index is normal.

* Investors following the "Good, bad, the ugly" investment strategy as discussed in chapter 4 could beat the investment performance of most financial managers.

* Between January 1, 1926,and December 31, 1995,according to *Stocks, Bonds, Bills, and Inflation 1996_Yearbook* published by Ibbotson Associates; Chicago, IL, common stocks as a group, offered a 10.54 percent average annual total return. Treasury Bills rendered the poorest performance at 3.72 percent annualized during the 69 years.

* Do not trade stocks; or, anything else based upon a cold call or hot tip information. Never make an investment until its potential performance return has been estimated. Profits must be identified before making the investment.

* Never buy a stock, until you understand why you are buying the issue; and, have the ability to set the sale price at the moment of purchase.

* Broker recommended stocks fit their game plan; not the investors. Ask them to give you a written guarantee against downside risk. They won't! Wonder why not?

* Every stock price will move in a price cycle. Do not try to guess the bottom or top of the cycle. Hold stock until

a sale signal is triggered. Limit losses to less than 7 percent below the initial buy point. Once a price performance up trend is confirmed, never allow the price to retrace back to below the initial purchase price.

* Purchasing stock is like riding an elevator. Imagine if you will, standing in a hotel lobby watching the elevator location indicator. Regardless of direction of movement, the elevator can stop and reverse direction without warning. From the lobby viewing point, it is impossible to determine why the elevator reversed course. However, passengers inside the elevator, have inside information. They know the answer! If you want the answer, they may share it for a fee; or, give it to you outright. Either way, when you jump aboard, you are taking a risk the insider was not lying and the elevator will function normally.

* Stock performance, should be monitored through utilizing a stock price weekly moving average. However, when all equity positions in a portfolio are above their moving average price, how can the investor determine which position to liquidate should the need for cash arise? The poorest performing stock over a specifically measured time frame should be liquidated first when all factors are considered. Selling the poorest performing stock, based upon market value quarterly percentage of gain, may be warranted. Formulating a stock performance table is easy. Lets assume four stocks were bought during the first quarter (January, February, March) of 1997. Each stock is above it's 15 week moving average line. Which stock should be sold to raise cash? A chart is helpful. Review the "Quarterly Allocation Chart" provided in chapter 4.

* Every stock is a market unto itself with its value driven by the auction process.

* Data and information are truly worthless; unless, put into a useful practical application, leading to experience. Experience leads to knowledge and knowledge is power. Power creates wealth and wealth begets wealth. We have been lead to believe, that it takes money to make money; and, that education leads to more money. Generally, that ideology is true; but, not necessarily so in every case. Traditional education falls way short of educating students in the art of wealth building. Educators are much like those they teach. Many have never invested in stocks. Most live from paycheck to paycheck; and, eventually will die flat broke. History is great. Trig is okay, English is so-so; but, investments are excellent. There is absolutely no excuse for high school students graduating without a practical knowledge of debt control; or, the ability to conduct their own stock analytical study. They should have begun their wealth building portfolio by the third grade. Many wealthy folks have a 6th grade education; whereas, many of super educated walk the aisle of the bankruptcy court. Do not assume for one minute, education is not important. We stress It is a major key to wealth building only if it is the correct education.

* Gender correlated investment returns are approximately equal between male and female mutual fund managers, according to a report in the June 1996 *Mutual Funds* magazine. According to the report; a two year study ending in 1995, indicated that female managed mutual funds yielded a 40 percent average total return when compared to the 39 percent total return of male managed mutual funds over the reported time frame. However, jointly managed funds returned 38 percent.

* BUCKLE-UP: Please! Wealth can vanish in a flash due to personal injury sustained during moving vehicle accidents. A second to snap that buckle cuts risk. NEVER DRINK ALCOHOL AND DRIVE!

* DO NOT SMOKE or use tobacco products in any manner. Businesses lose billions of dollars annually through lost employee productivity. Not until State governments stepped forward in 1995 and 1996 did the Clinton administration take action to address this problem. Tobacco tax and subsidy programs are big government "cash cows" bringing in large sums of tax revenue. Politicians allowed their greed to place the financial health of both workers and business at risk. Along the same line, the American drug epidemic will never be eliminated; unless,

parents take the initiative to resolve it. Law enforcement and the judicial system have too many employees whose salary is drug enforcement dependent for them to have a motivation to end the problem. Abuse of tobacco, drugs, and alcohol will continue to increase in a government controlled market place. Only in a free market place can competition drive the price of a product low enough to force suppliers out of business. Then and only then will the abuse epidemic cease. Until then, the wealth of every taxpayer will be drastically affected.

* Charge or not to charge. Is that the question? We have the answer. Do not Charge purchases!

* The Dow and S&P 500 have become the pulse of global economy.

* Legal cost could easily exceed medical cost when the unexpected *Summons to Appear* in court arrives unexpectedly. It's not necessary to be rich to have a personal attorney. A reasonable way to hire an attorney is through a legal service plan. Legal service plans are for personal or family litigation issues limited to family law, estate planning, civil rights discrimination, employment issues, contracts, consumer complaints; and, medical claim problems. Legal service plans usually cap the attorney hourly rate at 50 percent off the national average Investors interested in reducing litigation and attorney cost may contact either:

  Montgomery Ward Enterprises Legal Service Plan
  200 North Martingale Road
  Schaumburg, IL 60173

  Pre Paid Legal Services
  Ada, Ok
  1-405-436-1234

  NOTE: Most plans cost less than $20 a month.

* Financial freedom requires acceptance of responsibility.

* Financial independence does not necessarily mean being wealthy. It means, current investments are yielding returns high enough to support a selected lifestyle.

* Retirement does not mean financial independence. To the contrary, when retirement occurs, the retiree usually becomes totally dependent upon government and pension plan support.

* Remain debt fee. If not forcefully resisted, personal expenses will rise to eat away your income. Maintain a simple lifestyle. Should a true financial need arise, reach into the money shed only as necessary to withdraw emergency funds.

* Investment profits are not additional income. Profits should be cycled into other investments to allow leverage and compounding work to the investor's advantage.

* Ask the questions: Why do I impulse spend? Why have I not established a retirement plan? Why is my credit over-extended? Why do I not cover transportation cost when incurred? Why did my formal education fail to teach me wealth building skills? Why has society lead me to believe I should live above my means? Could there be a hidden agenda designed by big money and government to force workers into dying broke in order for their children to continue as an economic slave benefiting those in society who strive off the sweat equity of others?

* Dispel the myth that votes do not really count. Let your politician know about your concerns. They are not mind readers. Politicians will indeed listen to voters when their voice rises louder than that of big money lobbyist.

* Peace of mind does not come with ownership of material things; but, with the knowledge that you can purchase with cash anything desired.

* The average American is so debt overloaded and financial illiterate they have no real hope for a better future.

* Being rich does not ensure financial security. Financial security occurs the moment investments yield enough return to support a selected lifestyle. In fact, a homeless person may indeed be financially secure.

* Make a pledge to yourself to succeed. If you slip along the way, pick yourself up and continue onward.

* Avoid multi-level market scams requiring person contact recruitment. They are often difficult to monitor, take up valuable time, cost a lot of money to market long term; and, only truly benefits a few at the top of the level. You can be legally liable to supply the goods and products, if the multi-level sponsor bails out after you have collected the money, even if the money has been sent to the sponsor. Checkout all such schemes with your state Better Business Bureau and Secretary of State before spending a single dime promoting the goods, products; or, business of a multi-level marketing program. Never put personal assets at risk attempting to "get rich" and "retire in five years" with multi-level scams. You should earn money through selling and not through signing up down line associates. The best programs are those where the product provider closes the down-line deal on your behalf.

* Bankruptcy financially harms everyone. First, tax dollars are spent to hear the case. Second, creditors either up their product price to cover losses; or, they write off the loss. Either way, their earnings' base erodes. Every tax payer is forced to pick up the tab of a bankruptcy.

* Notes, bills, and bonds issued by the U.S. Department of Treasury are debt obligations backed by the full faith of the (middle class worker) federal government. Through these instruments, the federal government borrows money from citizens worldwide only to increase the tax base of American workers to repay the loan. It works like this: the investor loans the government money for a yield; say 6 percent. After the interest has been paid, the government sends the IRS around (except to foreign countries) to sweep away up to 35 percent of the 6 percent, leaving a 3.9 percent profit. The meager profit is then swept away with inflationary forces. Yields alone are not worth the investment. What is worth the risk; however, is equity growth in the bond principle value as yields drop. The principle of a 30 year bond generally increases by 10 percent for each 1/4th point drop in the yield. A one percent drop in yield can produce a 40 percent principle gain. Yields are locked in at the time of purchase and are paid upon bond maturity. To attract investors, Treasury debt instruments are usually sold at a substantial discount from face value. Yield compounding over a specific number of years pushes the market value to the maturity principle (face value). Taxes are paid on the yield annually even though they may not be accessible for years. The maturity and minimum evaluations vary with each instrument. Bonds purchased for growth do make excellent investments during periods of stock market over-evaluations. The market is considered over-valued when 85 percent of listed stocks are selling above their 200 day moving average.

  Checkout the latest yield and auction information with the Federal Reserve Bank of New York (1-202-874-4000) or, web site (http://www.ny.frb.org). Investors may also contact their district Federal Reserve Bank for information. We listed the bank telephone numbers in chapter 4. Request a copy of the booklet entitled *Direct to You.* The booklet explains in detail a new purchasing program the Treasury made available to the public in September 1997. Investors may buy and sell debt securities auctioned by the U.S. Treasury Department without conducting the transaction through a stock brokerage firm or bank. The "Treasury Direct Program" will prove well for wealth building.

* "Ultimately, when it comes to creating wealth, you have to become your own expert. You can draw upon the

collective wisdom of others experts; but, you will still be responsible for incorporating the information into your own framework." Robert Allen/ *Creating Wealth*

* Be as naïve as possible in order to get others to open up their thoughts to you. The only stupid question, is the one left unasked. The fastest route to the top of any endeavor is to discard all preconceptions, observe, listen; and, ask questions. After which, the information is put into useful application toward acquiring experience. Experience offers opportunity to gain personal knowledge; and, knowledge gives way to power.

* Naïve! Visit the Liberty Financial website (www.young.investor.com) for interactive teaching of money management, money terms, matters of financial awareness; and, money making opportunities.

* There is no such thing as "civil" or "human" rights! There are only "individual" rights. Individual rights should be equal among all members of the human species regardless of individual wealth level, gender, age, religious beliefs, educational background, physical or mental health condition; or, sexual life style. The recognition of individual rights would eliminate job bias discrimination quotes, jail over-crowding, Social Security; and, government supported charity programs. The recognition of individual rights, would also create wealth by eliminating the obstacles that destroy wealth. What a novel concept! Let the religious and charity organizations handle society problems' while the federal government correlate national security and state government programs. Was that not the intent of the *Bill of Rights* and the *Constitution of the United States of America*. What went wrong?

* "The greatest revolution of our generation is the discovery that human beings, by changing the inner attitudes of their minds, can change the outer aspects of their lives." William James.

* "The surest, fastest way to become enormously wealthy and exceptionally successful is to focus passionately, and unfalteringly on the process of achieving your goal." *The Cynergetics Sixty Minute Success/Wealth Guidebook*

* "The essence of success is that it is never necessary to think of a new idea oneself. It is far better to wait until someone else does it, and then copy them in every detail, except their mistakes." Aubrey Menen

* Believing in yourself is the key ingredient for successfully changing your lifestyle. To help, we offer the following six keys to change published recently in *The Power of Positive Thinking* presented through the courtesy of Kaiser Permanente, the "good people, good medicine" folks.

The Six Keys To Change

* True Desire- wanting something enough to be willing to face the fears you have about achieving it.
* Strong Belief- having the confidence to believe that you can have what you want.
* Knowledge- understanding the legitimate means by which you can accomplish what you want.
* A Plan For Change- plotting the specific methods and techniques for achieving your desired results.
* Setbacks- recognizing that the path of change is not a straight road and that it's only guilt and feelings of failure that stop your progress.
* Progress- learning to acknowledge and reward all accomplishments.

Don't Die Broke will agree that stocks offer the best investment around. Before jumping into stock investing, it is prudent to understand the stock market "auction barn" concept. Investors must know who is playing the game. Chapter 4 will show investors how to play the game to win. Winning Strategies eliminates the game (your) handy cap! Now chapter 3.

CHAPTER 3

THE AGIOTAGE PARADOX

A COMPLEX THEORY: Investing in the stock market is a very complex and controversial operation biased against the individual investor through ever changing market place and investment theories. Perhaps thousands of inexact theories have been formulated and fostered by the commission driven investment community over the past two hundred years. To no surprise, a majority of stock market theories are so flawed and complex that Wall Street professionals are theorist victims on about 4 out of every 10 stock transactions. To make a point; examine the stock holdings of almost any mutual fund portfolio. Do not be surprised to discover more stock price values declining than rising. Mutual fund managers generally will not admit their performance is often boosted, not by their stock picking ability; but, through dividends paid into their fund from companies sponsoring the stock held within the fund. The phase "total return," is used throughout the mutual fund industry to hide the true stock picking growth performance of fund management. Is there any college or university offering a Ph.D. in successful stock picking?

Review the most recent "New Issue" listing published by the *Investor's Business Daily (IBD)* (1-800-831-2525). Most likely you will notice that a majority of stocks listed are currently trading below their Initial Public Offer (IPO) price. An estimated 80 percent of all "new issues" trade below their IPO price within 18 months of going public. After reviewing mutual fund portfolio's and *IBD* "New Issue" listings, almost anyone could conclude that totally avoiding stock investing would be the best course of action. Do not be fooled! Although thousands of inexact stock market theories are floating around; historically, the stock market is by far the superior investment vehicle for long term wealth building.

Please don't be afraid to step-up to the investment plate and take a swing. Babe Ruth was the baseball home-run king until Hank Aaron came along. What many people fail to acknowledge is that Babe Ruth was also the world's baseball strike-out king. Ruth struck out about 30 percent more times than he hit the ball. When he did hit the ball, odds were in favor of a home-run. Investors; professional and amateur alike, are much like the "Babe." They strike-out on about 30 to 40 percent of their investment attempts. However, unlike the "Babe", investors strike-out not because they don't have the ability to win; but, because they play the investment game by ambiguous rules! Investors tend to rely on investment coaches who are perhaps no more qualified to coach than a Little Leaguer would have been to teach Ruth. The average investor, for a variety of reasons, can outperform the majority of investment professionals, once they understand the stock market game rules. According to the American Association of Individual Investors (1-312-280-0170), individual investors, can outperform the total investment return of the stock market pro's by approximately 4.4 percent annually. Individual investor superior performance is credited to a variety of reasons. For example, their trading isn't hampered with bias information, government regulations; or, with employer mandated commission quotas. Additionally, they can move with lightning speed when buy or sell signals are flashed.

Successful stock investors are usually well focused and motivated. They understand why they initially elected to invest; and, are generally smart enough to liquidate their position when conditions change. Most have the keen understanding, that a majority of stock market theories have been developed by the equity trade community to accommodate the investment needs of their preferred institutional clients. Institutional clients, such as, bank trust departments, insurance companies, mutual funds, and government retirement plans conduct 80 to 90 percent of total stock market transactions. The market is bias against individual investors. Despite the biases; historically, they are really the Babe Ruth's of the stock market investment game. Armed with information, individual investors can hit home-run after home run. One single solid hit can easily offset several strike out losses; plus, a whole lot more.

Investment success is a mind game won through education, focus, motivation, and strategy application leading to the formulation of a positive investment plan. Successful investors learn through practice and experience how to put the odds in their favor by eliminating traps guaranteed to create losers. The successful investor learns to keep their emotions in control. They learn how to successfully manage a personally selected portfolio in about one hour weekly utilizing basic supplies, a telephone, and research documents readily available either through a personal computer on-line service, mail order, or at most public libraries. Of course, the market will try to pitch a nasty curve or slide-ball. Most will draw upon their knowledge and perhaps will take a swing. With each swing, successful investors will evaluate their position and seek a better advantage point to swing again and again. Although there are no guarantees, investors willing to take a risk, should not be surprised when a grand-slam homer is knocked right out of the professional investor's game park. One solid hit can increase wealth substantially, if the investor understands all bases must be touched; and, the player has returned safely home before the investment comes crashing to earth. This chapter provides a brief introductory overview of stock market terms and game players. To be successful, investors must have a working knowledge of the market language and game players.

STOCK MARKET: Exchange markets of 1775, were originated to trade primarily in tea, gun powder, grain, and livestock commodities. Today these commodities are still traded; but, they have been over shadowed by a new commodity the financial community has termed "corporate stock". Although stocks have moved to the forefront, the exchange concept has changed very little. The American, Boston, Chicago, Midwest, New York, Pacific and NASDAQ stock exchanges represent the "1775 Auction Barn" concept of today. At the "auction," a stock commodity is traded between investors through a continuous "ask/bid" auction process. The auction is held at the request of stocktrader; arranged by their stockbroker, executed by a market maker or specialist; and, is controlled by oversight regulation enforcement administered either by the Federal Security and Exchange Commission (SEC); or, the National Association of Security Dealers (NASD).

At the stock auction, buyers set the price! Perhaps, that explains why stock trading transaction losses are associated with selling. Sellers loose money because they tend to sell their stock commodity position during the wrong price performance momentum cycle to buyer who is betting on the opposite performance cycle. A large percentage of novice and professional stocktraders, truly fail to understand the auction process. Traders will foolishly sell a stock rising in price, to fulfill an emotional need associated with perceived success (profits). When a stock they are holding enters into a price momentum performance downtrend, they usually hold their current position for fear of loosing money; or, buy more on the false assumption it is a cheap bargain. During a price downtrend, they simply can not accept the cold realization that losses have already occurred regardless if whether the position is retained or sold. They overlook the important fact that stock prices decline for a reason. Prices decline in a flooded market!

Typically, the emotional logic driven by profits, fear, and greed are usually wrong! Exceptions do exist in an imperfect auction system; however, the exceptions are rare. Stock price cycles, are created not only by political and economic conditions; but, through price manipulation by market makers and floor specialist. Generally; however, stock prices moving in an uptrend will continue up-trending. The same holds true for stock prices which are down trending. Regardless of the trend direction, a stock price will usually continue in the trend direction until the direction is altered through market forces. Only the exchange floor manipulators are true market "flow control experts." **Lesson to remember: To make money in the stock market, the investor must trade in sync with the market makers and floor specialist. Never invest against the house. You will lose, guaranteed!** Stocks purchased, based upon a stockbroker recommendation, are usually long term losers because the purchase is often investing against the flow control experts. Brokers tend to liquidate their house positions to remain in alignment with the position of their associate floor specialist or market maker; who is actually selling. For that reason alone, it is imperative for stock investors to learn how to pick stocks without assistance from anyone. Stocks being accumulated or distributed by the "flow control experts" are easily identifiable once the secret is learned.

UNDERWRITERS: Financial banker risk takers who underwrite stocks sold at the auction barn through the Initial Public Offer (IPO) process, are underwriters. They are market creators in the purest form. Underwriters purchase shares at wholesale from a company they have equity valued. The shares are then distributed through a market maker to affiliated brokerage firms, who in turn redistribute the shares at retail to the public through their stockbrokers. Once the stock begins to float, the underwriter and supporting company exit the auction process.

BROKERAGE FIRMS: Brokerage firms number into the hundreds. Several firms were founded more than a hundred years ago. They have a franchised right to represent traders on the auction floor. Not all brokerage firms are equal. Full service firms offer investment, analytical, and transaction services to their clients. Discount firms offer reports and transaction activity. Deep discount firms generally only execute trading . Deep discount firm commissions can be as low as only 10 percent of the commission fees charged by full service firms. A $10,000 trade through a full service firm may cost $300 in commissions; whereas, the identical trade placed through a deep discount firm could be as low as $9. What a difference a little knowledge can make! Stocktraders can conduct their own stock analytical studies and easily save a bundle of cash. A Deep Discount Brokerage listing is provided in chapter 2.

SPECIALIST AND MAKERS: The most savvy investors (flow control experts) are market markers and floor specialist. They control the commodity supply and demand equation. When they identify a stock being distributed (sold) accompanied by a price downtrend, they begin to throw curve balls in order to strike out investors. When fewer sellers come forward, trading slows and volume has a potential of halting. Should trading cease, the stock could be de-listed from the market or exchange. To prevent this from occurring; the flow control experts, kick in supply and demand economics. They begin to raise the stock "ask" price until potential buyers become greedy enough for perceived future profits to rejoin the auction fun. On each new purchase, buyer greed increases the stock "ask" price. As fewer and fewer buyers join the party, volume slows down. To keep the stock volume activity on going, the floor specialist or market maker reverses their position and now drops the "ask" price. Their position reversal will generally attract buyers. The cycle repeats time and time again for every listed stock several times daily, year after year. The concept isn't much different than when your local retailer puts something on sale at an attractive price to remove from inventory. Price manipulation magnifies when several specialist or makers trade the stock among themselves to keep the volume and "ask" price uptrend in place.

Sticking with stocks followed by at least 7 to 10 floor specialist or market makers tend to eliminate stock price manipulation. First, because inter-trading is reduced. Secondly, the stock price spread is held to a narrow margin due to competition between the groups for the spread commission. Remember, stocks move in price because of perceived future worth (greed) and rarely ever reflect the true underlying corporate assets or corporate management abilities. Prices go down because buyers lack confidence in future growth prospects. A down-trending stock price or daily volume should be a clear signal to the current commodity holder that something is very wrong. All stocks are risky unless they go up in value. The trading price reflects little upon the corporation it represents. Billion dollar corporations can and often do go out of business. Portfolio management is extremely important; but, it is only effective if positions held within the portfolio were initially purchased wisely and then sold at the correct profit point. Selling is the end product of the purchasing cycle, while profits and losses are the measure of portfolio management skills.

STOCKBROKERS: Stockbrokers are employees of brokerage firms. They have demonstrated through employer training and a series of security examinations to be fully qualified to ply their trade. Stockbrokers are necessary for investors to trade stocks on various exchanges, purchase new issues through IPO's; and, to receive investment information from the brokerage firm research analyst. The stockbroker may be commissioned or salary compensated. The broker is either employed by a full service brokerage firm, discount brokerage firm; or, a deep discount brokerage firm.

Salaried stockbrokers are compensated on a flat rate scale. They do not offer transaction recommendations and are paid to handle investor originated sell/buy orders. Their job is to place the transaction on the exchange floor. They may take sell/buy orders via computer, in person, or over the telephone. They will not bug you at home during your quite time with bogus hot tips.

Not true with commission stockbrokers! Commission driven brokers will telephone hot tips to anyone foolish enough to listen. Although, they may not be qualified as a stock analyst; they will talk 900 miles an hour with all their impressive facts about the hot stock. In reality, they perhaps know nothing more about the stock they are recommending than what they have read in a newspaper, analyst report, trade bulletin, or brokerage firm hot sheet.

Commissioned stockbrokers encourage buying stocks but rarely recommend selling; unless, their investor client purchases a replacement issue. They know that once a stock is purchased, sooner or later the investor will sell. The flip side of the investment coin is that commission driven brokers often give bad advice. In 1995, only approximately 71 percent of those taking the NASD series 7 test passed on their first attempt. Many new brokers have never experienced a "bear" market. Contact the National Association of Security Dealers (1-800-289-9999) for a background check on your broker. Crooked brokers can churn investor accounts to generate excessive commissions for himself or herself and their employer. Churning is a too often practice involving excessive trading of client accounts without regard to the clients financial well being. Alexander Woollcott (1887-1943) once commented; "A broker is a person who runs your future into a shoestring." Experience accumulated through millions of transactions may prove Woollcott correct. Suspect any hot tip when the caller does not state: the name of his/her firm, telephone number; or, the call is received around dinner time. Brokers should never call after 9 p.m.

STOCK ANALYST: Where do they get these people from? 22500 analyst are trying to figure out what companies are doing. Some will be recommending a hold (sell) while others are recommending a purchase of the same stock. If an analyst told half their clients to buy and the other half to sell, the analyst would always be 50 percent correct without knowing anything about the company whose stock they are hawking. Regardless of how they guessed, regarding earnings, a stock may react in a strong negative or positive way. No two analyst appear to evaluate stocks using the same rules. Confusing? You bet! Skip right pass the confusion by learning how to select winning stock yourself. Review chapter 4 for stock picking strategies proven to produce equity growth. To locate a winning stock analyst, look no further than yourself. If the investor is debt free; holding lots of cash, then they should search for a corporation which is managed the same way they have managed their personal affairs. It's really that simple!

STOCK VS SHARES: As previously suggested, drastic differences exist between the market of yesteryear and today. Not only has the commodity changed from tea, gun powder, grain, and livestock to "stock"; but, "stock" has been changed by the financial community to "shares." Before the turn of the 20th Century , it was typical for business owners to hire a broker to locate potential investors. Business owners would pay a finder's fee to the broker, if they could entice investors to buy into their business. Investors who bought into the business, actually received a "share percentage" of the business profits. Should management fail to produce profits for the "share" holders, they were often replaced by the investors and the business placed into receivership. Investor "share" holders had the option of either: installing new management, operating the business themselves; or, liquidating assets to pay off debts. If the business was liquidated, residual assets, after paying off the creditors, was then distributed among the share holders in an equitable manner.

Today, it's totally different! Currently, businesses usually do not sell actual share percentages. Instead, they hire stockbrokers to sell a stock, that should; but, rarely ever does, represent the underlying assets of the business. After stock representing a specific number of authorized shares are sold through an initial public offering, the shares are then traded among speculators. Perhaps, the business founder wants to pull out years of equity building. Perhaps the business wishes to expand and has been refused an extension to their line of bank credit. Maybe , management is seeking to establish a public value for their business. Stocks may be sold without a specific reason. Regardless of the explanation stated by management, a company benefits little from inter-trading by speculators, at least from a direct proceeds infusion point of view. Indirectly; however, corporate business may improve as management boast about how well their stock is performing in the market place. As previously reviewed, greed moves stock price. Greed has little to do with the investors faith in corporate management ability. Understanding investors could vote them out of their management position; managers at all levels of the food chain, especially those at the top, often refuse to operate the business without elaborate personal employment contracts, fiduciary insurance; and, golden parachute benefits payable for years after their employment terminates. In America, business managers rip-off stockholders with very little recourse afforded the investor. Federal rules protect crooks!

Within recent times, investors have lost millions of dollars with nothing more than lip service; or, minimum jail terms awarded to crooked management by the judicial system. Unlike the judicial system in America, China considers ripping off stockholders a very serious crime against society. In 1995, China publicly executed several business managers who defrauded their investors. Maybe the bankruptcy laws in America should be changed! Until they are, stockholders will continue to be placed at the bottom of the damage recovery list as inept management continues to operate the business under government protection. Investors should insist on management performance, by attending stockholder meetings and watching the corporate balance sheet. Safe companies should have increased earnings year-after-year with a positive balance sheet consisting of more cash on hand than long term debt. Remember, investors today are not usually given the front door key. They cannot review corporate books. They are not invited to use the corporate jet. They have little input into day-to-day business operations. Why? They own "stock of the business" instead of "shares in the business".

SHARE TO MARKET: What is the process for a company to sell stock through an IPO? The first step requires a management decision to offer stock of the business to the investing public. Next, an underwriter investment banker is invited to place an evaluation on all corporate assets. After the underwriter determines the "best guess" market value of the assets, they purchase a representative number of shares from the company at a deeply discounted (wholesale) price. The company receives payment for the shares. Funds received from the sale may be used by management to retire bank loans, business expansion; or, to give themselves a fat bonus.

Corporate stock owned by the underwriter is repackaged for retail sale. The stock is converted back into shares before being distributed across the various stock exchanges by market makers or floor trading specialist associated with the underwriter. The underwriter authorizes its associates to solicit buyers. After all shares, less underwriter reserves, have been distributed to the public through an IPO, inter-trading begins among the speculators. As marker makers and floor specialist auction the stock price up, the underwriter eventually liquidates their reserve position for substantial profits. At that point in the trading cycle, is usually where your friendly stockbroker telephones with the "deal" of the year. Investors are lead to believe they can't lose. The stock is presented as a real winner. Investors left on the side line will generally see the stock price rise; not, because it's a good deal, but because thousands of small lot investors are creating massive volume, as the flow control experts bid the price up. Eventually, the volume will dry up and the stock price will crash, leaving investors holding worthless stock. Everyone in the Wall Street food chain makes money, except investors who fail to realize when it was time to bail out.

Stocks sold through IPO's are created at cost (mark-up) usually well in excess of underlying corporate breakup asset value. Eventually, IPO's tend to retrace greed motivated gains by returning to a value more closely correlated with true corporate assets. A large percentage of IPO's will rise in value substantially during the opening trading session. Don't let your guard down! Approximately 80 percent of all IPO's sell below their initial offering price within 18 months after public distribution. IPO's are risky business and generally should be avoided. It is often wise, to wait until the price reversal occurs; and, the stock rebounds to a historical high price before plunging into an investment position. The company has established a performance track record not based upon the underwriters opinion; but, upon management performance. Management performance is reflected through earnings growth expansion supported by selling new products or services. Confirm the company management has a real interest in making the business work. The majority of new businesses fail within the first five years. Corporate failure, without a doubt does drag a whole lot of investors down the investment drain.

Secondary trading develops as the IPO buyers began to liquidate their position. When current holders wish to liquidate, they usually contact the stockbroker who initially sold them the stock. The stockbroker issues a sell order on behalf of the shareholder. The broker registers the order with an exchange trading specialist or market maker. The exchange logs the order and begins a computer search for a buyer. If a previous buy order has been registered, the flow control experts will fill the buy order at their "ask" price. Should a buy order not exist, the market maker or specialist may fill the sell order at their "bid" price while sweeping the stock into their house account. The shares remain parked until a buyer can be located. When the sell order is filled; and, the shares have a new owner, the exchange notifies the stock issuing company's registered agent of the transaction. The company is responsible for amending its stock registration ledger to reflect the current shareholder of record. The stock certificate issued to the former shareholder is canceled and another one reissued to the current owner. An option to actually issuing a stock certificate, is to place an electronic notation in the investors brokerage account, delegating the investors brokerage firm as custodian of the stock certificate. Stocks held on behalf of the investor by the brokerage firm is considered held in a "Street Name." Investors often prefer the brokerage firm act as custodian of their stock position. Stocks held in a "Street Name" allows trading flexibility while reducing transaction time. The downside; however, is the investor may never know when a commission greedy stockbroker trades the position through "Short Selling" or "Churning."

How does management profit from their corporate shares being sold to the public? Management benefits several ways. First, they receive money for the company stock from the underwriter. Secondly, the corporation does not need to increase debt through floating bonds or borrowing funds. Finally, management usually retain a stock reserve for themselves. To defer income and associated taxes, companies often grant performance stock options. Stock options authorizes management to purchase a specific number of shares at some future date for a pre-approved "strike" price. When the current stock price exceeds the option "strike" price, management floats a short term interest free loan from the company, to purchase the stock. They are then free to resale their stock at the current market price to repay the loan. Options do more than defer taxes, they provide a strong motivation for management to lie about true company performance. In the arena of trading stocks, bad news is often more truthful than good news. As investors began trading the stock in the secondary auction process, they tend to bid the stock price up. Likewise, as corporate earnings improve, the stock price will generally rise, especially if the earnings exceed analyst forecast. Either way, management's stock equity value increases dramatically.

WHO PAYS: Investors pay a minimum of two commissions for every stock transaction. The exception being when the stock is purchased directly from the offering corporation through a Direct Purchase Plan (DPP), Dividend Reinvestment Plan (DRIP); or, a qualified retirement plan. Review chapter 4 for details of the DPP and DRIP programs. Without a special program, commissions can destroy the best laid wealth building plan. First, the floor trading specialist or market maker collects a commission based upon the percentage difference between the stocks "ask" and "bid" price. The stockbroker and his employer are compensated through commissions when investors purchased the stock through an IPO and again when the floating secondary buy and sell transactions materialize. Brokerage commissions are paid regardless of whether the investor profited or lost from the transaction. Brokers are motivated through commissions to keep investors actively trading. They understand very clearly that every buyer automatically becomes an eventual seller. Brokers will generally not suggest selling a position until after they get the trader excited about purchasing another potential winner. A conversation between the investor and his or her stockbroker may appear to be friendly chit-chat. However, that is rarely what is really happening. Rest assured, the stockbroker's primary objective when contacting his or her client, is to close the deal!

Typical Conversation

Hello Larry, this is Bob. You got a few minutes.

Sure do Bob, What's up?

Well Larry, we got a hot tip a few minutes ago that will blow the lid off *AD2XCOT* company's stock. Look for a double over the next year.

(Larry) What do you think we should do?

We should sell your current holdings and buy 200 shares of *AD2XCOT* without delay! suggest Bob.

I agree, say's Larry. Do the deal.

Beware Investor Larry! Larry's stockbrokers excitement may not be in his best interest. Bob holds a distinct advantage as an expert in manipulation. Notice how Bob carefully used trigger words like: "hot tip," "look for a double," and "we." Notice how he addressed Larry by his first name. Bob has already computed the market value of Larry's current holdings; or, he would not have known he would have enough funds to purchase 200 shares of *AD2XCOT*. He has not told Larry what the hot tip was. He has not told Larry his employer has reason to suspect *AD2XCOT* is planning to file bankruptcy at the end of the month. Bob may not disclose to Larry that his boss ordered him to liquidate *AD2XCOT* stock out of the brokerage firm house account to avert substantial losses. Bob may not disclose that he was a commission under-achiever for the month and that his boss has placed him on notice of possible firing. Bob's excitement could be over how many hundreds of dollars in commissions he is about to milk out of Larry's account within the next few minutes. More on commissions later.

BID-ASK SPREAD: A "bid" stock price is the highest unexercised offer from a market maker or floor specialist to purchase a single share of a specific stock from the current shareholder. The "ask" price is the lowest stock price a market maker or floor specialist will offer to sell a single share of a specific stock to prospective buyer. The "spread" is the difference between the bid and ask price. Investors should always keep the spread as low as possible. Investors should limit spreads to a maximum of three percent. Spreads tend to be the widest before noon. The smallest spread generally occurs between 2:00 and 3:00 p.m. daily. Stocks trading above $10 per share; and, followed by no fewer than ten specialist or makers, generally have spreads well below 3 percent. S&P 500 and DOW stocks may have less than ¼ th percent spread. Information on the number of "flow control experts" handling a specific stock may be obtained from brokerage firms, the issuing company, Value Line; or, various other publicly available sources. Newspaper stock price quotes indicate the last "ask" price; therefore, the "bid" price of specific stock must be determined through another source. The spread is determined by subtracting the "bid" from the "ask" price and then divide the sum by the bid price. For illustration: Company *AD2XCOT* has an asking price of $10 with a bid price of $9.75. The spread is 25 cents; or, 2.5 percent of $9.75 (.25/9.75=2.5%). The floor specialist or market maker handling the exchange transaction earns a quarter for each share they handle. Should an investor purchase the stock at $10 per share and sell within a few minutes at $9.75, they would lose 2.5 percent of their investment; plus, the brokerage commission. As new Security and Exchange Commission regulations are introduced, investors may realize a commission break, due to a spread reduction for most stocks.

CHURNING: The act of aggressive account trading for the purpose of collecting commissions. Why does churning occur? There are many reasons. First, the Securities and Exchange Commission; nor, the National Association of Security Dealers conduct witch hunts looking for churners; unless, they are investigating a complaint filed by a ripped-off client. Secondly, churning occurs because clients make a drastic mistake when they put faith in their smooth talking stockbroker. Investors fail to realize that stockbrokers and used car salespersons have at least one commonality. Each are excellent at deal closing, by playing on human emotions; specifically greed. Stockbrokers always suggest investors purchase a specific stock because its the best deal going. They claim the recommended stock has the potential to be a big money winner. In the investors minds eye, dollar signs appear. While in a dream state of poor judgment, investors will generally allow greed make them a market victim. After all, everyone could use more money.

Estimates indicate up to perhaps 80 percent of all small capitalized investors lose money in the market place. The truth is clear! The direction of any stock price is a guess at best. Never bet against the position of the floor specialist, market maker; or, corporate insider. These market players have an insider advantage access to the corporate business strategy. Stocktraders should avoid bad advice and potential smooth talking churners. They should become free thinking investors with knowledge enough to ask the right questions. Crucial to wealth building, is to never invest into something you don't understand, or can not personally control. Churning should be suspect, if a broker suggest trading more than 2 or 3 times annually. It is not uncommon for a stock to price base for months before beginning a sustained upward price movement. "No person can serve two masters" is something to think about the next time you are contacted by a stockbroker. Something else to consider before jumping at a deal to good to be true, is that no stock suggested by a stockbroker is guaranteed to enhance the investors wealth. The opposite is likely to occur! Stockbrokers will sell anything for a commission, only to benefit themselves.

Whether, a broker suggest a trader acquire stock through an IPO, a secondary offering by an insider shareholder; or, inter-trading among speculators, the stock price will eventually bias downward. Why? IPO's (new issues) have a high probability of being below their initial offer price within 18 months after public distribution. Secondary stock offerings and large share grants to charity by a corporate insider (manager or director) indicates distribution out of a closely held position. Distribution by insiders regardless of their excuse, demonstrates lack of confidence in their corporate future. Their position liquidation will eventually create havoc with supply and demand economics until the additional stock infusion can be absorbed into the floating market auction. Insider stock liquidation will generally result in share prices biasing downward. The absence of management stock ownership is negative for future price appreciation. Insider buying; however, is very bullish for long term price appreciation.

Shares purchased after insiders release shares into the secondary market may initially trend higher; however, they will eventually down trend as volume dries up. The stock price will remain trending downward until the stock is covered by a floor account; or, the company bankrupts. Investors should pay very close attention to the stock price of any issue liquidated regardless of the excuse offered by corporate insiders. A stock trending down over several trading sessions after an insider distribution should be a sell candidate. Insiders, are the most informed group of investors with regards to the future direction a company will go. Therefore, if a "red flag" is not waving in the economic winds of the companies future, why should they sell? After all, doesn't the Wall Street pro's suggest stock investing should be considered a long term strategy! As with any commodity, why should anyone pay top dollar during a flooded market; or, when management is having their personal going out of business sale. Keep an eye open for churning. Report any unauthorized trading within your account to government authorities without delay.

STOCK SPLIT: When a pine board splits; it's strength is weakened. A split marriage weakens family values. Oil tankers destroy the environment when they split. "Split" is the word to remember! Wall Street manipulators would have investors believe a stock split is good. A split is necessary to bring the price into a trading range affordable to the average investor. In reality, stock splits occur when price has topped. Splits, is a tool used by the market to control the supply and demand equation. More shares on the market will boost volume. Stocks splitting can experience a short term price appreciation as more odd lot traders enter into the action. A post-split price boost of up to 20 percent may occur immediately after the split is announced. However, such growth is rare. Some market observers recommend liquidating out of a position the moment a split is announced only to repurchase if the stock recovers to investment quality. It may be more difficult to find buyers for 200 shares than for 100 shares.

DIRECT SHARE BUYING: Stockbrokers, market makers, and floor specialist receive commissions on every buy and sell stock transaction they process. Several methods exist to bypass the typical stock purchase process; thus, reducing or avoiding commissions. First, stocks can be bought directly from another investor through a private deal. Secondly, stocks can be purchased directly from the company issuing the stock provided they have a DRIP; DPP, or an employee stock option plan. Finally, stocks can be traded via personal computer at substantial commission discounts. The NASDAQ Small Order Execution System (SOES) provides investors equal access to small lot sell orders (1,000 shares or less) before the marker maker and floor specialist have the opportunity to manipulate the stock price up. SOES became law in 1987 and appears to be popular with deep discount brokerage firm clients. SOES are not popular with commission greedy brokerage firms. At least one New York based securities firm has complained to the SEC. The complaint stems from losing fat commissions. Apparently, the Wall Street SOES professional traders have employed the system to profit at the expense of NASD member firms. Tough! Chapter 2 contains a partial listing of deep discount brokerage firms. Chapter 4 offers a listing of companies offering DRIP and DPP stock purchase programs. Purchase direct and eliminate the middleman!

MORE ABOUT COMMISSIONS: "A fee or percentage allowed to a salesperson or agent for his services" (*The American Heritage Dictionary*). At first glance, the definition seems straight forward. Do not be fooled! Commissions make a significant difference in whether the investor makes a profit or loss. Upon a casual review, commission rates may appear to be similar; but, with close scrutiny, notable differences emerge. For the individual stock investor working with limited funds, picking the wrong commission rate creates market place losers. Commission rates must carefully be considered when establishing a personal wealth building plan. To illustrate, we invite you to take the following quiz. You pick out the best deal.

<u>Quiz</u>

* *XYZ* Brokerage Firm has a commission rate of $300 for trading $10,000 worth of stock.

* *ZYX* Brokerage Firm will conduct the identical transaction for $18.

QUESTION: Which company offers the best commission rate?

ANSWER: The best commission rate depends upon how much profit is realized upon selling. Since nothing a stockbroker recommends is guaranteed to enhance wealth, the real dollar best commission rate would be the $18. Why? Because the average person can learn to analyze stocks well enough to beat the pro's of Wall Street. Even if the investor knows absolutely nothing about stock selection, the odds are biased in their favor of beating the pro's.

Investing into a mutual fund or depository receipt which mirrors the Standard and Poor's 500 Index (S&P 500) during the "good" investment months often beats the long term performance of professional Wall Street. The point being: when considering all the facts, the lowest commission rate possible is usually the best deal. Higher rates often buys poor investment advice. Not one stockbroker or brokerage firm have enough faith in their recommendation to issue a written contract guaranteeing their recommendation will indeed make the investor a profit. Brokerage firms won't even consider accepting the investors account application; unless, the investor agrees not to take the brokerage firm into court over losses incurred as a result of their employee selling bad advice. Examine it from another view. The brokerage firms hired gun talks the investor into buying junk only after the investor agrees not to sue the brokerage firm for losses as a result of pressure from their employee! High commissions do not guarantee higher investment returns or quality service. The National Association of Investors, Inc. (1-313-543-0612); like so many other groups, advocate small investors who conduct their own basic analytic research can beat the total returns obtained by market place professionals.

Additional proof indicating small investors may have the clear investment advantage, is that in 1995 there were about 5,756 professionally managed mutual funds registered in the United States. A combined average total return of all listed domestic funds yielded around 30 percent; whereas, the S&P 500 returned about 34 percent. On December 18, 1995 the *Investor's Business Daily* published a listing of the top 25 growth funds for the year to date. Only 9 out of 25 (36 percent) of the funds reviewed actually outperformed the unmanaged S&P 500 Index. Investors purchasing an indexed mutual fund from Fidelity, Vanguard, U.S. Government FERS; or, a S&P Depository Receipt listed on the American Stock Exchange (Ticker symbol *MDY* or *SPY*), at the beginning of 1995, would have beat 64 percent of all Wall Street pro's. Nothing has changed since 1995. Historically, the S&P 500 Index total return outperforms the investment performance of professional money managers. Commissions do not guarantee equity growth performance; therefore, investors must keep investment cost as low as feasible.

Commissions charged by brokerage firms are split with the stockbroker who initiated the transaction. Firms will often terminate brokers who are low commission producers. It is not unusual for a stockbroker to earn a $10,000 monthly salary pushing junk with no guarantees. Remember: market place rules are geared for institutional investors. Full service brokerage firms are geared up to serve them even, at the expense of individual investors. To collect high commission salaries, full service brokerage firms usually charge a commission based upon the total dollar value of the transaction. For example, a $10,000 stock transaction could easily trigger commissions exceeding $300. The commission is then split between the brokerage firm and the stockbroker. Who can blame anyone for trying to make that kind of money within a matter of minutes? The individual investor can, that's who! An identical total dollar value transaction through a deep discount brokerage firm; who does not pay a stockbroker to give out bad advice, would cost between approximately $18 to $48. It does not take investors with the IQ of a brain surgeon to realize that a commission savings of up to $282 for each transaction adds up to possibly thousands of dollars saved annually. Dollars which can be applied toward substantial wealth building. Brokerage firms justify high commissions allegedly for providing a service associated with conducting a particular buy or sell transaction. "Spreads" are fees charged by the market maker or floor specialist for services related to arranging a buyer or seller necessary to fill orders. Investors should strive to keep commissions as low as possible.

Understand this! Commissions are bias against small investors; and, when combined with bad advice, could explain why a majority of investors loose money with stocktrading. At several full service brokerage firms, millionaire clients appear to be exempt from paying any commissions. The majority of full service brokerage firms offer their privileged clients a reduction in commissions for increased investment deposits, while socking it to investors with transactions of less than approximately $50,000. Small capitalized investors often pay up to 3.3 percent in commission fees for every trade, while their rich peers escape unharmed. There is little doubt small investors are helping the rich get richer through subsidizing their investment cost. Commissions may also limit the small players in competition with the rich. A large percentage of stock prices will fluctuate 2 to 4 percent daily. With commissions set at the average fluctuation percentage, small players would lose money day-trading short term price swings; whereas, the big money traders would make money, due to their commission break. If the small Investor is not invited to get the same break as the wealthy, they should take their business elsewhere. Deep discount brokerage firms and DRIP/DPP companies are waiting with open arms!

ALTERNATIVES: Every investor should take their hat off to Mr. Charles Schwab. Many years ago, he leveled the playing field by founding Charles Schwab and Company (1-800-540-6713). To the benefit of the independent investor, Schwab paved the way for substantial cost savings in commission rates. Mr. Schwab opened the flood gate and dozens of firms similar to Schwab were formed practically overnight. Individuals, at last could receive excellent stock trading execution service while eliminating full service stockbrokers from their wealth building equation. Fortunes could then be built through commission savings alone; and, without account churning or bad advice. Investors no longer need to waste investment money in order for their friendly stockbroker to be provided with fancy cars, big offices, French cooked meals; or, dozens of other commission driven perks. Should a stockbroker telephone, watch how fast they hang-up should the investor suggest they sign a contract guaranteeing a profit; or, refund any losses on the transaction the broker represented as being good for you. It would be unfair to scare investors away from stockbrokers, high commissions; or, wide spreads without providing an alternative. Before preceding; however, we should illustrate the importance of alternative investment concepts. Read the following two true stories carefully. Hopefully, the message they portray will help other investors side step similar traps.

TRUE STORIES: The nightmare began for two unlucky investors on May 14, 1984. On that day, little did they know what was about to unfold when they accepted an unsolicited telephone call from a stockbroker representing a well known full service brokerage firm. The stockbroker convinced one investor to open an account with him, valued at approximately $10,000. The second investor opened an account valued at approximately $5,000. The stockbroker traded both accounts, as an "Account Executive" until April 29, 1992. During the time he managed the two accounts, the stockbroker aggressively recommended 85 transactions with commissions exceeding $9,578. The sad part, is the broker also made 76 transactions without the knowledge of his clients. Commissions from unauthorized trades netted the stockbroker and his employer another $7,946. Between the two accounts, the broker took in over $17,524 in commissions for his firm. Although the accounts realized an annualized growth, they grossly under-performed the broad market. 161 trades occurred during the 8 year period. The stockbroker victimized his clients simply because they trusted him. Feeling betrayed, one client wrote the stockbroker a letter outlining what had been discovered. The "Account Executive" telephoned the client and complained that if his boss saw the letter he could be fired. Well, he was fired by his clients. Both accounts were moved to a deep discount brokerage firm. The incident sparked motivation within the investors. They became very interested in how the stock market really worked. As a result of their motivation, the investors established a strong financial investment plan; and, dedicated their experience toward helping others avoid similar wealth destroying situations (*Don't Die Broke*). They never recovered the ripped off commissions, because the broker hid the complaint from his boss. Remember! No stockbroker will give you a written guarantee.

The second story: On March 21, 1986, the telephone rang at an investors residence around dinner time. The call was from the same stockbroker involved in the previous horror story. The investor was told of a promising company named Corvus Systems, Inc. Based solely on the telephone contact, the investor purchased 385 Corvus shares for $2,402 including commissions. The commission was at 3.9 percent. The transaction statement contained a very important clue that should have alerted the investor of forthcoming problems. First, the statement indicated the transaction was an "unsolicited order." Secondly, in very small print was a notice indicating the brokerage firm was a market maker of the stock; and, a dealer for its own account regarding "odd lot" trades. Odd lot trades are more expensive to package, carry higher commission rates; and, consist of less than 100 share blocks: i.e., 50, 125, 1,058 shares are examples of "odd lot" transactions. The investor was not informed by the stockbroker of neither of these facts. The investor was an odd lot trader with 385 shares.

On July 11, 1986, the stockbroker once again contacted the investor with a recommendation to purchase shares of yet another unheard of company. Based upon information provided, the investor purchased 1,250 shares of Onyx IMI, Inc. for a net cost of $2,497. The commission rate and fees hit a whopping 6.48 percent. Thirty-nine days later, on August 19, 1986 Onyx merged into Corvus. Another fact, the broker should have known; but, failed to disclose on May 14; nor, July 11, 1986. The transaction statement once again indicated the transaction was an "unsolicited order". Another lie!

Based upon information received from the stockbroker, the investor made two additional purchases of Corvus through a local bank trust department. One purchase of 115 shares was valued at $582 including a 6.4 percent commission. A third purchase of 100 shares was valued at $229 with a the commission rate hitting 18 percent. The fixed dollar minimum commission rate paramounted into an extremely large percentage of the total transaction cost.

The soliciting broker never telephoned the investor with a warning that Corvus was in financial trouble. August 2, 1988 was a wipe-out for the investor. The investment was lost when Corvus filed Chapter 11 bankruptcy. Why did the stockbroker not telephone the investors advising them to sell the troubled stock? Was it because his employer, as the market marker, dumped the stock from the house account because they knew of the forthcoming bankruptcy! How good was the stockbrokers original advise? Very bad for the investor and bad for the brokerage firm.

BAD ADVICE: Individual investors are not the only ones who loose money based upon bad expert advise. For example: (1) The Orange County, California retirement plan filed bankruptcy due to massive losses within the plan after its broker "Account Executive" lost millions on improper investments. Orange County allegedly filed a two billion dollar lawsuit against the stockbroker and his employer. (2) Pier-1, Inc., claims $20 million in losses because of inappropriate trades after they hired an advisor to manage $37.5 million (*Investor's Business Daily* 12/27/95). (3) Fidelity Investments has been allegedly accused of wrongdoing; and, sued by an investor who claimed Fidelity manipulated the stock price of Mieru Technology, Inc., by touting the stock (encouraging investor to buy) while selling from a Fidelity house account. (4) "Adviser Goldlinger is sued by two New York clients" reads another report by the *Investor's Business Daily*. Allegedly the advisor collected substantial commissions from trading activities after being aware losses of $4.8 million had occurred. Law suites by cheated investors deserve serious consideration. Investors do have rights. They should fight against anyone breaching those rights.

Stock Investor Rights

* The right to never allow a cold caller stockbroker rip them off.
* The right to refuse signing a brokerage arbitration agreement.
* The right to hire a professional advisor with market place experience.
* The right to consult with an attorney regarding a stockbrokers conduct.
* The right to become self educated and motivated.
* The right to diversify across several different type of investments.
* The right to never pay for something they can get for free.
* The right to keep all their money working to their advantage.
* The right to conduct independent stock research.
* The right to learn from success as well as from mistakes.

Sadler and Associates (1-800-587-2570) of Atlanta, Georgia have attorneys with government regulatory agency and/or brokerage firm management experience. Sadler may provide assistance in the preparation of presenting a case before a securities arbitrator.

Securities Arbitration Commentator (1-201-761-5880) will provide for a modest fee, a national list of arbitration attorneys. They also publish an arbitration newsletter. A law suite may be the only recourse for a swindled investor; but, it's usually far from the minds of managers with golden parachute contracts containing huge stock option quotas. Management stock option performance award contracts were never designed to benefit long term buy-and-hold investors.

STOCK OPTIONS: The loaded gun dirty trick, designed through federal tax law, to protect the compensation interest of corporate America management, to the long term detriment of shareholders. A "stock option" is a management grant authorizing to them a right to purchase a specific number of shares at some future date for a predetermined price. Stock options may or may not be offered to the general investment community under the privileged management terms. Stocks having unexercised option grant, exceeding 5 percent of the market float should be suspect. Watch the stock price very close especially if the price has began an uptrend within the 60 days preceding the option expiration date. The stock could be under manipulation by either management or the "flow control experts."

Lets review how an option could effect a stock price. Assume Mr. Corporate President has been granted an option to purchase 1 million shares (5 percent of the float) at a strike price of $6.00 per share three years hence. The current price is at $4.75. Mr. President is now motivated to accelerate the stock price as high above the $6.00 strike price feasible possible. To achieve that objective, he must generate greed among the current floating stockholders. Stockholders of record, the date the option package was granted will generally do well as the option expiration date approaches. Their risk of a price downtrend (loss) increases only after the options are exercised. Why? As previously stated, Mr. President needs to generate greed among the players. To meet that objective, he could attempt to show a rosy corporate picture though manipulation of corporate earnings reports, glowing press releases, and the use of countless other dirty tricks. If he is successful, and they usually are, as the price moves well above $6.00, he will exercise his option rights.

Where does the stock he purchase come from? The optioned stock is usually released from corporate reserves. Although not in the floating pool yet it soon will be. Mr. President is often allowed to borrow from the corporate general fund, at arms length (no collateral), a short term interest free loan to purchase the stock. During the loan term, he sells his position at current market prices to cover the loan. He keeps the difference and walks away rich while the equity value of other stockholders plummet. The additional flood of stock infusion into the floating stock pool dilutes the existing equity per share. The price will continue to retrace until market makers move in and limit supply through reducing the float. They remove stock from the shelf and store it in their house account warehouse.

To conclude this chapter, it is very important to understand term and game players of the market place. Never invest against the "flow control experts!" Experienced investors protect their investment through every "trick in the book." The agiotage paradox clearly emerges when evidence points to a conclusion that secrets written in "the book" have only been shared with a few. Students of *Don't Die Broke* have a clear asset management advantage based on the experience of dozens of investors that have made personal fortunes through equity investing. These people were just like most Americans. They were perhaps no different than you are right this moment! They graduated from high school investment illiterate. They were motivated to learn the stock market game after being burned by instigated stockbroker greed. They were and still are the average "Joe", so to speak. In fact, they could even be your neighbor. Now to chapter 4

--NOTES---

CHAPTER 4

WINNING STRATEGIES

Let's get down to the business of successful investing. In this chapter, investors will be introduced to several investment strategies which have historically offered superior investment returns. Although there are no guarantees, strategies reviewed have proven to be winners throughout both bear and bull stock markets. Best of all, investors will be shown how to slip the grip of stockbrokers, hot tipsters; and, so called market guru's. Individuality is the name of the game! To make the individual choice a reality, we will share with aspiring investors the secret of selecting the best performing stocks the market can offer. Short selling, DRIP, DPP, dollar-cost-averaging, real estate investment trust (REIT), exponential moving averages, bonds, Dow theories, overhead pressure; and, much more will be reviewed in detail. Any single strategy standing alone, could aid any investor in acquiring skills necessary to accumulate substantial wealth. The publisher of *Don't Die Broke* utilizes one or more of the illustrated strategies on every investment selection. We would not share them with our readers, if they had not historical performed well.

<u>STOP HERE UNTIL YOU COMPLETE THE APPENDIX WORKSHEETS</u>

For the strategies to perform, investors must be prepared mentally and financially to accept the risk associated with success. The wealth building road is very bumpy. There are a lot of potholes to navigate around. Do not even consider taking that road; until, an evaluation of your net worth is completed. At regular mile post along the wealth building road, the investors net worth will need to be reevaluated. Wealth building is only measured through net worth growth. Anyone earning a million dollars annually while experiencing a net worth reduction of $1 is a loser! Complete the worksheets provided for your convenience in the Appendix. They will aid in the development of a wealth building financial plan. Investors wishing to earn an excellent commission marketing this publication should review the Publishers offer also located in the Appendix.

Never place investment funds at risk, until you understand the investment strategy; and, have developed investment skills well enough to reward yourself with winning transactions 80 percent of the time. Keep personal debt load under control. Practice with a "play money" portfolio until portfolio management skills provide winning results on the majority of investment transactions. A target annual net worth growth should be approximately twice the 30 year U.S. Treasury bond yield percentage. In October, 1997 the annualized net worth growth target was 12.76 percent. Should the growth objective experiences a shortfall, do not become disappointed. Investing is not by any stretch of the imagination an exact science. *Mutual Funds* (Oct '97) drives that point home very well. They report that only 77 domestic stock funds over the past 10 year investment period actually beat the S&P 500 Index. 84 percent of managed mutual funds fell short of the benchmark!

The accumulation of investment funds is one penny at a time. $10,000 appears to be the ideal minimum amount for entry into an individual stock selection wealth building plan. Some experts recommend investors remain in mutual funds until a net worth of $100,000 is obtained. We do not subscribe to that philosophy. Instead we recommend starting with $500, while limiting investments to a percentage of net worth. It is very important to remain focused on your objective not to die broke. Avoid commissions whenever possible. With a $10,000 entry point, commissions can be so low, that gross profits are possible after the stock price increases by a fraction of a percent. Limiting commission rates to a mere fraction of one percent is essential. Do not waste time and money purchasing small odd lot blocks of shares. 100 shares of a $8 stock, for example. After factoring the transaction for commissions, administrative fees, inflation, and taxes; foolishly investing into low priced small order transactions, generally traps the investor into becoming a victim of their own greed! Smart investors stick with equity investing while limiting exposure to debt (loaning money) instruments. As previously mentioned, we recommend that investment funds be allocated and controlled by a percentage of net worth. To our knowledge there has never been an investment allocation formula devised, which has provided 100 percent protection from net worth downside risk. Hundreds of asset allocation formulas do suggest risk protection through diversification of assets across several investments. One recommended asset allocation model; however, does appear superior to others we have reviewed. Investors are encouraged to consider the following allocation model. It was designed to reduce downside investment risk while protecting net worth.

Net Worth - Investment Allocation

Investment	Percent of Net Worth
Margin Account Limit	2%
Single Stock.	5%
Single Mutual Fund.	10%
Total Investment Real Estate.	30%
Maximum Debt Load	37%
Maximum Bond Holdings:	.80 (x) Age
Maximum Stock Holdings	100 (-) Age

NOTE: Net worth is total assets less total liabilities. 15.7 percent of career reported earnings should equal the investors social security account value. Social security should be considered a bond (debt) investment when factoring a bond allocation too net worth. Investors are encouraged to obtain a *Statement of Benefits* from the Social Security Administration semi-annually. Total all the reported earnings listed on the statement. Multiply the sum by 15.7 percent. That figure should be very close to your social security account bond holding market value. The maximum stock investments include the value of all stocks owned regardless of where they are held. In addition to allocating investment assets to net worth, investors are encouraged to abide by the stocktrader golden rules.

Stocktrader Golden Rules

* The only good investment are those which make money.
* Limit investments to 3 or 4 proven strategies.
* Investing is like raising chickens. Eventually everyone gets plucked.
* Always invest into an uptrend.
* Fads, bad news, demographic change; and, new technology create opportunities.
* Keep investments properly allocated to net worth.
* Compute net worth quarterly.
* Control margin usage temptations. Never borrow money to roll craps.
* Dump losers. Keep winners until they become losers.
* Avoid the temptation to follow the crowd. They are usually wrong!
* Nothing is new in a free market. No investor is a consistent profit taker in a free market.
* Adjustments will be necessary to invest in sync with the "flow control experts."
* Markets are never wrong, only the investors are.
* Seek investment concept knowledge. You can't play the game without knowing the rules.
* Limit losses to 7 percent below the initial purchase price <u>before</u> a positive uptrend is confirmed.

* Once a positive uptrend is confirmed, through a 15 week exponential moving average computation, limit the stock price downtrend to two consecutive plots below the moving average value; or, 15 percent below the highest price point, whichever is less. Never allow a profit to convert into a loss.
* Wealth is accumulated one penny at a time. Go slow and grow.

The *Stock Traders Golden Rules* naturally give way to a positive equity portfolio having characteristics that include:

* Simplicity.
* Liquidity.
* Individuality.
* Low net worth risk.
* Low commissions.
* Low Spreads.
* Peace of mind.
* 24 hour daily trading convenience.
* Steady long term growth potential.
* Diversification.
* Fully Invested during market up trends.
* In a cash or alternative investment on downtrends.

A personal investment plan must always consider the expenses associated with income production, too include:

* Total debt limited to 37 percent of annual gross income.
* Revolving charge account balance limited to 20 percent of annual gross income.
* Emergency cash reserve equal to three months gross income.
* Transportation account established with funds set aside for the account each paycheck.
* Tax deferred retirement plan established.
* Home ownership with the equity equal to a minimum of 15 percent of the appraised value.
* Continued education.

Armed with the golden rules plus a proper allocation to net worth, investors can sidestep conflicting investment theories. They can make individual choices trade after trade. Leave speculation to the gamblers while moving onto the historically proven *Winning Strategies*.

DIVIDEND REINVESTMENT PROGRAMS (DRIP'S): DRIP's exceed the basic requirement for successful wealth building. They offer the elements of time, compounding, capital appreciation, low originating fees; and, peace of mind. They guide investors into a circle of top quality corporations. DRIP investing is easy to understand. Simplicity. The concept is straightforward. Investors purchase a single stock share through a brokerage firm of their choice. After which, they take delivery of the stock certificate. Next, the investor request and file a DRIP application with the host company. Finally, additional shares are purchased directly from the host company. Dividend distributions are reinvested into additional shares. DRIP shares can be purchased in fractional share quantities. Shares purchased from the DRIP provider have low administrative fees, no odd-lot charges; and, never a commission. DRIP's can easily be started with very little money; however, it is very important to make purchases into a positive market uptrend; and, to plot the stocks 15 week exponential moving average weekly. Practically the only long term downside risk is the problem of short term liquidity. To eliminate that problem, investors are encouraged to request the provider issue a stock certificate equal to 80 percent of the outstanding shares assigned to their account semi-annually. The stock can then be sold, at the investors convenience. Hopefully, through a deep discount brokerage firm at a low commission cost, should a sell signal be triggered. More than 1000 corporations across America and around the world extend DRIP's to investors. To identify DRIP companies within your neighborhood follow these steps:

<u>Drip Company Search</u>

* Search for companies whose products or services you enjoy.
* Inquire with their shareholder representative about the feasibility of offering a DRIP.
* DRIP sources include *Drip Investor* (1-800-711-7969); and, *The Money Paper* (1-800-388-9993).

To assist our readers in establishing their DRIP investment plan, we offer the following selected DRIP company listing. Included is the company name, stock ticker symbol; and, telephone number.

NAME	STOCK SYMBOL	TELEPHONE #
Abbott Laboratories	ABI	617-575-2900
ALCO Standard Corp.	ASN	215-296-8000
Allied Signal, Inc.	ALD	201-455-2127
Aluminum Co. of America	AA	412-553-4708
Amerada Hess Corp.	AHC	212-997-8500
American Brands, Inc.	AMB	800-524-4458
American Express Co.	AXP	800-647-4273
Amoco Corp.	AN	800-446-2617
Anheuser-Busch Inc.	BUD	314-477-2039
Atlanta Gas Light Co.	ATG	404-584-3794
Ball Corp.	BLL	317-747-6472
Baltimore Gas & Electric Co.	BGE	800-258-0499
Bank of New England Corp.	NEB	617-742-4000
Bank South Corp.	BKSO	404-529-4238
Bank America Corp.	BAC	800-642-9880
Barnett Banks, Inc.	BBI	800-524-4458
Bausch & Lomb Inc.	BOL	800-526-0801
Bell South Corp.	BLS	800-631-6001
Black & Decker Corp.	BDK	410-583-2890
Block, H&R Inc.	HRB	816-753-6900
Campbell Soup Co.	CPB	609-342-3585
Carolina Freight Co.	CAO	704-435-6811
Caterpillar Inc.	CAT	309-675-1000
Chemical Waste Management Inc.	CHW	708-218-1500
Chervon Corp.	CHV	415-894-7700
Chrysler Corp.	C	313-956-3007
Citicorp	CCI	800-342-6690
Clorox Co.	CLX	510-271-7000
Coca-Cola Bottling Co.	COKE	704-374-2697
Coca-Cola Company	KO	800-446-2617
Colgate Palmolive Co.	CL	212-791-6422
ConAgra Inc.	CAG	402-595-4000
Cooper Industries Inc.	CBE	713-739-5400
CSX Corp.	CSX	800-521-5571
Cummins Engine Co. Inc.	CUM	800-446-2617

Dana Corp.	DCN	800-537-8823
Dean Foods Co.	DF	312-625-6200
Deere & Co.	DE	309-765-8000
Delta Air Lines Inc.	DAL	404-897-3464
Detroit Edison Co.	DTE	313-237-8757
Dial Corp.	DL	800-453-2235
Disney	DIS	818-560-1000
Dow Chemical Co.	DOW	517-636-1463
DuPont E.I. de Nemuurs & Co.	DD	800-488-3853
Duke Power Co.	DUK	800-488-3853
Eastman Kodak Co.	EK	716-258-5853
Emerson Electric Co.	EMR	314-553-2197
Energen Corp.	EGN	800-654-3206
Engelhard Corp.	EC	212-791-6422
Equifax Inc.	EFX	404-885-8000
Exxon Corp.	XON	212-791-3409
Fay's Inc.	FAY	800-526-0801
Fina Inc.	FI	212-791-6422
Fleming Companies Inc.	FLM	405-840-7200
Flowers Industries Inc.	FLO	800-772-5364
Food Lion Inc.	FDLW	800-633-4236
Ford Motor Co.	F	800-521-1190
Foster Wheeler Corp.	FWC	800-524-4458
Freeport McMo Ran Inc.	FTX	504-582-4458
Gannett Co. Inc.	GCI	703-284-6000
General Electric Co.	GE	203-373-2816
General Mills Inc.	GIS	800-445-4802
General Signal Corp.	GSX	203-357-8800
Genuine Parts Co.	GPC	404-588-7822
Georgia-Pacific Corp.	GP	212-791-6422
Gerber Products Co.	GEB	312-461-2549
Giant Food Inc.	GFS-A	301-341-8480
Gillette Co.	GS	617-421-7000
Goodyear Tire & Rubber	GT	216-796-3751
Handy & Harman	HNH	212-707-2690
Harland (John H) Co.	JH	800-772-5564
Harris Corp.	HRS	305-727-9283
Heinz, H.J. Co.	HNZ	800-233-3399
Hercules Inc.	HPC	212-613-7147
Hershey Foods Corp.	HSY	717-534-7526
Home Depot Inc.	HD	770-433-8211
Home Stake Mining	HM	415-624-4100

Honeywell Inc.	HON	800-647-4273
Hudson's Bay Co.	T:HBC	416-981-8997
Ingersoll-Rand Co.	IR	800-524-4458
Inland Steel Industries Inc.	IAD	704-383-5183
IBM	IBM	212-735-7000
Int'l Multifoods Corp.	IMC	800-446-2617
Int'l Paper Co.	IP	914-397-1500
Johnson & Johnson	JNJ	800-446-2617
Johnson Control, Inc.	JCI	414-287-3956
Justin Industries Inc.	JSTN	817-390-2415
Kellogg Co.	K	616-961-2765
Kerr-McGee Corp.	KMG	405-231-6711
Kimberly-Clark Corp.	KMB	800-442-2001
Kmart Corp.	KM	800-257-1770
Kroger Properties Inc.	KOG	800-633-4236
Lay-Z-Boy Chair Co.	LZB	212-936-5100
Lance Inc.	LNCE	704-554-1421
Lilly, Ell, & Co.	LLY	800-833-8699
Limited, The Inc.	LTD	614-479-7000
Liz Claiborne	LIZC	212-676-3822
Louisiana Pacific Corp.	LPX	503-221-0800
Lowe's Companies Inc.	LTR	919-651-4000
Luby's Cafeteria Inc.	LUB	512-654-9000
Lukens Inc.	LUC	215-383-2601
Lyondall Petrochemical Co.	LYO	800-524-4458
Manufacturers Hanover Corp.	MHC	212-613-7147
Manufacturers National Corp.	MNTL	800-521-1190
Marsh Supermarkets, Inc.	MARS	317-594-2647
Martin Marietta Corp.	ML	301-897-6000
Maytag Corp.	MYG	515-791-8344
McDermott Int'l Inc.	MDR	504-587-5682
McDonald's Corp.	MCD	800-791-6422
McGraw-Hill Inc.	MHP	212-512-2000
McKesson Corp.	MCK	415-983-8367
Mead Corp.	MEA	513-222-6323
Medusa Corp.	MSA	800-678-6338
Merck & Co. Inc.	MRK	908-594-6627
Merrill Lynch & Co. Inc.	MER	212-510-6834
Midwest Resources Inc.	MWR	800-247-5211
Minnesota Mining an Manufacturing Co.	MMM	612-450-4064
Mobil Corp.	MOB	800-648-9291
Monsanto Co.	MTC	314-694-1000
Morgan, J.P. & Co. Inc.	JPM	212-791-6422

Morrison Knudsen Corp.	MK	208-345-5000
Motorola Inc.	MOT	312-461-5335
Nashua Corp.	NSH	603-880-2323
National Standard Co.	NSD	800-777-1618
Neiman Marcus Group	NMG	617-232-0760
New York Times Co.	NYT-.A	212-791-6422
NICOR Inc.	GAS	708-305-9500
Nordson Corp.	NDSN	216-892-1580
Norfolk Southern Corp.	NSC	804-533-4810
Northrop Corp.	NOC	212-613-7147
Norwest Corp.	NOB	612-450-4180
Occidental Petroleum Corp.	OXY	800-622-9231
Ohio Edison Co.	OEC	800-736-3403
Old Stone Corp.	OST-N	401-825-3564
Olin Corp.	OLN	203-356-2000
Outboard Marine Corp.	OM	800-442-2001
Pall Corp.	PLL	516-484-5400
Penney, J.C. Co. Inc.	JCP	800-524-4458
Pennzoil Co.	PZL	713-546-4000
Pep Boys- Manny, Moe & Jack	PBY	215-229-9000
PepsiCo, Inc.	PEP	914-253-3055
Pfizer, Inc.	PFE	212-573-3704
Phelps Dodge Corp.	PD	602-234-8100
Phillip Morris	MO	800-446-2617
Phillips Petroleum Co.	P	800-356-0066
Piccadilly Cafeteria Inc.	PIC	504-293-9440
Quaker Oats Co.	OAT	800-344-1198
Quaker State Corp.	KSF	814-676-7676
Questar Corp.	STR	801-534-5885
Ralston Purina Co.	RAL	314-982-3000
Raytheon Co.	RTN	617-575-2900
Reynolds Metals Co.	RLM	804-281-4765
Rockwell International Corp.	ROK	412-565-7120
Rollin's Inc.	ROL	404-588-7817
Rouse Co.	ROUS	410-992-6000
Rubbermaid Inc.	RBD	216-264-6464
Safety-Kleen Corp.	SK	708-697-8460
Savannah Foods & Industries Inc.	SVAN	912-234-1261
Schering-Plough Corp.	SGP	201-822-7436
Scott Paper Co.	SPP	800-752-0771
Sears, Roebuck & Co.	S	312-875-6705
Sherwin-Williams Co.	SHW	216-687-5745

Snap-On-Tools	SNA	414-656-5200
Southern Co.	SO	404-393-4498
Standard Products Co.	SPD	216-575-2532
Stanley Works	SWK	800-526-0801
Super Valu Stores Inc.	SVU	612-450-4075
Tambrands Inc.	TMB	914-696-6543
Tenneco Inc.	TGT	800-446-2617
Texaco Inc.	TX	800-283-9785
Textron Inc.	TXT	212-791-6422
Thomas & Betts Corp.	TNB	201-685-1600
Thomas Industries Inc.	TII	502-893-4600
Tidewater Inc.	TDW	504-568-1010
Time Warner Inc.	TWX	212-484-6971
Timkin Co.	TKR	216-471-3376
Toro Co.	TTC	612-887-8526
Transamerica Corp.	TA	800-446-2617
Trans Canada Pipeline Ltd.	TRP	403-267-6806
Travelers Corp.	TIC	800-288-9541
Tribune Co.	TRB	800-222-9100
TRW Inc.	TRW	800-442-2001
Tyco Laboratories Inc.	TYC	603-778-9700
Union Camp Corp.	UCC	201-628-2000
Union Carbide Corp.	UK	203-794-2212
Union Electric Co.	UEP	800-255-2237
Union Pacific Corp.	UNP	212-791-6422
Union Planters Corp.	UPC	901-523-6656
United Technologies Corp.	UTX	203-728-7000
United Telecommunication	UT	913-624-2541
Universal Corp.	UW	804-254-1303
Universal Foods Corp.	UFC	414-271-6755
UNOCAL Corp.	ULL	800-252-2233
Upjohn Co.	UPJ	800-253-8600
USF & G Corp.	FG	410-547-3311
US West Inc.	USW	800-537-0222
Vulcan Materials Co.	VMC	205-877-3204
Wachovia Corp.	WB	919-770-5787
Walgreen Co.	WAG	708-940-2936
Warner-Lambert Co.	WLA	201-540-2000
Waste Management Inc.	WMX	708-572-8800
Wells Fargo &Co.	WFC	415-396-0560
Wendy's International Inc.	WEN	614-764-3100
Westinghouse Electric	WX	412-244-3654
Whirlpool Corp.	WHR	800-526-8762
Winn Dixie Stores	WIN	904-783-5000

Woolworth Corp.	Z	212-553-2000
Wrigley	WWY	800-824-9681
Xerox Corp.	XRX	800-828-6396
Zurn Industries	ZRN	814-452-211

DRIP companies tend to market products or services well known among consumers worldwide. Utility companies are also excellent DRIP target corporations. With a little research, even the smallest capitalized investor, can begin a life long investment relationship with their favorite corporation. DRIP investing is an excellent way for children to began an investment portfolio. It is a long term investment approach. As with any investment, it needs managing no differently than any other business. Diversify across several companies and market sectors. DRIP investing may be started with as little as $100. Of course, the initial investment has to be placed through a stock brokerage firm; however, that requirement is rapidly changing. The Direct Purchase Program was introduced to investors in 1996.

DIRECT PURCHASE PROGRAM (DPP): Created in 1996, after the Securities and Exchange Commission (SEC), along with several state securities regulators, gave qualifying corporations the authority to bypass regulatory procedures mandating investors to purchase all initial public offering stock through a brokerage firm. The State of Georgia, for example, authorized small venture companies, having less than $1 million in stock market value, to offer for sell their IPO directly to investors. California authorized similar securities regulations. Check with your local Secretary of State for DPP companies approved within your state. If the authority has not yet been approved, investors are being denied an excellent investment opportunity. They should consider petitioning their elected officials to implement DPP. A word of caution, please. DPP's are often representative of companies without a proven track record. Anyone venturing into this arena, must do so with extreme caution. The potential profits equal the risk of loses. Small capitalized companies can offer big returns as well as gigantic loses. DPP's are spreading very fast as larger corporations open their investment door to welcome investors. Mr. Carlson, publisher of *DRIP Investor* hit it on target when stating; "It doesn't take a lot of money to assemble a starter portfolio of no-load stocks." (*Atlanta-Journal Constitution* 12-2-96). We Agree! Direct purchases can begin a wealth building portfolio for as low as $50. Constant expansion of the DPP concept offers diversification across both domestic and international boundaries. Many DRIP and DPP companies are so well diversified across international boundaries, they actually represent what amounts to an international mutual fund. An international corporation selling a multiple product line across several economic, political, and monetary subdivisions, are perhaps one of the safest long term "buy and forget" investments around. Investors must never forget that regardless of how tempting an investment may appear, the only good investment is the one going up in value. As with any stock, monitor the DPP trend through computation of the stock's 15 week exponential moving average based up on the Wednesday closing price.

Investors may request a listing of more than 180 DPP companies from National Corporation Services Inc., website (http://www.csn.net/ir/direct.html). Another source of DPP companies, is the Direct Stock Purchase Plan Clearing House (1-800-774-4117). Review the current stock price of the DPP stocks listed. As with any stock, select only the best performing stocks. Search for stocks whose price is hitting a new high. New products. New management. A relative strength and earnings per share *IBD* ranking above 79. A review of the Analytical Study section of this chapter will be helpful in the selection process. As with the DRIP investment, request your company issue to you 80 percent of the shares held within the account at least twice annually. Track the price performance moving average as detailed within the *15 week Exponential Moving Average* section of this chapter, to identify the sell point of the issued stocks. Hold 20 percent in the account as a base to build from when a buy signal is triggered.

DPP Company Search

NAME	STOCK SYMBOL	TELEPHONE #
ABT Building Products	ABTC	800-286-9178
Advanta	ADVN	800-851-9673
AFLAC	AFL	800-227-4756
AirTouch Communications	ATI	800-233-5601
Amoco	AN	800-821-8100
Atmos Energy	ATO	800-382-8667
Bard, C.R.	BCR	800-828-1639
Barnett Bank	BBI	800-328-5822
Bob Evans Farm	BOBE	800-272-7675
BRE Properties	BRE	800-368-8392
CMS Energy	CMS	800-774-4117
Capstead Mortgage	CMO	800-358-2323
Carpenter Technology	CRS	800-822-9828
Central and South West	CSR	800-527-5797
Crown American Reality Trust	CWN	800-278-4353
DQE	DQE	800-247-0400
DTE Energy	DTE	800-551-5009
Dominion Resources	D	800-522-4034
Duke Realty	DRE	800-278-4353
Eastern Company	EML	800-633-3455
Energen	EQN	800-286-9178
Enova	ENA	800-307-7343
Entergy	ETR	800-225-1721
Equitable Cos.	EQ	800-437-8736
Exxon	XON	800-252-1800
First USA	FUS	800-482-8410
General Growth Properties	GGP	800-774-4117
Guidant Corp.	GDT	800-537-1677
Hillenbrand Industries	HB	800-286-9178
Home Depot	HD	800-928-0380
Home Properties	HME	800-278-4353
Houston Industries	HOU	800-231-6406
Illinova	ILN	800-750-7011
Integon	IN	800-826-3978
Johnson Controls	JCV	800-524-6220

Home Properties	HME	800-278-4353
Houston Industries	HOU	800-231-6406
Illinova	ILN	800-750-7011
Integon	IN	800-826-3978
Johnson Controls	JCV	800-524-6220
Kerr McGee	KMG	800-395-2662
Madison Gas & Electric	MDSN	800-356-6423
McDonald's	MCO	800-228-9623
MidAmerican Energy	MEC	800-247-5211
Minnesota Power & Light	MPL	800-535-3056
Mobil	MOB	800-648-9291
Montana Power	MTP	800-245-6767
Morton International	MII	800-990-1010
NorAm Energy	NAE	800-843-3445
Norwest	NOB	800-813-3324
Owens Corning	OWC	800-452-2210
Penney, J.C.	JCP	800-565-2576
Peoples Energy	PGL	800-228-6888
Pharmacia & Upjohn	PNU	800-286-9178
Piedmont Natural Gas	PNY	800-633-4236
Portland General	PGN	800-808-2233
Proctor & Gamble	PG	800-764-7483
Reader's Digest	RDA	800-242-4653
Region's Financial	RGBK	800-922-3468
SCANA Corp.	SCG	800-763-5891
Southern Company	SO	800-554-7626
Southern Union Corp.	SUG	800-793-8938
Tenneco	TEN	800-446-2617
Texaco	TX	800-283-9785
Tyson Foods	TYSN-A	800-822-7096
U.S. West Communications	USW	800-537-0222
Urban Shopping Centers	URB	800-992-4566
Utilicorp United	UCU	800-647-2789
Viad	VVI	800-453-2235
WPS Resources	WPS	800-236-1551
Wal*Mart	WMT	800-438-6278

Western Resources	WR	800-236-1551
Whitman	WH	800-660-4187
Wisconsin Energy	WEC	800-558-9663
York International	YRK	800-437-6726

Direct stock purchases of foreign companies are normally through the purchase of an American Depository Receipt (ADR). ADR's are receipts which represent a specific number of shares in the foreign business. One Emerson Electric Corporation ADR, for example, may represent 5 shares in the Emerson Electric Corporation. Typically, ADR's are purchased from the various stock exchanges through a brokerage firm. However, DPP ADR's are not listed on the exchange. They are sold directly to the investment public. Morgan Guaranty Trust Company (1-800-749-1687) represents dozens of foreign DPP corporations. Contact Morgan for their fee schedule and DPP list.

DRIP and DPP investing has tremendous advantages. A simple portfolio may be started with minimum funding. The portfolio tends to be global, well diversified, and offers simplicity. Direct investing into 3 to 5 companies could easily provide risk protection while enhancing equity appreciation normally associated with no-load or low load mutual funds. For clarification "load" is a fancy word for commission. "Mutual" is the coming together for the purpose of a common goal. "Funds" is the money needed for the mutual goal. The concept is based on the idea there is safety in numbers. Don't bet on it! To get the point, look no further than the October, 1997 market crash!

MUTUAL FUNDS: A very popular investment for the past 60 years. Mutual funds with just about any investment objective imaginable, flourish today. According to Lipper Analytical Services, Inc., more than 9000 mutual funds were operating within the United States during 1995; plus, another 11,000 operating outside the USA. Many mutual funds are small; but, there are giants in the business. Fidelity Investments of Boston, offer approximately 180 funds, including the fifty billion dollar Magellan Fund. Not all mutual funds are listed in the newspaper. Funds with less than 25 million in net asset value (NAV)are currently omitted. Website (http://www.mfmag.com) of *Mutual Fund* magazine list mutual fund prices for funds having a NAV of less than $25 million. Funds listed on the website are often not advertised. They may be small; but, many are extremely well managed and profitable. To locate the telephone number, recent performance; and, current net asset value (NAV) of funds with a NAV exceeding $25 million, review the mutual fund tables provided in the latest edition of the *Investor's Business Daily*.

Mutual funds are either "load" (commissions charged) or "no load." Load bearing funds may either be front or aft-end loaded. Funds are either "closed-end" or "open-end" registered.

Shares of closed-end funds are listed on the various stock exchanges and are traded through the auction process similar to stock. They either sell at a discount or at a premium to their NAV. Closed-end mutual funds have a limited number of authorized shares. They may represent a single country, sector, or concept. One reported profitable method of trading close-end funds is to buy the fund when it is at a 20 percent discount and then liquidate the position when the discount narrows to 15 percent. Another trading strategy is to buy shares when the current discount from the NAV is greater than the historical moving average discount. For example, a buy signal is flashed if the current discount is 20 percent; but, the average discount is 17 percent. A sell signal is flashed when the actual discount to the average discount spread is eliminated. Avoid funds selling at a premium to the NAV. Profits can be realized when the discount is removed as a closed-end fund converts to open-ended fund status.

Open-end mutual funds; unlike their closed-end counterparts, sell and redeem their shares directly to investors. They will always sell either at a premium (commission load factored into the price); or, at their net asset value. Open-end mutual funds number into the thousands and represent just about any investment objective imaginable. Each fund has its own trading rules and limitations. Investers with limited funds are wise to start investments here.

Investing through mutual funds can be rewarding, if the traps are avoided. Pass up funds with 12b-1 fees. 12b-1 fees are charged by some fund managers to compensate them for advertising the fund. Limit loads (commissions) to zero when possible. Loads and fees of any description never guarantee performance results and should be avoided. No-load and closed-end funds perform just as well. Limit management fees to 1 1/2 percent of the funds NAV. Select funds which authorize direct deposits; and, a minimum of 4 telephone exchanges annually. Initially enter into the mutual fund family through a companion money market account, offering check writing privileges. The money market should pay a dividend yield of not less than 80 percent of the current 30 year treasury bond yield. For example, if the treasury is yielding 7 percent, the seven day yield of the money market fund should not be less than 5.6 percent annualized (.07 x .80 = .056). Also:

* Fund total return performance should be superior to the S & P 500 Index 3 out of the most recent 5 years.

* Fund management should have at minimum a 3 year track record managing the specific fund.

* The fund should report low rollover cost. A reduced rollover cuts associated brokerage fees the fund must pay to trade stock in order to meet the management's investment objective. Avoid funds experiencing consistent roll over. Funds trading more than 50 percent of the shares held annually may be doing so to generate commissions for a stockbroker buddy.

* The fund should be investing into a long term trend. Investing into a long term economic trend will generally reduce fund portfolio rollover transaction cost. Total administration cost will be lower and that is very bullish.

* Ask the fund, the date of their next dividend distribution. If it's within 30 days, wait until after the distribution before investing. The funds NAV value will bias downward to absorb the distribution. Investors will be taxed on their own money because the IRS treats dividends as income.

* Track the funds price moving average before buying. Buy after a price uptrend has been confirmed. Check the performance of other funds holding similar investments. The majority of similar objective funds should be experiencing similar performance.

* Except for subscribers to the *Mutual Fund Forecaster* (1-800-442-9000), investors should always read the funds prospectus. For a modest subscribership fee, the Institute for Econometric Research does an excellent job screening out the dogs.

* Check out the Mutual Fund Council (1-212-768-2477) website (http://networth.galf.comm.council) for a current list of 100 percent no load funds.

Mutual fund investing is generally a long term investment strategy. Therefore, it is important to ask questions.

<u>Mutual Fund Questions</u>

* How do I purchase shares?
* How do I sell Shares?
* What services are provided?
* What is the investment objective?
* Has management outperformed the S&P-500 Index 3 out of the past 5 years?
* What are the fees and expenses?
* What are the trading restrictions.

* How are dividend distributions made and taxed?
* What is the five year total return track record?
* How long has the fund been managed by the current manager?
* What is the current management strategy (individual or group)?

Mutual fund total returns tend to outperform returns offered by checking, savings, bonds, certificates of deposits; or, other debt investments by a wide margin. Discounting inflation and taxes, equity investments have the potential of doubling the investors money every 7.2 years. Over the past century, common stocks have averaged an annualized total return of approximately 10 percent. Dividend compounding, time; and, capital infusion are the ingredients which create fortunes. None of the ingredients will occur, if the potential investor is so debt over loaded they never realize the opportunity to invest into equities. With an investment portfolio doubling each 7.2 years, a single $10,000 investment can develop into substantial wealth over a long investment horizon. This is one of many reasons children should be taught at the earliest age, the importance of debt, asset, and investment management.

Investment 7.2 Year Doubling Factor

AGE	INVESTMENT
20	$ 10,000
27.5	$ 20,000
35	$ 40,000
42.5	$ 80,000
50	$160,000
57.5	$320,000
65	$740,000

Factoring into a mutual funds total return, 31 percent federal tax plus 4 percent for the historical annualized inflation rate, an investment beginning at age 20 could easily exceed an after tax value of $375,000 (1997 dollars) by age 65. Not a bad deal by any measurement! A retirement draw-down of 10 percent could provide a lifetime annual retirement income of $37,500; plus, social security and pension income. Another thought! Why doesn't the federal government deposit $10,000 into an individually numbered equity account the next business day after a child is born and forget about social security, and other programs which tax away the quality of life?

Investors seeking information on asset allocation among mutual funds have many sources of information available through newsletters, banks, and brokerage firms. The *Mutual Fund Forecaster* (1-800-442-9000), the International Association for Financial Planning (1-800-945-4237); and, Schwab Advisor Source (1-800-777-3337) are excellent sources for asset allocation information. Telephone numbers for mutual fund families are published daily in the *Investor's Business Daily*.

Investing through DRIP, DPP and mutual funds, should be considered a long term wealth building strategy. Holding the investment position 3 to 5 years or longer is acceptable. After the original share purchase, additional shares are accumulated throughout the holding period either through regular cash infusion, or dividend reinvestments. Purchases at regular intervals in fixed dollar amounts will provide a moving average price through "dollar-cost-averaging." The alternative to "dollar-cost-averaging" is to remain invested in mutual fund equities during a general performance uptrend; but, moving investment funds into and out of the equity position based upon the mutual funds 75 day (15 week) exponential moving average performance. A long term investing strategy does not imply anyone should make an investment and then forget it. Never make the false assumption, it will be professionally managed to the investor's benefit. Mutual fund managers do frequently sell stocks. It is not uncommon for a fund manager to sell 100 percent of their portfolio annually. Long term investing does not mean for the investor to hang onto a sinking ship. Think of a mutual fund as a single stock with many economic subparts. If it's loosing money, sell! Park the funds in a money market until your favorite fund begins a price performance up trend. Once the uptrend is confirmed, buy shares. Hold the position until a sell signal is flashed. Limit investment funds into a single mutual fund to 10 percent of your total net worth, including a "best guess" value of social security. Understand this: people with a negative net worth should avoid investing until they develop a positive net worth and the recommended cash reserves. Investing requires asset management. The only logical reason to invest is to increase net worth.

The individual social security account value should be approximately 15.7 percent times total reported accumulated earnings, with a 40 calendar quarter minimum. For example: assume social security reported earnings were $200,000 over 10 years. The social security account value should be approximate $31,400 ($200,000 x .157=$31,400). When computing net worth, use the social security account reported earnings accumulated after age 26. Social security is a real account having real value and should not be discarded lightly. Limiting a single mutual fund investment to 10 percent of net worth reduces risk associated with over-diversification while decreasing the probability of owning too much of a single stock through different mutual funds. Generally, stock ownership in 3 or 4 funds will provide maximum diversification. To reduce over-diversification complications, mutual fund investors should consider membership either in the Mutual Fund Investors Association (1-800-638-1987); or, the Institute for Econometric Research (1-800-442-9000). Adhering to their recommended asset allocation models, reduces the risk of owning the same stock through different mutual funds.

Investors willing to risk capital for potentially higher returns carrying associated downside risk may consider single country, region; or, industry sector funds. Sector funds focus on a particular economic sector. Investors, can purchase gold, food, natural gas, banks, real estate; and, dozens of other products through sector funds. Fidelity Investments (1-800-544-8888) offer the widest selection of sector mutual funds. Before considering sector investing, investors must have a working knowledge of which economic sector is up-trending. Is new housing purchases increasing? Are biochemical stocks moving up? Will cold weather create a demand for heater oil or natural gas? Will flooding in the grain belt create a bread shortage? Answers to questions of this nature can generate tremendous wealth through sector investing. Three methods are available to answer these and other sector performance questions. Although, past performance does not guarantee future performance, it can be a key indicator of momentum performance direction.

The first method, we at *Don't Die Broke* use to identify the performance trend of a specific sector, is to compare the target sector's percent of gain to other sectors since January 1st of a specific year to date. The sector with the highest percentage point gain is worth further investigation.

The second method we use to determine sector performance, is to identify which sectors have the highest percentage of stocks within the sector reaching "new high" historical price levels. New 52 week high price information is published daily by the *Investor's Business Daily*. Sectors with stocks hitting price levels never previously obtainedare worth serious investment consideration. The *Standard and Poor's Stock Guide* provides the information necessary to determine if the current 52 week high price is indeed the historical high price.

Finally, the performance of a fund can be determined between any two dates. Website (http://www.mfmag.com) is accessible for performance calculations. The service is provided by *Mutual Funds Magazine*. Once a sector is identified as being in play, the next step is to compute the Wednesday 15 week exponential moving average to confirm trend performance and direction. The procedure for computing the exponential moving average is explained later in this chapter.

Mutual fund investing requires flexibility. Telephone redemption and dividend reinvesting are essential. Dividend reinvestments force investors into dollar cost averaging. Telephone exchange authority provides a downside protection escape route during a rapid broad market decline, if the switchboard is not overloaded. Major market corrections generally occur over a very short time frame after an extensive long uptrend. A 10 percent year to date return can be wiped out in a single day! Investors should become a student of the market place. *Don't Die Broke* aids the independent investor in meeting that objective. As a student of the market, it is critical for investors to learn the importance of limiting equity investing during the historical months that a single day wipeout is most likely to occur. A strategy to capitalize from "good, bad, the ugly" annual economic cycles could prove to be a very wise long term investment decision. Do not be suckered into increasing investment activity during the "**JASON**"months. The market historically corrects sharply downward during these months while leaving market victims scattered along it's destructive path. Every market cycle is greed motivated; and, "flow control expert" manipulated to benefit a few, at the expense of everyone else. Investing against the experts will make any investor a loser! A strategy to capitalize from the stock market "good, bad, the ugly" cycles could prove to be a wise decision.

GOOD, BAD, the UGLY: Economic cycles repeat year after year; and, are driven through consumer based greed repetitive demands. Each spring the marriage cycle occurs. Summer brings on the housing construction and vacation travel boom, at the expense of a slump in corporate earnings as inventories are depleted. By August or September the stock market begins correcting to absorb the earnings shortfall. Each winter, consumers cycle into higher heating requirements. Retail sales increase through the holiday season. The stock market is downward biased by tax motivated selling, starting around the middle of September. Mid- December generally sees the market cycle bottom with a rebound accelerating into January. As a result of the way Americans conduct their lives, most gains in the stock market are realized over a mere 80 to 90 trading days between November and June. Throughout the "JASON" months stock prices generally enter into a price base consolidation or trend downward. Either way, stockholders are losing money due to missed opportunities available elsewhere. The cycle repeats year after year!

Extensive studies have been conducted into the American consumer economic cycles and their effects on wealth building. *The Wall Street Digest (1-941-954-5500)* suggest there are good and bad investment months created through consumer demand. One forty five year back-test study, compared the total investment return of a single lump sum "buy-and-hold" investment strategy verses equity trading based on consumer driven market cycles. Researchers divided the calendar year into two test month groupings for evaluation. One group included the dates between November 1st and April 30th. The remaining group included the dates between May 1st and October 31st. The "buy-and-hold" strategy was measured across the entire forty five years. A $10,000 lump sum invested on November 1st through April 30th annually and held in cash the remainder of the year appreciated to an amazing $190,526 during the forty five years. $10,000 invested over the same years between May 1st and October 31st annually, appreciated to a measly $17,204. The "buy-and-hold" strategy appreciated to approximately $88,000. Why the difference? First, major market corrections were avoided during the November-April investment months. During the forty five year research period, there were three market corrections between the November-April "good" months exceeding five percent. Equity growth during the "good" months averaged approximately 15 percent annually excluding the interest when compared to the "buy and hold" investment return of approximately 10 percent. Additional growth was enhanced by earned interest while the investment was held in cash between May 1st and November 1st annually.

"Good" month superior equity growth is supported by several factors. Retail sales generally improve as inflation lowers during the year end holiday season and spring recovery cycle. Thanksgiving, Christmas, New Years Day, Easter, Martin Luther King Day; and, Valentine's Day when combined with the Spring marriage cycle, crop planting, signing of summer merchandise delivery contacts, temporary help employment demands, new home purchases; and, related economical events push corporate earnings higher. Earnings beating Wall Street estimates generally push stock prices higher. Experts have discovered that approximately 85 percent of stock equity growth occur during the "good" months. There have been exceptions to the research findings. For example, economic cycles have either started late or earlier than forecasted for a variety of reasons. For example, the month of May between 1990 and 1997 has returned an excellent 4 percent annualized equity growth, beating the annualized total return of most bank accounts. In 1997, the DOW rose 19 percent during the "bad" months to eventually reverse direction on August 6th as the majority of stocks traded above their 200 day moving price average. "Good" months of December and February also have a tendency to develop into down-market due to tax selling and holiday charge card covering. How-be-it, overall the "good" months remain intact, as the best stock investment months.

"Bad" months witness the absence of the corporate earnings found during the "good" months. Profits reported during the "good" months are generally generated through the use of plastic debt which not only effects future corporate earnings; but, practically every other category of investments. Money removed out of circulation to pay off debt simply can not be used for investments. Fewer holidays, more vacations, more school breaks, fewer political elections; and, increased lazy-hazy days of summer lure shoppers out of retail shops and into the local swimming hole. As a result, the S&P 500 Index experienced 11 major corrections during the 45 year research period. The market returned negative growth during the "bad" months 37 percent of the time. Market downward corrections were usually very steep and fast while upward corrections are long and smooth, except for periods of price consolidation. Due to the high potential of a downward market correction during the "bad" months; and, the liquidation delay time of up to 45 days for some retirement plans to process exchange request, investors should consider the risk and remain in cash during these months. Hold onto your strategy even if the market continues up. Do not try to squeeze every ounce of yield out of the market. Make every effort to protect your investments against downside risk. Investors are rewarded by knowing when not to bet against the house. In the "bad" months, take a break! It can get mighty ugly if you don't have the forthwith to stand your ground and stick with proven winning strategies. Equities will generally rise in value during the "good" months. Investors should think of protecting their net worth and not equity growth during the May to November cycle.

"Ugly" is the wealth lost by investors when they fell their duty to become a student of the market prior to entering into an investment. No investor will be consistently correct 100 percent of the time! For example, analyst routinely error on their estimates of corporate earnings projections. Wait a minute! Aren't these the pro's most brokerage firms depend upon for accurate information? You bet! Incorrect analyst projections emphasizes the importance of why every stock investor must be able to conduct their own stock analytical research. Investors must learn how to pick the best stocks or mutual funds without having to be spoon fed erroneous analyst information by some slick talking stockbroker.

Avoiding commissions is very important to wealth building. For mutual fund investors, Vanguard Investments (1-800-662-7447) historically offers the lowest possible mutual fund total management and commission fees. Additionally, for the independent stock investor, the deep discount brokerage firms we have listed in Chapter 2 offer investors the lowest possible commission cost. Investors wishing to obtain a reasonable return while limiting downside risk need only a telephone, a deep discount brokerage account; and, a current copy of the *Investor's Business Daily* (1-800-306-9744). The *IBD* has a complete section devoted exclusively to mutual funds.

What to do *now!* Plan on investing up to 10 percent of total net worth into either a depository receipt; or, an indexed mutual fund on November 1st of the current year. As November approaches the investment selected should be tracking above; but, very close to its 15 week exponential moving average. If they are, purchase a position provided the general market is also above its 200 day moving average; and, 45 to 65 percent of all listed stocks on the New York Stock Exchange are trading below their 200 day moving price average. **Do not buy, if the market is down-trending or is topping out!** Review the market trend charts published daily on the market page of the *IBD*.

Should the market check out and a purchase is made, hold the position until the Wednesday closing price falls below the 15 week exponential moving average for two consecutive plot points. Sell on a confirmed downtrend either when the price falls greater than 7 percent below the initial purchase price without first establishing an up trend above the moving average; or, if the price falls below the moving average. Expect a downtrend to occur in December due to tax sell off; and, again after May 1 due to the ending of the "good" month economic cycle activity. Government employees enrolled in the *Federal Employee Retirement System* can take advantage of "good" month S&P 500 Index investing by telephone switching from the "G" fund into the "C" fund on October 14th and back to the "G" fund on April 14th annually. Due to transfer request delays of up to 45 days, do not attempt to exchange funds based upon moving average computations. Trying to second guess the market during the "bad" months is simply not worth the risk of a wipeout. It could take years, to recover from a 10 percent downward correction that could have been avoided. CAUTION: Wait until the market corrects during the "bad" months before switching funds! For the sake of repeating, research indicates the Dow will generally top out when approximately 80 percent of all listed stocks on the New York Stock Exchange (NYSE) are trading above their 200 day arithmetic moving average. A market bottom occurs when the percentage drops to approximately 20 percent. It hit 85 percent in October, 1997.

Does research confirm market cycles exist? You bet! Between January 1, 1996, and May 1, 1996, the S&P 500 Index rose 16 percent, eventually peaking at 18 percent on May 24th. After absorbing a substantial 11 percent correction between May 24th and July 12th, the Index tracked horizontal through the lazy-hazy days of summer. On September 10th' the S&P 500 broke out of a 15 week consolidation base. During the next seven weeks, the general market advanced 7 percent. Between November 1, 1996, and January 27, 1997, investors realized additional equity growth of 8.4 percent; plus, dividends. The S&P advanced another 23.6 percent through July 18, 1997 before entering into a "bad" month correction. Peaking on August 6, 1997 the market began a sustained general downtrend. By October 29th the Dow had retraced 10 percent off the August 6th high point.

"**JASON**" the character in the *Friday 13th* movie series was one bad dude. Fear was instilled into the minds of many movie goers. Investment months of **J**uly, **A**ugust, **S**eptember, **O**ctober; and, sometimes **N**ovember (**JASON**) are also bad dudes. With the exception of November (the market is in a positive uptrend) the "Jason" months should be avoided. We will not be so bold to say the market will perform poorly during "**JASON's**" rule. We will say; investors exposing their assets to the market during these months do so at the risk of substantial losses.

JASON: A Bad Dude

* The majority of major stock market corrections occur during "**JASON**" months.
* Piece of mind during "good" months is important.
* Holding cash during down corrections allows purchase power on the rebound.
* Individual performance can beat the pros.
* "Good" month simplicity.
* When a **JASON** correction occure, market stops are triggered. Trading halts and all stock is worthless until market trading resumes.

THE NEW AMERICA: Profits can be made from something new. Investors entering into a stock position at the beginning of a new concept or idea often gains the winning edge over the Wall Street pros. Suggestion: Review and clip out for future reference, "The New America" page of *Investor's Business Daily* each issue. Request from the featured company, their latest annual report. Companies featured may be future big winners, especially if they are holding more cash than long term debt. Buying into "New America" stocks can build a substantial portfolio. Apply the stock selection strategy outlined the *Analytical Study* section found in this chapter.

Rotate issues out of inventory based upon the exponential average 15 week computation. Mr. William O'Neal, founder of *IBD,* has also co-founded a mutual fund consisting of stocks similar to those featured on "The New America" page. The New USA Growth Fund (1-800-222-2872) may be worth consideration, for a long term investment. Direct your questions regarding the fund to your discount broker; or, contact the fund directly.

INITIAL PUBLIC OFFERING (IPO): This is one investment which should be avoided by the novice investor. Investors in ignoring this warning, should consider purchasing the IPO at the opening bell on the first day. Research discovered that most IPO profits occurred early on the first trading day, as the stock float expanded. The average IPO produced an 18 percent gain during the initial trading day. However, within 18 months after going public, more than 80 percent of all IPO's were selling below their IPO entry price. The investors edge mandates investing at the IPO entry point and selling later the same day. Recent IPO filings are published daily in the *IBD*. Investors spotting a company of interest should contact their brokerage firm for details on how to get in at the opening bell. "True grit" are the words to remember! IPO investors are real snake-eye crap shooters.

VOLUME vs. FINAL TICK: Correlation between a stocks final daily tick and the probability of a price gain during the next trading secession has been well documented by the Institute of Econometric Research (1-800-442-9000). According to the Institute, a 74 percent probability exists for a stock price to up trend the next trading session, if the final daily tick (price) rose from the previous tick; and, the trading volume remained above the historical daily volume moving average. Typically, volume moving averages are computed using a 50 day arithmetic moving average. Stock prices are published at 15 minute intervals, if the stock traded during that interval. Stock price quotes are known as "ticks" by professional tape readers. "Ticks" appear in the form of stock prices moving across the bottom of financial network television screen reviews. Computer programs can be used to monitor the stock ticks quoted during the final hour of trading. Stocks identified as tracking a high volume with an uptrend price movement between the final trade and the previous trade warrants serious purchase consideration.

TWO CONSECUTIVE TICKS: Like it's sister investment strategy, the *Two Consecutive Tick* theory, implies a stock price which has risen on two consecutive daily final ticks, regardless of the volume trend, has a 74 percent probability of a price uptrend during the next trading session. Investors can utilize the concept to potentially profit by merely selecting a group of stocks and plotting their final tick daily. When a stock is identified as meeting the requirements, the investor would purchase a position.

NOTE: Substantial profits are possible by using the final tick investment strategies. Identify a few stocks within an up-trending economic sector which are hitting higher consecutive daily closing prices. Purchase maximum shares at the lowest possible commission. Sell the position when the most recent closing price falls below the previous day final tick. With commissions held to less than 1 percent, a 3 percent return realized over a day or two yields an excellent annualized return. It only takes a few 3 percent days each year to create substantial wealth.

THE BURNING MATCH: Devised by investor Mr. J.L. (Jim) Straw of Dalton, Georgia to keep investors out of the stock market when the risk of loses are the greatest. Mr. Straw advises against stock investing; unless, the market has guided the investor as to when to buy and sell. According to *The Burning Match*; buy and sell signals, for every listed stock are telegraphed slightly before the actual signal is flashed. Investors taking advantage of the signal can beat the crowd by either buying or selling before the crowd does. Investors not recognizing the signals will get burned! Is Mr. Straw's observation of the market correct? You bet! Trading the *Burning Match* theory can be profitable; but, also very risky.

A burning match buy signal is flashed when a stock price is trending up accompanied by the daily volume remaining constant; or, increasing. The volume must be above its short term (5 to 10 day) historical moving average. *The Investor's Business Daily* lists the percentage relationship between the current volume and the stocks historical 50 day moving average volume. Stocks hitting new high prices, especially those who's volume are at least 50 percent above their 50 day moving average are always of interest. A sell signal is flashed, regardless of the price direction of movement, when the daily volume crosses to below the volume short term historical moving average by 15 percent.

To implement the burning match theory, investors need to look no further than the most current *Investor's Business Daily*. Investors should search for stocks indicating a rise in price; plus, a volume above the volume moving average by at least 50 percent. Investors should be searching for real short term money maker opportunities created by large block investors trading large share blocks over very short trading secessions. The profit phenomena appears to be closely associated with companies whose quarterly earnings report has beaten analyst projections. The concept strongly supports the theory that surprise earnings push volume; and, volume pushes stock prices.

Earnings drive the machine; but, volume is the locomotive transporting the commodity to market. Almost without exception, a stock price will tumble hard and fast very shortly after the volume crosses below its historical moving average line. Selling the moment it does can cut losses.

We do not recommend *The Burning Match* investment concept be utilized by investors with limited resources. The theory is best used during day trading with large sums of cash. Commissions must be held to a minimum. We suggest investors initially enter into the market place through a more conservative approach with an objective of matching the S&P 500 Index performance; or, at minimum beating the Dow's total return. Do not get burned by holding a stock during a burnout phase. Not only is it important to know when to holdem', it's more important to know when to foldem'.

BEATING THE DOW: This is an excellent long term low risk investment strategy developed by Mr. Michael O'Higgins, President of Michael B. O'Higgins & Company (1-518-786-1854). *Beating The Dow* (Harper Collins-1992), reveals a simple, low risk investment approach to stock investing with a potential of beating the total return of the Dow Jones Industrial Average year after year. Mr. O'Higgins explores many back-tested Dow investment concepts which has easily beaten the Dow. Each concept reported varying results. "The closest an investor can get to a sure thing," reports *US News and World Report*. "A conservative investment strategy" writes the *Kiplinger's Personal Finance* magazine. "By using this approach, it is possible to be successful regardless of the direction the overall market takes." acclaims the *New York Times*. What's the secret? Low downside risk and simplicity!

Mr. O'Higgins illustrates three basic and nine advanced strategies anyone can use to beat the Dow's total return performance. Each strategy provides for a diversification of equity and risk management. Portfolio management time allocation can be as low as 30 minutes annually. It does not appear to matter, when the equities are purchased. Commissions are held to the lowest possible cost when trading transactions are conducted through one of the "flat fee per share" deep discount brokerage firms listed in Chapter 2. Capital gains tax is deferred until the portfolio annual adjustment date. Once annually, investors do a simple price and yield calculation to adjust equities held in the position. There will never be more than 10 stocks owned at any one time: and, the stocks which are owned represent companies whose products have worldwide consumer demand.

Total return performance of a back-tested *Beating The Dow* portfolio between 1973 and 1991 was reported to have exceeded 9915 percent equity growth. The Dow Jones Industrial Average (DJIA) over the same 18 years yielded approximately 515 percent. The DJIA total return has clearly outperformed the professional money managers, as a group, during the extended bull market starting in 1982. We will not attempt to go to deep into each of Mr. O'Higgin's Dow theories. We prefer to encourage investors interested in the concept, to review Mr. O'Higgin's book which has been available at most book retail outlets and public libraries for several years. In a June 17, 1997 advertisement by *Beating The Dow* newsletter published by the Hirsch Organization, Inc. (1-201-767-4100), they correctly concluded, *Beating The Dow* was "The most amazing stock strategy ever devised...$10,000 to $989,450...last 24 years." Who can argue against that level of return?

Dow stock prices and yields are published in each Friday issue of the *Investor's Business Daily*. The stock symbols are published daily. A Dow performance chart is also published daily. Dow stocks are also published monthly in the *Standard and Poor's Stock Guide*. A DJIA listing, including current yields, can be provided by most brokerage firms. DJIA information is readily available. The starting point to invest for beating the Dow, is to align oneself with the best professional investors the market has developed. To become a winner, the investor must think like a winner. In order to think like a winner, investors must learn how to identify a potential market winner. Stock analysts, generally are not market winners as evidenced by two facts. First, when analysts are wrong on their earnings estimates, the stock will generally reverse price momentum direction. Secondly, professional money managers generally rely upon stock analyst projections. Professional money manager performance often falls way short of the S&P 500 Index and DJIA total return performance. Although beating the DJIA can be a reality, one fact must never be forgotten. No investor can actually beat the market simply because they are the market! Hot tips and recommendations from stockbrokers only help the broker improve their commission performance. Stockbrokers have reportedly been fired for making negative comments about a stock their employer was hawking to the investment public.

A single stock investment strategy will not guarantee a positive future performance. To be a market winner, investors must become a student of the best market professionals the industry has developed. Throughout *Don't Die Broke* , readers will find reference to the market great's the author has followed for years, while successfully operating a personal stock trading business. They are: William J. O'Neil, founder of *Investor's Business Daily*; Peter Lynch, the number one money manager of all time, according to *Time*; Donald H. Row, publisher of *The Wall Street Digest*; Norman G Fosback, President and Research Director of The Institute for Econometric Research; Michael O'Higgins, one of America's top ranked money managers and President of Michael B. O'Higgins & Company. And, those darn motley fool investors, David and Tom Gardner, author of *The Motley Fool Investment Guide*. Each are within their own right, are highly respected within the investment community. However, when their strategies are combined, opportunities for wealth building beyond anyone's wildest expectations materialize. The following information is accredited to these fellows. Thanks!

The DJIA represents a group of international industries whose products are in demand worldwide. They are stocks many investors believe represent safety. Dividends supplement social security and retirement income for millions of retired folks. Yet, as with any stock, they reflect the truest measure of the market place: greed! Assuming the dividend payout dollar value remains constant, the dividend yield will vary on every price tick change. Yields will trend higher, as the stock price falls; thus, attracting retirees and other investors seeking yield income. The greed for yield present tremendous opportunities for equity investors. According to Mr. John Downes, editor of *Beating the Dow* (1-800-477-3400) newsletter, the 10 highest yielding Dow stocks, held in equal dollar amounts through the 1996 calendar year, returned 30.5 percent compared to the 28.6 percent total return of the DJIA.

Investment strategies proven to be successful in specific market cycles include all the strategies covered within this material. However, a strategy most favored by the author, is actually a combination of several strategies presented to the investment community by Norman Fosback, David and Tom Gardner; and, Michael O'Higgins. They are: (1) the 10 highest yielding Dow stocks, (2) five highest yielding stocks with the lowest price, (3) the second lowest priced stock of the 5 highest yielding stock group having the lowest price, (4) those foolish four; and, (5) the 15 week exponential moving average to monitor the investment performance. The moving average can automatically trigger a buy, hold; or, sell signal of any equity regardless of the market direction. Let's review the stock selection process of each strategy, then illustrate the usefulness of the exponential moving average to guard against loses.

Ten Highest Yielding Dow Stocks

Substantial funds are required to make this strategy successful. We recommend the entry point be no less than $100,000. To keep commissions as low as possible, $10,000 is the minimum amount to invest on each stock. Investors not having the recommended entry level money are encouraged to work through the selection process in order to identify the best single potential growth performance DJIA stock to purchase. The O' Higgins "Penultimate Profit Prospect" (PPP) stock can be purchased in odd lot quantities with a very small investment. Of course, it will need watching very closely. Odds are very high this stock will be sold within weeks of purchase. It is very simple to identify the next (PPP) candidate through the selection process in order to began the cycle anew. Who can complain of buying 2 or 3 stocks annually, especially when each equity could easily appreciate by 15 to 30 percent! The stock selection steps are:

* Review the most recent Friday *Investor's Business Daily* for stock price and yield information.

* Tip: A quick method to find a stock, is to scan the stock column for the stock symbol.

* Using graph paper, list the stock yield and price for all 30 DJIA stocks.

* A priority ranking #1 is assigned to the highest dividend yielding stock, with ranking numbers increasing to #10 with decreasing dividend yields. For stocks having equal yields, assign the lower ranking number to the lowest priced stock. We suggest that if the unlikely situation arise where two or more stocks have both equal price and yield, assign the lowest ranking number assigned to the issue having the highest cash to long term debt ratio, lowest number of stock floating, and the highest annual earnings growth.

* After ranking the top ten Dow stocks, purchase all 10 stocks. Invest an equal dollar percentage amount into each equity. Expect to pay a slightly higher commission due to odd-lot trading.

* Contact each company shareholder representative. Inquire about their DPP or DRIP. Investing through these programs will eliminate commissions. The majority, if not all, have 800 telephone numbers. The alternative, is to open a deep discount stock brokerage margin account Review the brokerage listing in Chapter 2.

* Track each stocks performance by one of two methods. First, establish a moving average plot for each stock.

* Next, once annually, rank all DJIA stocks according to their price and yield. Replace any stock failing to meet the selection criteria or falls below its 15 week moving average.

NOTE: Do not liquidate a stock simply because it has been removed from the DJIA. Wait until the annual update; or, a sell characteristic has been triggered by the individual stocks 15 week Exponential Moving Average. Stocks removed from the DJIA often outperform their replacement. Update the DJIA stock list whenever companies are removed from the list. Check the DJIA quarterly to keep the stock list current. Your brokerage firm can provide a current listing. Additionally, a symbol list is provided daily on the Dow tracking chart published by the *IBD*.

Stocks purchased through the 10 highest yielding dividend strategy between 1973 and 1991 was reported to have appreciated the initial investment by 1926 percent. The strategy returned an annualized yield of 17.16 percent compared to the Dow's 10.92 percent annualized return. Investors seeking higher returns with a slightly increased risk, can reduce the number of stocks to five through additional screening. By selecting the five highest yield-lowest priced stocks, potential higher total returns exist. From 1973 to 1993, five highest yield-lowest priced stocks, of the 10 highest yield group, returned an annualized growth of 20.38 percent. Purchase the stocks in equal percentage dollar amounts. Limit a single stock investment to 5 percent of net worth.

Five Highest Yield - Lowest Price

* Prior to commencing this strategy, investors should have already ranked the 10 highest yielding low priced stocks from the Dow group.
* Select from the 10 stocks, the 5 stocks having the lowest price.

* Rank the lowest price stock #1 with the highest priced stock of the group #5.

* Rank stocks of equal price according to their yield, assigning the stock with the highest yield the lowest ranking numerical number.

* Invest equal percentage dollar amounts into each of the five stocks.

* Monitor the stocks according to buy and sell rules discussed throughout this publication.

Higher historical returns have been achieved through a critical; yet, slight modification to the Five Highest Yield Lowest Price group. Additional ranking of the group identifies a single stock proven to be a true market winner. Investment returns have been phenomenal. Mr. O'Higgins refers to this stock as the "Penultimate Profit Prospect."

O'Higgins Penultimate Profit Prospect

The Penultimate Profit Prospect puts the investor into a single stock with associated risk. Cumulative total returns from 1973 to 1991 of the Penultimate Profit Prospect, according to Mr. O'Higgins, hit whopping 9918.7 percent. The annualized growth rate was 27.44 percent. A single stock investment is very risky. During twenty test years, the selected stock took four negative hits of which three exceeded 10 percent. Quoting O'Higgins, "I wouldn't put my grandmother in one stock." We agree; unless, grandmother had a safety net and was dedicated enough to monitor the stock weekly. The safety net is the stocks' 15 week exponential moving average computation.

Investors wishing to locate a very high potential profit stock can do so on any given trading day in about ten minutes utilizing publicly available information. Review the following Penultimate Profit Prospect selection process.

* Follow the procedure to locate the 10 highest dividend yield stocks. Continue the selection process to locate the 5 highest yield-lowest price stock. Rank the stocks as previously instructed.

* Identify the #2 ranking stock from the 5 highest yield-lowest price group. You have located the O'Higgins Penultimate Profit Prospect!

* Buy at the market! A slight odd-lot commission premium can be expected. A wise investor may choose to make the purchase on Monday afternoon. Wall Street "flow control experts", as with many employees across America, appear to lack work motivation after stuffing themselves with a noon lunch. As a result, stock prices appear to fall a few pennies per share during the mid-afternoon. After the slight price dip, prices will tend to rise in the final hour as the "flow control experts" manipulate prices up in an attempt to close the market up-trending.

* Plot the 15 week Exponential Moving Average as illustrated within this chapter. Begin the plot cycle on the next Wednesday closing price. The initial moving average plot will be the same as the stocks Wednesday closing price. If the Wednesday price is missed, use the Thursday morning opening price; or, contact your broker for the Wednesday price.

* Monitor the stock price twice each day until the stock price either: (1) falls to a price greater than 7 percent below the initial purchase point, (2) has established a price performance up trend tracking above; but, very close to the moving average price; or, (3) until fifteen weeks has past and the stock is still forming a price base. It is most important to understand that stock prices could easily fluctuate from the purchase price by 3 to 5 percent throughout the day. However, price fluctuation exceeding 7 percent below the initial purchase price is abnormal and unacceptable. Once, the stock price remains above the moving average price for two consecutive weekly plots, it is generally safe to watch the price weekly.

* Do not panic if the Wednesday closing price is below the initial purchase price. A 7 percent downtrend from the purchase price is within the daily fluctuation acceptable limits. Under no circumstance purchase additional shares until an uptrend develops! Many stocks will trend down from a recent high point, before a rally begins.

<u>Sell Quickly: When</u>

* The stock downtrend exceeds 7 percent below the purchase price. Hanging on could cost plenty. Do not register a loss-stop order with your broker. Just watch the price.

* If the stock price does not trend above the 15 week exponential moving average price within 15 weeks after the purchase date. Why? Stocks moving sideways are not appreciating. If the price isn't moving up, the investor is loosing money through lost opportunities elsewhere. A short base consolidation is usually very positive. Odds appear to favor a price breakout to the upside from an extended consolidation base. Once out of the base, an uptrend exceeding 10 to 20 percent is not uncommon before the price takes a break and reenters basing. Fifteen weeks will allow the stock price pass several option expiration and quarterly earnings reporting dates. It is plenty of time for good news to push the price up. No movement upward warrants a sell.

* If the Wednesday closing price falls below the moving average price, after trending above the average price; and, remains below the average price for two consecutive plots.

* If the price, at any time falls below the initial price, after an uptrend above the initial price has occurred. Never let a profit convert to a loss! Finally,

* Stocks experiencing a rapid appreciation can reverse course with devastating results. Liquidating a position when a divergence of 15 to 20 percent develops between the current price and the moving average price often hits close to a price peak, signaling a reversal. Do not confuse a stock price rising from the buy point by 20 percent with a price diverging above the moving average by 20 percent. Healthy stocks can rise 100 percent and never be more than 1 or 2 percent above the moving average along the way.

* Repeat the selection process each time a position is liquidated.

<u>Those Gardner Foolish Four</u>

Investors have been instructed on how to select from 1 to 10 stocks having a high potential for out performing the Dow Jones Industrial Average regardless of the market direction of movement. A word of clarification is warranted. Beating the Dow does not mean equity growth in every situation. For example, if the DJIA corrects down 20 percent; and, your selected stock corrects down 15 percent, the investment still beat the Dow by simply not correcting as much. Investors have been instructed to consider investing equal percentages of investment funds into each selected DJIA stock. They have been advised to limit each stock investment to 5 percent of their net worth; and, to make portfolio adjustments to remain invested in the best stock. The O'Higgins strategies are perhaps as close to investment perfection as possible. As with any near perfect product, someone always comes along to challenge the concept. No different here! Those darn fools; the Gardner brothers; David and Tom, have slightly modified the O'Higgins Five Highest Yield-Lowest Priced Stock strategy with reported successes. Their strategy has been back tested over a 20 year test period and beat the O'Higgins' performance by approximately 100 percent.

According to *The Motley Fool Investment Guide*, the Gardners modified the O'Higgins Five Highest Yield-Lowest Price strategy by dropping the #1 ranked stock from the portfolio. Next, they doubled their investment percentage (40%) on the #2 ranked stock. As previously reviewed, that stock is the O'Higgins "Penultimate Profit Prospect." Each of the three remaining stocks, received 20 percent of the investment funds. The "Foolish Four" concept appreciated $20,000 into $1,791,000 as compared to the $856,000 O'Higgins return over a twenty year back test period. Exceptional by any measurement!

It must be emphasized, both the O'Higgins and Gardner strategies were based upon theory back testing. We all know the saying "hind sight is 20/20." We at *Don't Die Broke* have tested both strategies with real dollar short term success. To limit down side risk, we traded and replaced stock within the portfolio utilizing both the equity to net worth ratio and the 15 week exponential moving average. Based upon our results, both strategies were successful. Our success is not isolated. At least one international brokerage firm, has committed millions of dollars to *Beating The Dow* strategies through a managed mutual fund.

Investors wishing to acquire additional information about the "Foolish Four" strategy may address their questions to "Ask The Fool" at website Fool@fool.com; or, write to *The Atlanta Journal-Constitution:* Box 4689, Atlanta, Georgia 30302.

HOT OFF THE PRESS-September 9,1997: O'Higgins Asset Management, Inc. released a report indicating Mr. O'Higgins has out done both himself and the Gardner brothers. *Beating The Dow With Bonds, Treasury Bills and Stocks* (BTDWB) is the latest report by Mr. O'Higgins. At the date of this publication, the book had not been released. When it is released, it should be placed on every investors reading list! In a letter we received from Mr. Michael B. O'Higgins he wrote: "We feel compelled to notify you that we are not recommending the use of the *Beating The Dow* (BTD) stock selection strategies at this time." He further explained the reason behind his recommendation was due to a current under evaluation of 30 year treasury bonds. He recommended investing 100 percent into 30 year Treasury Zero Coupon Bonds until the end of 1997. At which time, the portfolio and market position will be re-examined. The next day, the *Don't Die Broke* portfolio followed his recommendation!

Looking long term, every investment strategy must be re-examined periodically. Mr. O'Higgins based his recommendation on...you guessed it...a moving average. He summarizes in his letter that "if both stocks and bonds return to the average valuation levels of the past 70 years, the DJIA will fall over 50 percent and long term 30 year treasury bonds will return over 40 percent." On September 17,1997 bonds made the largest gain for a single day in recorded recent history. How did he know that would happen?

As reported by Mr. O'Higgins, back testing the bond and stock strategy combination for 24.09 years resulted **in amazing** results. When compared to the total return of the DJIA (2,640 %), *Beating The Dow* 5 Stocks

(12,377 %); Beating the Dow with bonds returned **47,886 percent**! Enough said. Watch for the book. Until we can obtain more information; however, we will limit debt investing and stick with trading the "Foolish Four" monitored through their Quarterly Allocation; or, moving average performance. The Quarterly Allocation stock rotation strategy is detailed later in this chapter.

No two investors will have the exact same results, because yields change with each price tick. Therefore, do not become despaired, if your selection differs from someone else's. The system works, according to the experts, regardless of which day the investor chooses to begin the process. Again, expect to pay a slightly higher commission rate due to odd lot buying.

Why do *Beating The Dow* stock theories function so well? They work primarily due to a yield divergence developing between the Dow median yield; and, the selected representative stock yield. The Dow Jones Industrial Average (DJIA) for more than 100 years has been the most published measurement of the United States stock market performance. Stocks within the DJIA 30 stock group represent international merchandisers who provide an array of products and services to practically every household worldwide, especially those of industrialized nations. In general, they are the household names representing the global economy. Many of the Dow companies were formed early in the American industrial age, by descendants of the first pioneers to the New World. Being formed by true "blue bloods", the "blue chips" have long histories of uninterrupted dividend distributions and growth. Companies within the DJIA group trade merchandise among themselves; and, their management is under extensive shareholder pressure to equal the equity growth performance of their peer companies. DJIA stocks are found within practically every retirement fund. A Dow stock reducing it's dividend distribution, is paramount to burning the *Trojan Horse*; or, slaughtering the *Sacred Cow*. TABOO! Companies who reduce their dividend either through a percentage reduction; or, through a stock price runaway, destroys public confidence often for many years. The stock price generally suffers, as retirees dependent upon a fixed income, shift assets into higher yielding investments, such as CD's, bonds, and money market accounts. Only after the stock price falls so low, it pushes the yield higher than alternative investments, do the fixed income "yield seekers" rejoin the party. As they climb aboard, the "flow control experts" take advantage of the new capital influx to bid the equity value up.

Dividend values are usually set at a fixed dollar amount per share. For example, a dividend payout could be $1.00 per share. Assuming the current stock price is $10, the dividend represents 10 percent ($1 / $10= .10) of the stock price. Therefore, considering a constant dividend value, the yield changes with each change in the stock price. As yields become attractive to income seekers, they flock to the stock in numbers great enough to influence the stock price. Massive trading is reflected by the daily volume pushing above its 50 day arithmetic moving average. Price upward performance potential will soon follow. As the price trends up, assuming no change in the dividend dollar value, the yield percentage lowers. The flip side, is that stocks beaten down by bad news, or a negative earnings report, force dividend yields to higher evaluations. It's from among this group, we pick the ten highest yield-lowest priced Dow stocks. As previously discussed, the Dow, as a group, has a median yield percentage. Every stock within the group, will eventually trend toward the median yield of the group. The DJIA median yield hit a five year low of 1.63 percent on July 25th, 1997.

Historically, major market corrections have occurred when the DJIA yield dropped to below 2 percent. Bond yields become more competitive, while carrying much less risk, when the DJIA median yield drops below 2 percent. The historical DJIA yield information; however, may not continue as a gauge for predicting future market corrections. As DJIA stocks become more globelized, during an era of low inflation and rapid growth, it would be a wise corporate business decision to forego yield payments in order to foster corporate expansion from internal cash flow. During high inflationary economic periods; however, it would be wise to pay higher yields in order to attract new money instead of paying expensive interest to banks. Historically DJIA dividend yields below 2 percent have been negative for the stock market. Investors can *Beat The Dow* by taking advantage of opportunities materializing as a yield divergence develops between individual stocks within the Dow group and the median yield of the group.

Consider for example, the yield and price performance of the International Paper Company (IP) between February 26th and July 25th , 1997. On February 26th, IP's price final tick was $43.00, carrying a dividend yield of 2.3 percent. The dollar value of IP's yield was about 99 cents per share ($43.00 x .023 = .989). The DJIA group median yield was at 1.85 percent. In order for IP's yield to align with the DJIA yield, the 2.3 percent yield would need to retrace .45 percent (2.3-1.85=.45). To accomplish the retrace, IP's stock price would need to rise by 24.3 percent ($43.00 x .023 = $.989 / .0185 = $53.45. $53.45 - $43.00 = $10.45 / $43.00 = 24.3 percent). The stock blew past $53 like a tornado as it hit $59.18 on July 25th. IP's yield had adjusted downward from 2.3 percent to 1.7 percent as the stock price appreciated. However, the DJIA yield had also fallen to a five year low of 1.63 percent. IP's yield was still above and divergent to the Dow's yield by a mere .0007 percent. To wipe out the divergence, IP's price would need to appreciate to $61.00 per share; or, the Dow's yield would need to increase either through Dow price drop or increasing dividends. The opposite would need to have occurred, if IP's yield had been in divergent below the DJIA median yield. In that situation, IP's stock price would have needed to correct substantially lower to bring the yield into alignment with the DJIA yield. IP is used as an illustration to show that it is very realistic to forecast a future stock price based upon the current yield divergence from the historical yield.

Risk associated with this theory, is that the entire Dow group could crash in order to bring the median yield up to around 3 percent. It is not uncommon for a general correction to occur, once the median yield drops below 2 percent. A broad market adjustment is more likely to occur than for an individual stock price to appreciate 100 percent. This highlights the primary reason for tracking every purchase with a 15 week exponential moving average. As the market falls, so does every correlated stock. The exponential moving average will limit downside risk by automatically triggering a sell.

15 WEEK EXPONENTIAL MOVING AVERAGE: Moving average trading systems are very popular among professional stock and mutual fund traders and investors. The effectiveness of moving average systems is based upon a comparison between the current equity price as it relates to its historical average price when measured over a specific time period. Every stock, commodity, precious metal, bond; or, real estate price will eventually develop a moving average price performance trend identifiable through a price wave cycle. The cycles are identified through plotting points identifying where the current price and moving average price intersect. Points of intersection are dependent upon the price volatility; and, the selected time span of the moving average computation.

The ideal moving average, should have a time plot long enough to eliminate excessive trading; yet, short enough to automatically signal a buy; or, sell transaction within 7 percent of the wave reversal. Moving average computations are simple to compute while offering excellent single stock ownership with downside risk protection. They are especially attractive when used to track a single Dow stock. Each stock within an investment portfolio should be monitored through a moving average. The moving average tends to smooth out the price value wave while eliminating minor price volatility. To calculate a price average, the computation may can either be arithmetical, or exponential.

Arithmetical averages are determined through the sum of a selected number of price plots divide by the number of plots. For example, to find the average of 5 trades totaling 100, simply divide 100 by 5 to obtain an average of 20. To get the average to move; however, when adding the sixth trade, it would be necessary to drop the first trade position in order to compute a new average sum. Let's assume the new sum is 110. The new average is 110 / 5 = 22; thus, the average is moving higher. The process is repeated with each new plot while limiting the total plot points to a maximum of 5. Of course, there are an infinite number of plots from which to choose. The last plot price has actually more value than the first because it is the plot which results in the average moving. Arithmetic moving average calculations assign equal weight to each price plot. Point to point price fluctuations are controlled by the new price being plotted while the oldest price is being dropped. To plot an arithmetic moving average of sufficient length beneficial to stock investors, could take weeks. Valuable investment opportunities could be lost. The alternative is for investors to plot an exponential moving average. The exponential moving average assigns a fixed value "smoothing constant" to the current price while assigning a "balance factor " to the previous moving average price. The process arbitrarily establishes a moving average equal to the initial plot price through updating the current price. Although the exponential moving average, is not a true moving average, it is closely correlated to an arithmetic moving average of an identical cycle length. The advantage of using the exponential average, is the ability to compute any time cycle utilizing a single price plot entry point. A second plotting point will provide the "balance" and "constant" corrections. Unlike the arithmetic moving average, it is never necessary to drop a price from the computation. Instead, by adjusting the previous average and the current price with the "balance" and "constant" factors starts the exponential static average moving while slightly deviating from the arithmetic average. The divergence is too small for concern.

The advantages of moving average systems are simplicity, automatic buy and sell signals, unlimited upside potential; and, limited downside risks.

The major disadvantage, is that moving average strategies are a trailing technical indicator and will never trigger a buy or sell transaction at the exact bottom or top of the cycle. Another disadvantage, is that an infinite number of moving averages exist. Additionally, moving averages should never be used as a stand alone stock selection tool. Investors must also use caution when selecting a moving average cycle length. A moving average cycle for a specific investment may not work well with a random selected arithmetic average; whereas, it could perform quite excellent with a 5, 10, or 75 day plot. Real estate REIT's, for example, may require a 6 month plot cycle; whereas, gold and bonds may require a plot cycle of several years. Low volatile investments may benefit from a short moving average cycle while more volatile issues may require a much longer cycle to smooth out the average price. To help stock investors resolve which moving average could provide the best return performance, Mr. Norman Fosback at the Institute for Econometric Research (1-800-442-9000) published an extensive special research report dealing with the moving average concept.

The Institute released their excellent report in the early 1990's. They tested both the arithmetic and exponential moving average concept. After reviewing hundreds of arithmetic moving average trading results, when compared to a "buy and hold" strategy, it was discovered that a 15 week moving average returned a 12 percent more profit with 31 percent less risk than all other evaluated averages. Between June 30, 1982 and June 30, 1991 a "buy and hold" mutual fund position returned 282 percent while the 15 week arithmetic moving average returned an outstanding 316 percent. The study found the 15 week moving average limited transactions to about 2.6 round trips annually. Based upon the Institutes' report, investors are encouraged to consider the investment benefits associated with a 15 week (75 day) moving average strategy. Since there is a very little performance difference between the arithmetic and exponential moving average, we at *Don't Die Broke* adopted the exponential concept to monitor stocks held within our personal investment portfolio. Our choice has been very profitable. The computation formula is easy to implement. Once started it must be followed weekly until the position is liquidated.

15 Week Exponential Moving Average

Formula	Example
Step 1: 2 / (C + 1) = x	2 / (15 + 1) = .125
Step 2: 1.00 - x = y	1.00 - .125 = .875
Step 3: CP (x) + PMA (y) = EMA	$10 (.125) + $10 (.875) = $10

* (CP) = current price. * (X) = current price smoothing constant. * (PMA) = previous moving average.
* (Y) = pma factor. * (EMA) = exponential moving average. * (C) = selected plot cycle: i.e. 15 weeks.

NOTE: Previous week (EMA) becomes current week (PMA).

CAUTION: * Never use a moving average as a buy indicator.

* Convert fractional prices into whole numbers prior to computing the average (5 5/8 = $5.625 etc.). Stock splits, price gaps, dividend distributions, and the purchase of additional shares will effect a stocks median price and the price relationship to the (PMA). Adjust the previous (PMA) for stock price corrections prior to computing the current (EMA). For example, if 100 shares were purchased for $10 each ($1000) and later another 100 shares were purchased for $13.37 each ($1337), the median price of the total portfolio would be $11.685 per share. The (PMA) would need to be adjusted upward by the difference between the current price of $13.37and the new median price of $11.685. In this instance, the adjusting factor would be $1.685, ($13.37- $11.685 = $ 1.685).

Illustration

Week 1 (PMA) is adjusted for additional shares purchased during week 2 for $13.37 per share. Week #3 is adjusted for a $1 dividend distribution paid during week #2. To find the median share stock price, of a portfolio divide the total portfolio value by the shares held.

Week	CP	(X)	PMA	(Y)	=	EMA
#1	$10.00	.125	$10.00	.875		$10.00
#1	$10.00	.125	$11.68	.875		$11.47
#2	$13.37	.125	$11.47	.875		$11.70
#3	$12.00	.125	$10.70	.875		$10.86

NOTE: The price at week #1 reflects additional shares. Week #3 reflects a $1 dividend payout. Adjust the previous weeks (EMA) to obtain the current (PMA). The relationship between the CP and EMA remains constant. The investor has already made 8.5 percent ($1/$11.685 median price) on their investment through dividends.

* The (CP) suggested is the Wednesday closing price. Why? The market rarely, if ever, closes during normal business hours on Wednesday. Prices have generally recovered from previous holiday; or, weekend market closing. A price base has begun to build for the forthcoming market closing. Regardless of the day of purchase, reserve the following Wednesday closing price for plotting the weekly (EMA). Once again, if you miss obtaining the Wednesday price, use the Thursday opening price, or contact your broker for the Wednesday closing price. Stock prices are kept practically forever. During vacation trips, the use of a 1-800 number to acquire stock prices is very helpful. Your brokerage firm must have a method for investors to obtain free of charge stock information, 24 hours a day from anywhere on the Earth. We recommend avoiding firms who can not service their customer needs.

Moving Average Buy Signal

The moving average strategy should never be used as a stand alone buy signal. The investment is selected through one of the several selection strategies detailed throughout this chapter. After the investment is bought, use the moving average strategy as an investment performance momentum trend indicator. Plotting the indicator will eliminate the stress associated with watching a stock price continuously. HOLD the position until a sell signal.

Moving Average Hold Signal

Hold the investment position as long as the Wednesday (CP) is tracking slightly above the (EMA). Remember! The position was not purchased based upon the moving average; therefore, a moving average bullish signal may not materialize for several weeks after the purchase date.

Moving Average: Any Single Sell Signal

Investors lose money by selling an investment during the wrong price cycle. Purchasing a stock at the right moment does not mean much if emotions control selling. Eliminate the emotional roller coaster associated with selling.

Do not hold past any single sell signal!

A moving average sell signal is triggered when: (1) the (CP) has not moved above the (EMA) within 15 weeks of purchase, (2) when the (CP) is developing a wide divergence above the (EMC), and when the Wednesday (CP) crosses below the (EMA) and remains there for two consecutive Wednesday closing price plots. The price down trend must be confirmed. However, other situations do occur, warranting sell considerations.

* Should the (CP) on any given day close down from the initial purchase price by greater than 7 percent. Seven percent falls way outside of the median daily price fluctuation range for most stocks. Stocks retracing more than 7 percent off an initial buy point could take years to recover. SELL BUT FAST!

* If a bullish up trend has not been confirmed within 15 weeks after the initial purchase date, sell. The (CP) must cross above the (EMA) and remain there for two consecutive Wednesday pilot points for a bullish signal to be confirmed. Fifteen weeks give management plenty of time to prove their management skills. Failure of equity growth clearly indicates the wrong investment. Holding the stock could cost plenty as opportunities are lost elsewhere.

* If the (CP) has diverged above the (EMA) by 20 percent within 15 weeks. The (CP) is moving too fast. Stocks developing a wide divergence between the (CP) and the (EMA) can experience a price collapse as traders capture profits at the top of the price cycle. The best stocks have a low (CP) weekly price volatility while tracking slightly above the (EMA) week after week. Why? Stocks experiencing a raid price run-up tend to be more volatile when they correct back toward their moving average. Every stock CP will eventually correct toward the EMA.

CAUTION: It is very important to note the 20 percent divergence is between the (CP) and (EMA) relationship and not between the (CP) an initial purchase price (IPP). Stocks moving up 20 percent off a previous historical high price within a few weeks of purchase, generally warrants the purchase of additional shares.

For the sake of repeating, do not forget to adjust the previous EMA for splits, gaps; dividend distributions; and, average purchasing. The (CP) must remain correlated with the (EMA). Hold the equity until a sell signal is flashed. Once the sell occurs. Do not keep tracking the equity.

Test Question: Review week #3 and determine the correct action. The question is, should the investor buy more shares, hold; or, sell?

Week	CP	(X)	+	PMA	(Y)	=	EMA
#3	$12.00	.125		$10.70	.875		$10.86

Hint: (CP) is overextended 10.4% above the (EMA). ($12.00-$10.86 = $1.14. $1.14 / $10.86=10.4%)

Answer: Buy more shares; or, hold the position. The stock is performing very well!

* A price "Gap" occurs when the stock opens at a price differently than the previous closing price.

* A stock "Split" can be forward or reverse. (2 for 1) means the investor now owns 2 shares for each 1 original share. 100 shares x 2/1 = 200 shares. $10.00 share / 1/2 = $5.00 share, etc. Additional split examples are:

(5 for 3) equals 100 shares x 5/3 = 500/3 = 166 shares.
(3 for 5) reverse split 100 shares x 3/5 = 300/5 = 60 shares.

In summary, moving averages are used by professionals to gauge the broad market, as well, as to successfully manage client accounts. According to the December 7, 1995 *Investor's Business Daily*, Mr. Frank Gretz of Shields and Company observed that the stock market appears to peak whenever 80 to 90 percent of the stocks listed on the New York Stock Exchange are trading above their 200 day moving average. He observed the market bottomed when 10 to 20 percent of the listed stocks were trading above their 200 day moving average. The percentage of stocks trading above their 200 day average is reported daily in the *IBD*. Mr. O'Higgins mentions a 75 year bond average price in a recent letter to clients. Other advisors use a 39 week arithmetic moving average. The *IBD* utilizes both a 50 and 200 day moving average to review stock charts. Use of moving averages to monitor investments is well documented.

Opportunities exist in the market place only to the extent the investor knows how, when; and, where to identify them. Finding stocks to purchase is similar to panning for gold. Investors will throw a whole lot of rocks away before finding a single nugget. Throughout this publication, strategies have closely adhered to the advice of professionals. We believe every investor can beat the pros at their own game, once the game rules are understood. Stock selection need not be a complicated task requiring lots of time and costly equipment To keep stock selection simple and inexpensive, for the "do it your self investor," we suggest investors learn in-depth our recommended *Stock Analytical Study*. The *Stock Analytical Study* presented next will aid investors in locating the "mother load" of profitable stocks. Investors will be provided useful information absolutely essential in locating the best stocks the market has to offer outside the Dow grouping. Stocks located through the study have a potential of outperforming the Dow by a wide margin. Many will be the rising star of tomorrow!

STOCK ANALYTICAL STUDY: A learned skill giving the independent stock picker a winning edge. Never again will investors need the services of over 22,500 stock analyst; or, 150,000 professional investment guru's plying their under-performance expertise against the wealth building attempts of the independent thinker. Investors can shake forever the shackle of confusion and discrepancies found throughout the investment advisory community. As previously discussed, your friendly stockbroker recommends a transaction usually based upon advice from an analyst hired by his employer. Investors must never forget, it is not uncommon for rifts of disagreement to exist among analyst regarding future earnings performance of a specific stock. One analyst may be advising investors to buy while another is advising clients to hold. "Hold" is the industry code word for "sell." There have been reports of management, who's company stock was underwritten by a specific brokerage firm, demanding a stockbroker be fired over a "sell" recommendation. Therefore, a "hold" recommendation is about as low as the Wall Street gang will brave to go; unless, they need to liquidate their house account to prevent personal losses. One analyst may upgrade their recommendation while another downgrades the same stock. Confusing? You bet! Yet, both analysts and stockbrokers believe, in their greedy minds, they are performing a valuable public service.

They are. Not by being correct; but, by being wrong regarding their recommendation. Investors moving in an opposite investment orbit to that of analyst and brokers often have the winning edge. Stocks will almost always move up in price when analyst underestimate (wrong) a company's earnings. It will usually drop in price, if corporate earnings fail to beat analyst estimates. Until stockbrokers back their recommendations with a guarantee against losses with profit sharing in lieu of commissions, pass them up. Investors need to learn and apply stock analytical studies in order to be truly successful in the inexact science of stock selection. The service value of both the analyst and stockbroker has rapidly diminished with the introduction of DPP, DRIP, mutual funds, deep discount brokerage firms; and, the arrival of *Don't Die Broke* onto the stock investment scene. The day has arrived for investors to learn how to conduct the independent stock analytical study.

We have stressed the necessity of building a strong financial base, the elimination of debt, higher education; and, the utilization of several different types of investment strategies. Investors have been shown how to monitor stock price trend performance through the utilization of moving averages. They have been shown back-tested DOW investment concepts proven through actual trading, to be profitable trade after trade, at cheaper cost with less downside risk. This section provides critical information necessary for investors willing to wade through the trash searching for the best stock. Pure and Simple! True, not every stock selected will prove to be a winner. Winning on every trade is not necessary. It only takes two stocks moving 10 fold each to appreciate an initial $10,000 investment into a cool pretax million bucks.

Independent stock pickers can achieve predictable results. They can determine the stock price selling point upon entering the investment. Tricks of the trade will practically eliminate investment judgment errors caused by the "short squeeze" trap, overhead pressure, cold callers, hot tipsters; and, emotional knee jerk reactions. Investors can sidestep churning, stock brokerage firm dumping, bias press releases; and, the endless number of factors influencing stock investment decisions. Having a healthy body, clear drug free mind; and, a storehouse of knowledge, enables investors to absorb small bits of information necessary to be profitable. For example, President Bill Clinton stated during an October, 1996 White House press conference that Mexico had repaid a 1994 bail-out loan plus interest 18 months ahead of schedule. A quick Mexico stock market review indicated the Mexico market was up 44 percent year to date at the time of Clinton's comment. The Mexico Fund (MXF) was up year to date by 45 percent while the Mexico Equity Income Fund (MXE) had risen 33 percent respectively. 1996 exports into Mexico from the United States had soared to $4.57 billion. It was clear by the evidence, Mexico was rebounding and the potential for investors to capitalize on the rebound existed. A ten second comment by the President triggered substantial movement into Latin American investments. Following the crowd at this point would have been a drastic mistake. As new money poured into Mexico and Latin America, investors who had ridden the profit wave prior to the Presidents observation bailed out.

Greed for profits clouded the judgment of many new money investors from realizing Mexico's economy was still very weak; and, the loan was repaid by money borrowed from other sources. Profits were made prior to Clinton's announcement; but, to reap the rewards of a 44 percent market rise, Mexico equity holders needed someone like Clinton to trigger investor greed so they could sell out. Investors keen enough to translate data into information;

and, information into action, could have still profited from Clinton's remark. Not by investing into Mexico; but, by investing into companies doing business in Mexico. Data indicated Wal*Mart held ownership interest in 18 superstores in Mexico; and were planning to expand. A commitment of millions of dollars for the expansion give investors a clear signal the stock was posed for a rebound. Wal*Mart stock began to appreciate in value shortly after the Presidents remark. Do other Latin American opportunities for wealth building exist? Most certainly. Take into consideration the billions of export dollars flowing into Latin America and Mexico from the United States.

Tools necessary for conducting an independent analytical stock review are simple to use. Simplicity is the game. With confidence, investors over time can develop excellent stock picking skills. Developed skills bring success; and, success brings forth investor positive characteristics. With a reasonable amount of practice, investors can develop their own unique ability to spot trends, set sell points; and, locate the cream of the crop stocks. They can quickly identify stocks with low debt, excellent returns on equity, reasonable management ownership, earnings; and, the stock price momentum performance. Investors can learn all the tricks in less time than it took them to read *Don't Die Broke* too this point.

The analytical study of a particular stock through the utilization of up to 15 stock characteristics will aid investors sort through the rocks searching for a true market winner. For a stock to qualify as a true winner, it must have a strong potential of outperforming, not only the professional money managers; but, also the S&P 500 Index and the Dow. Stock selection is critical; however, profits and losses occur by knowing when to holdem' verses when to foldem'. Sadly, stock investors are often trapped into becoming gamblers without fully understanding the game rules. Ignorance of stock selection rules generate millions of dollars for commission greedy stockbrokers and professional money managers daily. A wise investor will know the game rules; and, set a stop-loss limit prior to playing the game. To that end, investors are wrong on their investment choice a majority of the time. That need not be the situation. Study the buy and sell stock characteristics. Review each characteristic with seriousness. Your financial well-being could depend on it. Use the characteristics to develop both buying and selling skills.

Create a play stock portfolio. After the play portfolio is consistently returning an annualized yield of at least twice the current 30 year treasury bond yield; its time to consider putting real money into play. For example, should the current 30 year treasury bond yield 7 percent, seek a 14 percent annualized total return. It is realistic to achieve 14 percent within a few days. To illustrate, consider a $10 stock appreciating, to $10.12 over a one month period. The annualized yield hits 14 percent ($10.12 - $10.00 = .12 / $10 = .012 percent (x) 12 months = 14.4 percent annualized). Its very obtainable to hit several such short term gainers annually. Should the investor lose money on 3 out of every 5 trades (60 percent of all trades), by keeping losses low, investors still have the potential of doubling their portfolio market value every 5 to 7 years. One single 20 percent gainer when offset by three 7 percent losers is a break-even. The odds favor the investor, that gainers will out number the losers long term. Do not be surprised to hit three or four stocks gaining 12 to 15 percent annualized during a calendar year. What keeps the investor in the game long enough to succeed, is an ability to replenish losses with new capital. That is why a job and emergency funds are so important.

The study of stock characteristics is not a complex science; nor, is it exact. Sources of stock investment information available for public review include analyst reports, press releases, Security Exchange Commission forms 10-K and 10-Q, earnings reports, *The Investor's Business Daily*; and, the *Standard and Poor's Stock Guide.* Additional sources are also available at the public library, brokerage firms, the host company, computer websites; as well as, most local newspapers. Investors utilizing the *Investor's Business Daily* (*IBD*) as an investment source can screen thousands of stocks within only a few minutes. *IBD* is basically a grouping of historical investment information computer screens printed daily for mass distribution; thus, eliminating the need for each investor to build a personal computer data base. The point being, to become a successful stock investor, it cost very little to locate a reliable information source. Tools of the trade include the information source, calculator, telephone, pencil, note pad, time, and money.

Before preceding, investors should have before them the most recent copy of the *Investor's Business Daily*. An *IBD* dated within the past 10 days will work; but, the most current issue is a better choice. Screening for potential winners may be accomplished either through reviewing the stock columns; or, the stock charts. Each daily *IBD* format is slightly different; therefore, we recommend keeping close at hand a minimum of 5 back issues in order to track important buy and sale characteristics of a specific stock.

`Caution:` The saying "a picture is worth a thousand words" do not apply to stock selection; unless, the investor has the whole picture. Taking into consideration incorrect analyst projections, crooked management, greedy stockbrokers, and market manipulators; investors see the whole picture through cloudy vision. No matter how attractive a stock chart appears, always check out the story by reviewing the stock columns.

Lets take a look at the Analytical Buy Characteristics that will narrow the search for a potential winner. Eighty-five percent of all listed stocks (rocks) will be discarded right up front. Many more will be eliminated through analytical screening. Investors will be screening only the best stocks while searching for the golden nugget.

Analytical Buy Characteristics

* First, review the latest issue of the *Investor's Business Daily (IBD)* 52 week high stock columns for the notation "NH." Stocks hitting new high (NH) points are very positive; if, the "NH" is a confirmed historical high price and the recent price is approximately 90 to 105 percent above the previous 52 week low price. A historical high price wipes out the negative aspects of overhead pressure and short squeezing. For now, it is not necessary to determine the stocks historical high price. Write down only those stock who's "NH" is 90`to 105 percent higher than the 52 week low. The IBD "NH" is looking back 52 weeks. Investors need to look much further. Next step!

* Eliminate from you list, all stocks failing to meet an *IBD* earnings per share (EPS) growth ranking 79 or greater. EPS is the *IBD* ranking of each stock according to its earnings growth compared to the earnings growth of other stocks. Look at the top of the stock column to locate the EPS header. Follow the column down to your stock pick.

* Next, eliminate from your list all stocks failing to meet an *IBD* relative strength (RS) ranking 79 or greater. RS is the *IBD* ranking of each stock according to their price per share growth over the past year when compared to the price growth of other stocks. The RS header is next to the EPS header.

A RS or EPS ranking of 79 places the selected stock within the top 21 percent performance grouping and automatically eliminates the underachievers from your list. A top 21 percent EPS/ RS ranking often identifies the best managed companies. Through the accomplishment of the three previous steps, investors have created a listing of the market hottest performers. The next step is very important. It will cull out the rocks from the golden nugget!

* Is the "NH" of all stocks remaining on your list, the historical high price for that specific stock? To locate the historical high price of a stock, review the "price range" column of the most current issue of the *Standard and Poor's Stock Guide (SPSG)* (1-800-221-5277) located in the reference section of most Libraries. The *SPSG* is published monthly and provides the latest information provided by the companies listed. Not all companies are listed in the *SPSG*. Should a stock on your list not be covered in the *SPSG,* contact the company; or, your discount brokerage firm for the historical high price information. We can not over emphasize the importance of the correlation between the current stock price to it's historical high price. A $10 stock will never hit $100 unless

it reaches new high points along the way! Eliminate all stocks from your list <u>not</u> at the historical high price. Remember, the "NH" is between 90 and 105 percent higher than the stocks previous 52 week low price. Considering that fewer than 100 stocks double annually, those that do have done so based upon demand outpacing supply. Jump on that train for a 10 to 20 percent equity increase ride. It only takes a hand full of these stocks annually to make an investor wealthy beyond any expectations. Don't stop yet, the selection process is not finished.

* From the listed stocks, in the historical high price grouping, select companies who's cash and cash equivalent investments exceed long term debt. Cash to long term debt information is located in the current *SPSG*. Again the information may be obtained directly from the company or a discount stock broker if it is not available in the *SPSG*.

ALERT: Do not be surprised nor disappointed to discover all the stocks on your list have been screened out. The market is telling investors to remain on the sidelines for their wealth sake. Repeat the stock selection steps day after day. Eventually, stocks will remain on the list. Should the lucky event occur where several stocks remain listed, return back to the *IBD* for additional screening. You are still searching for the single best performer of the group.

* Look for a 30 percent minimum annual earnings growth; or, twice the Price-Earnings Ratio (PE) which ever is the highest. Growth rate excludes earnings not associated with income derived from the sale of products or services. For example should; Wizbangitsme company report a 1997 earnings of $32 million compared to a 1996 earnings of $20 million because the company sold 4000 acres of land for $6 million. The $6 million must be subtracted from the reported $32 million to realize an operational earnings of $26 million. The $26 million less the $20 million reported 1996 earnings should be exceed the $20 million by at least 30 percent. However, if the current PE of Wizbangitsme is 29, the earnings growth rate would need to be 58 percent or greater. Additionally, earnings growth must be accelerating over the past five years. Earnings for the most recent quarter should also exceed the reported earnings for the previous quarter and also beat or equal the annual growth rate. The most single powerful characteristic of a strong stock is perhaps a strong earnings growth.

<u>Annual Earnings Growth Rate Formula</u>

Current Year Adjusted Earnings (-) Past Year Adjusted Earnings (=) Net Earnings Difference.

Net earnings Difference (/) Past year Adjusted Earnings(=) Annual Earnings Growth Rate.

<u>Example</u>

1997 reported earnings: $32 million
(-) 6 million land sale
(=) $26 million (1997)
(-) $20 million (1996)
(=) $6 million net earnings difference
$6 million (/) $20 million (=) 30 percent annual earnings growth rate.

* Next, compute the Price to Earnings Ratio (P/E) for Wizbangitsme. Wizbangitsme has 26 million shares outstanding. The adjusted earnings for 1997 represents $1 per share: (26 million shares / $26 million adjusted earnings). Assuming the stock is selling at $15 per share the price to earnings is 15: (Price $15 / $1 earnings = 15). Is the annual earnings growth twice the P/E value: (P/E 15 times 2 = 30)? Yes, both the PE and earnings

annual growth rate, represent 30 percent. That would be is very positive for future price appreciation of Wizbangitsme stock. The P/E represents the number of years it will take the investor to recoup their investment based on the current earnings level. P/E numbers are widely published; but, if not you now know how to compute it.

* Avoid cheaply priced stocks! Share prices of $10 or greater is preferred. Stocks trading at $10 or higher tend to have a greater following of floor specialist and market makers. "Spreads", the hidden commission, are generally lower and liquidity is enhanced. Never own anything you can not liquidate! According to the *Wall Street Digest*, stocks priced in the $20 to $30 price range appear to double more than any other price level stocks. Never forget! Stocks setting at 50 percent off their highs are not cheap, if they are still above their book value. Low priced stocks are usually not a bargain, they're often cheap underachievers. The stock market is a auction barn. Anything of value brings higher prices. All stocks are bad unless the market demand runs the price up! Stocks and other investments go down in price due to lack of demand. The buyer always sets the price!

A review of thousands of listed stocks will only take a few minutes. Stocks selected using the previously discussed buy characteristics will fall within the best performance group on the stock market. However, to narrow the selection field further, it will be necessary to go inside the corporate makeup.

Excellent Corporate Stock Fundamentals.

* Annual sales growth rate of 25 percent. Compute the sales growth by using the Annual Earnings Growth Rate formula principle. Annual sells of less than $200 million often identifies a merging growth company which is the preferred choice of many professional investors.

* A positive cash flow is essential. Adjusted earnings must exceed spending.

* Market capitalization value of between $200 million and $1.5 billion. Lower capitalization generally increases the risk of losses associated with liquidity while higher capitalization increases the risk of losses due to stagnation. Mid-cap stocks are generally in the growth phase of their corporate life cycle. We at *Don't Die Broke* find stocks in the $20 to $30 price range with 10 to 75 million shares outstanding having a float of between 5 and 50 million shares, very attractive.

Market Capitalization Formula

Current Price (CP) x Shares Outstanding (SO) = Market Capitalization (MC).

$10 (CP) stock x 26 million shares (SO) = $260 million (MC).

A (MC) below $50 million = micro capitalization.
$50 mil to $200 mil (MC) = small capitalization.
$200 mil to $1.5 billion (MC) = mid capitalization (Our best group)
$1.5 billion plus (MC) = large capitalization.

* Net profit margin 10 percent or greater. Profit margins of this level are almost non-existent in the airline, trucking, insurance, retail; or, hotel industries. Technology companies reach profit margins of this magnitude during the introduction phase of new products and usually until the completion catches up.

* The daily share volume is above its 50 day arithmetic moving average with a daily volume dollar value less than $3 million. To compute the volume daily dollar value, multiply the daily volume by the current stock price. Double check the figures to assure a correct computation. Volume is reported by a factor of 100; therefore, when 300 is listed, the actual volume is 30,000 (100 x 300 = 30,000) shares exchanging hands.

<u>Daily Volume Dollar Value Formula:</u>

Daily volume (x) share price = daily average dollar value.

The daily volume is generally either above or below its 50 day arithmetic moving average. To determine the trading "average dollar volume value," mathematical corrections are necessary. To obtain an average volume, add together the normal historical daily volume and the 50 day arithmetic moving average volume. Divide the sum by two. Volume, like a stock price will eventually trend toward its average. A volume falling 10 to 15 percent below a short term average could flash a sell signal. A volume drying up is bad for stock price appreciation.

Volume is a greed barometer. It represents the level of perceived future equity, investors believe will be forthcoming. Should volume dry up, the stock price upward momentum will stagnate and pricing generally enters into a base line; or, corrects sharply downward. Either way, the stock price will eventually cross below its historical moving average and flash a sale. Corporate bosses hate negative stock price performance. Their bonuses and stock options could suffer. To please the boss, market makers may attempt to boost the price by artificially creating a floating supply shortage through purchasing the stock off the open market for their floor account. As they back fill their house account, the volume begins to move. The investing public will note the volume boost and almost without exception will resume trading activity. Stocks listed in the *IBD* indicating trading well above their 50 day volume moving average are well worth further study especially if the last two final price ticks were up from the tick 15 minutes earlier.

* Return on equity (ROE) should exceed twice the 30 year treasury yield; but, in no case less than the P/E ratio.

* Stock float between 5 and 50 million shares. The "float" is a measurement of the number of shares available for trading on the open market. It represents the shares outstanding less those held by management. For example, a privately held corporations has a zero float; whereas, a publicly held company may float several hundred million shares. A stock split may or may not change a "float" percentage to outstanding shares. Stocks representing a 5 to 50 million share float often represents a growth company opportunity having a strong potential to outperform larger capitalized companies.

* Management stock ownership of between 15 and 45 percent is preferred. Management ownership must be substantial enough to tie management's wealth to the company's stock price performance; yet, low enough to prevent them from installing their own puppet Board of Directors. A publicly held corporation ceases to be a public company the moment management is allowed to install their good-ole boys from the country club onto the board for personal gain instead of for the management of shareholder business interest. As a side note, before voting on installing a board member, check out their relationship to management. If there are any business, personal; or, family connections, vote a big fat "NO!". The surest way to lose money, is to allow the good- ole boys award Buba manager a "golden parachute" as an escape route for inept management.

* Long term debt should be of a lower valued than cash and cash equivalent holdings; and, must never exceed 85 percent of the market capitalization. Companies holding more cash than long term debt will not generally go to

the court house to file bankruptcy while the investors are asleep. Short term debt is usually offset by inventory and is not a consideration in the stock selection process.

Cash exceeding long term debt is an excellent gauge of how management is performing. It is difficult to understand why performance bonuses are tied to increased sales; or, earnings if those sales or earnings are accomplished by driving the company further into debt at the expense of shareholder equity. Stick with companies having a debt to cash ratio of less than one: (Long term debt / cash = <1). Remember, the risk of loss increases with higher debt to cash ratio's. Obtain the information from the most recent quarterly stockholder report. Both cash and debt are listed in the *SPSG*, if the company is tracked.

Debt is bad. Cash is king! Why? First, when buying a stock underwritten by substantial cash, the true cost of the stock is reduced by the cash per share value. For example, if a company has 1 million shares outstanding; but, is holding $1 million in excess cash greater than long term debt; and, the shares cost one buck, in effect, the shares are free. Secondly, cash can be used to either buy down debt, conduct research, expansion; or, for a dividend distribution. Either case, it will eventually benefit the share price. Another reason, it is very important to keep an eye on the cash pile, is because a large cash position may attract takeover specialist attempting to raid the company for the money. Investors wise enough to get out when given a tender offer for their stock usually profit.

* Total corporate assets should exceed the sum of total long term debt; plus, all other liabilities.

* The stock price trending above its 15 week exponential moving average. Review the 15 week exponential moving average within this chapter.

* Look for a charted stock price spike accompanied by a volume well above the volume 50 day moving average, especially if the price is moving off an extended consolidation base.

* Earnings reported to the stock holders must be the same as that reported to the Internal Revenue Service. Tax cheaters make poor business partners. The Z-Seven mutual fund listed on the New York Stock exchange has been reported to utilize this strategy successfully.

* The broad market should be in a general up trend. How the market goes; except in rare situations, so does practically everything else. The *IBD* provides a market trend chart daily. The market should be above its 200 day moving average. Investors must use caution when more than 80 percent of all the listed stocks on the New York Stock Exchange are trading above their 200 day moving average. Historically, stock price levels of this magnitude indicates the market is topping.

Additional *Investor's Business Daily* information

* Group strength: How is the group your stock belongs to doing? The *IBD* ranks each stock by group strength. Stick stocks with a ranking of "A" or "B". The strength compares the stocks group price performance over the previous six months versus the price performance of the 196 stock groups monitored by the *IBD.*

* Accumulation/ Distribution: The measurement of daily price change factored by the stocks daily volume indicates whether a stock is being accumulated or dumped (distributed). Price upward momentum is pushed by high volumes relative to the historical volume moving average. A ranking of "A" is positive.

* Sponsorship: A sponsorship of "A" or "B" indicates the stock has become attractive to institutional, retirement;

and, large investors. Since this group as a whole, conduct perhaps more than 85 percent of all stock transactions, their involvement is positive.

To conclude buying characteristics, do not become discouraged if the selection process appears complex. It's not! As with any new skill, it will require a little practice before expertise emerges. Likewise, it is not an ironclad rule that every stock must meet all the buy characteristic. Few stocks ever will. Search for stocks meeting the majority of the characteristics. When a specific stock is identified, Buy it that day, then track its performance with the 15 week Exponential Moving Average beginning the following Wednesday.

Now that it is known what to buy, investors will never acquire wealth if they fell to understand the importance of when to sell. No stock is a good investment unless it makes money. Holding onto a stock for years is often an unwise decision. Every stock will eventually experience a price collapse. Perhaps, someone in your neighborhood purchased Eastern Air Lines stock back in 1979 when Eastern's Great Silver fleet was number one in the world only to lose their investment when the carrier cease operating after a devastating strike 12 years later. Dozens of publicly held corporations fade away annually. So much for security! Consider very carefully management controlled retirement stock accounts. The 1997 United Parcel Service strike, by the Teamster represented employees took this issue very serious, as well they should. Keep your investments, private affairs; and work separate.

"Those who fail to make a plan; will fail," is a sad fact of reality. Avoid the temptation to run over the cliff with the pack. The market will alert investors on which stocks to purchase through subtle signals. Mega-computer programming is not necessary; and, in fact should be avoided. Simplicity is the profit route. William O'Neil's *Investors Business Daily* and the *Standard and Poor's Stock guide* has already done the work to provide information vital to selecting future potential market winners. Allocate investment resources across bonds, real estate, DRIPs, DPPs, the DOW theory; and, mid-cap stocks identifiable through the aforementioned buy characteristics. Investor now know when to buy. How about when to sell!

Analytical Sell Characteristics

Never enter into a stock position without first setting a target sell point. The self induced emotional roller coaster stress experienced by a majority of stock investors must be eliminated, if the joy of profits are to be realized. Investors should never fall in love with a stock. If you do, expect disappointment. The only good stocks are those that go up in value. The objective is to make money. Holding a position to avoid taxes is often a mistake. Speaking of taxes. Capitol gains tax was revamped in 1997 to reward investors for long term holding. Do not believe for one second that investor financial well being was given consideration. Long term, the majority of professional traders will benefit much better by trading to profit while paying the tax due quarterly. Think of taxes as an expense of doing business. Holding a position longer than necessary to profit will often cost more than paying the tax simply because of missed opportunities. **To control losses, sell without hesitation if any single sell characteristic is triggered.**

* The stock fails to break out of an extended basing price range within 15 weeks after the initial purchase. A base formation can generally be identified when the price remains within 7 percent of the original purchase price week after week. Holding 15 weeks gives the company ample opportunity to produce a positive earnings follow through.

* The price trends greater than 7 percent below the initial purchase price prior to establishing a positive up trend. Stock prices falling will tend to continue falling, often taking months or even years to recover. As prices fall, overhead pressure increases, as current investors hold the position; or, even foolishly purchase more because they

fail to realize they made a wrong stock selection choice. **Never buy stock (average down) below the initial purchase price! Investors only make money in a rising market. They lose in a sideways or downward trend.**

* The *IBD* Relative Strength (RS) purchase point ranking drops by 15 percent; or, to 74 whichever is highest. EPS has no bearing on selling. After the stock is purchased, forget about the EPS. The price RS will trail a weak EPS.

* *IBD* group strength, accumulation/distribution; or sponsorship correcting to a ranking of "C" from A+, A, or B.

* After a stock price is confirmed by it's 15 week exponential moving average to be in an up-trend; and, the current closing price drops to and remains below the moving average reference line for two consecutive plots, sell quickly.

* The current price has overextend by approximately 20 percent above the Wednesday 15 week exponential moving average price.

  Healthy stocks follow a gradual pricing up-trend which tracks very close; but, slightly above the moving average line. The current stock price relationship to its historical average price is very important. To compute the stock price divergence, subtract the moving average price from the current price and divide the remainder by the moving average price: (CP - EMC = x / EMC = d).

* Dow theorist should sell based upon the annual portfolio readjustment requirements outlined within that section of this chapter. The actual date is unimportant; however, investors should remember that major market corrections exceeding 10 percent generally occur in the "**JASON**" months. Mid-December appears to be an ideal entry point. A properly valued market would be helpful. Investors considering using the Dow theories could project to do very well if they entered the investment when 40 to 60 percent of all the listed New York Stock Exchange stocks were trading above their 200 day average. Liquidate the position when 85 percent of all the NYSE stocks trend above their 200 day average. The October 1, 1997 stock market experienced evaluations of that magnitude.

  The *Don't Die Broke* stock portfolio was liquidated and the assets were moved into 30 year zero coupon bonds shortly after the broad market triggered over-evaluation limits. No one can predict the market direction; but, mathematically, every market will trend toward its historical median average. From the October 1st evaluation, the market would need to pull back 29 percent to reach a correct evaluation: (85% above 200 day average less the median average of 60% equals 25/85 = 29.4%). A correction of that magnitude will push long term bonds up. Our choice to move into bonds was a correct one even if the market never corrects down. Why? First, the threat of a substantial correction over a long base line is tremendously high. Secondly, the market began trending sideways on August 6,1997. A side moving market is just as bad for wealth building as a downward moving market. Finally, a stock market correction will flush investors into the safe haven of dividend paying treasury debt instruments. As they do, demand will out strip supply, forcing bond prices up until the government issues additional bonds to absorb the demand.

  The flood of investors into the treasury market will increase the debt owed by the government to its lenders (bond holders). Increasing the federal debt obligation will not allow the bureaucrats to balance the budget by the year 2002. To reduce the federal debt load, the Feds will monkey around with the interest rates. Congress and the IRS will monkey around with the corporate and individual tax structure, which they did eventually accomplish in September 1997. The bottom line will be a reversal in the stock market as increased corporate earnings and favorable tax breaks push corporate earnings into new high levels. Stocks will push to higher levels to relieve the debt load of America as investors jump out of bonds back into stocks. Stocks will also trend higher as the government tries to fix the failed social security system. Under current cash flow levels, the system will enter a negative cash flow position in the year 2012. Long before that date, the government will attempt to convince investors to not expect funds from the program to support their retirement. We agree!

Along with higher corporate profit levels will come the demand of increased wages by the work force. The very government wishing to balance the budget will side rail the effort by bending to the whims of organized labor in an effort to strengthen party funding. Put another way, the Congress and Office of the President will sell out the future of our children, for many generations to benefit their political self interest, if not watched very carefully. Ever wonder why the American bald Eagle is the symbol of America? Eagles have keen eyesight. The American investor had better learn to keep watch over their investments with the eye of an Eagle. More valuable to the average worker is the skill to manage their assets than to receive higher wages. DEMAND YOUR EMPLOYER OR UNION INCLUDE ASSET MANAGEMENT TRAINING INTO YOUR CONTRACT OR WORK BENEFIT PACKAGE! A good bet is the Dow will exceed a lackluster level of 18000 before the Social Security bust of the year 2012 occur. Along the way, investors can benefit through a combination of investment and asset management strategies. Let's continue with the sell characteristics.

* Earnings growth rate retracing to the P/E level, either through P/E expansion; or, growth reduction.

* Never allow a post inflation / tax / commission profit revert into a loss. A penny profit beats a loss! Of course, a stock may be sold any time to make a net profit.

Lots-o-wealth has been accumulated through stock trading. Investors should commit only funds not required for current living cost plus emergency reserves. Expect to stick with an investment plan 3 to 5 years. That doesn't mean sticking with a single stock or mutual fund. Don't fall in love with a stock. The moment it doesn't perform, it should be fired. As Jim Straw put it, "a stock is like a burning match, once lit, it's passed around until someone gets burnt." We agree! Regardless of the strategy used to select an equity, at some point it will become prudent to liquidate. Never let a profit turn into a loss; and, for goodness sake, do not under any circumstances average down a stock losing value. Prices drop because the "auction barn" fails to recognize future value. Never bet against the house; you'll lose.

QUARTERLY ALLOCATION: An alternative to our preferred moving average stock strategy is the quarterly allocation strategy. Quarterly allocation evaluations will automatically weed out stock under-performers. The steps to implement the quarterly allocation are:

* Log the share price and the number of shares for each stock when purchased.
* Log the gross purchase market value of each stock.
* As stocks are purchased, place the stocks initially in alphabetical order.
* At the end of the current calendar quarter, multiply the number of shares by the most recent closing price to arrive at the current share market value.
* Reorganize the stock with the highest market value at bottom.
* At the end of the second quarter, recalculate each stock market value again.
* Compute each stocks percent of change since the last quarter.
* Rearrange the stocks so the one with the highest percentage of gain for the quarter is at the top.
* Sell the lowest percentage of change stock and replace it with another choice.
* Place the new issue at the bottom of the list. It will have a zero quarterly growth.
* Stock performance comparison should not occur until after a full quarter cycle. Review the following illustration.

Current Quarter Stock Holdings

DATE	STOCK	PRICE	#SHARES	MARKET VALUE	% +/-
1/23	A	10.00	1000	10,000	0
2/2	B	6.00	500	3,000	0
3/4	C	12.87	300	3,861	0
3/10	D	9.75	1000	9,750	0

Following Quarter Stock Holdings

DATE	STOCK	$ PRICE	#SHARES	$ MARKET VALUE	% +/-
4/1	B	8.75	500	4,375	+45%
4/1	D	10.75	1000	10.750	+10.2%
4/1	C	12.87	300	3,861	0%
4/1	A	9.00	1000	9,000	-10%

Sell stock company "A" and replace it with a new stock. The percent growth (+/-) of the replacement stock will initially be zero. The stock may be purchase anytime within the quarter. The stock price appreciation illustration of 45 percent quarterly is not unrealistic when selecting stocks through the analytical stock characteristics.

Appreciation of 2 to 4 percent monthly is more realistic, however. quarterly allocation stock selection assumes several basic factors. First, stocks are selected through an identical selection process. Secondly, under-performers have failed the performance expectations. Finally, stocks are sold and systematically replaced without emotional conflict.

DIVIDEND ELITE: Investors seeking dividend income perhaps should not consider stock selection through either the Analytical Study or Beating The Dow strategies. They should emphasize total return stability through consistent dividend distributions; plus, a modest price appreciation Dividends are an important supplement to retirement income. Do not be fooled into investing into any company just because their dividends are high. Be suspect of any dividend exceeding the 30 year Treasury Bond Yield. The yield of any equity will fluctuate in percentage on every trade. Additionally, as the stock price trends up, the yield will fall. Sell any stock whose price rises high enough to cause a dividend pull back of 30 percent. Income seekers should search for companies having characteristics of the dividend elite. Dividend elite companies are those with:

* At least a 50 year history of dividend payouts. Dividend information is listed within the monthly *SPSG.*
* Corporate cash position exceeding long term debts.
* Total assets exceeding total liabilities including the long term debt.
* Earnings growth 30 percent annually with current quarter beating the previous quarter.
* Dividends increased annually 3 out of 5 most recent years.

We have been discussing how to locate the best stocks the market offers. In our thoughts along that line, Real Estate Trust (REIT's) stocks can prove to be big winner especially when purchased during the topping phase of an up-trending market. REIT's are an excellent alternative to bonds. Both are highly liquid.

REAL ESTATE: Real estate investing excludes your home simply because good old Uncle Sam disallows home owners from taking depreciation cost associated with true real estate investing. For example, if an investment were made into a business complex, tenants would pay rental fees (Income). Business expense plus depreciation could be used to offset the income. Everyone riding the elevator, using the rest room; or, opening the front door generates depreciation. Through the depreciation factor, every person utilizing an investment property, extend tax benefits to the investor owner.

Except for raw farm land, real estate historically has under-performed equity (stock) investments across practically every measurement period. The reasons for under performance are many; but, one thing is clear to many investors. The forced payment of property tax on the same product year after year creates losers through up-surging wealth to the government. Property tax, standing alone, is an excellent argument for voting into existence a value added sales tax or lottery to support the local education system. Money raised through these mediums could be distributed to both private and public schools through a grant process based upon attendance projections. Children could be educated in their own neighborhood instead of being institutionally kidnapped and forced to travel often an excessive distance by a federal judge who sends their child to a private school across the street.

Closely correlated to unjust property tax is the real estate problem of liquidity. Real estate value is controlled by demand, utility, scarcity, transferability, social patterns, building codes, street designs, property tax mill rate, and location... location...location. Property selling by the acre within 3 to 5 miles beyond a point where property is selling by the square foot has a potential of creating extreme wealth, as the property transitions from the acre valuation to the square foot cost base, if it can be sold.

Knowledge of your community growth path is very important not only from a monetarily point of view; but, also from a personal comfort viewpoint. Americans hate discomfort. To ease the pain of employment, working socialites systematically expand communities toward the Northeast. Socialites commuting to and from the central business district despise looking into bright sunlight while driving. Who doesn't? Their discomfort presents a wide array of real estate opportunities. A word of caution. Never purchase investment real estate without first identifying the profit source before entering into the deal. Reduce the frustration often associated with real estate investing by hiring a professional management company to serve your best interest. A Real Estate Investment Trust (REIT) may best serve the average investor by assisting them in reaching an important wealth building goal.

REIT's offer professional management throughout a wide property diversification to include apartments, regional malls, shopping centers, healthcare facilities, factory outlet stores, storage warehouses, lodging facilities, health clubs, and much more. The total return yield, is generally very close to the prime rate yield. REIT's may be purchased through both closed and open ended mutual funds. Additionally, they may be purchased through real estate firms set up to renovate and rent property under terms set forth within the *Federal Housing Tax Credit Act.* of REIT's selling at wholesale (discounted below net asset value) are very attractive because they tend to move toward their retail evaluation range, as the real estate sector improves.

Closed End REIT Listing

Agree Reality	ADC	Hospitality Properties	HPT
Beacon Properties	BCN	HRE Properties	HRE
Bedford Property Inv.	BED	MGI Properties	MGI
Bradley Real Estate	BTR	Mid-Atlantic Reality	MRR
CALI Reality	CLI	Parkway Properties	PKY
Camden Property Trust	CPT	Storage Trust Reality	SEA
Centerpoint Properties	CNT	Trinet Corporate	TRI
Columbus Reality	CLB	U.S. Restaurant L.P	USV

Essex Property Trust	ESS	Voranado Reality Trust	VNO
Equity Residential Properties	EQR	Weeks Reality Trust	WKS

Open End REIT Listing (1-800)

CGM Reality	345-4048	C&S Reality	437-9912
Colombia Real Estate Equity	547-1707	Crabbe Huson Real Estate "P"	541-9732
Evergreen Global "Y"	807-2940	Evergreen USA "Y"	807-2940
Fidelity Real Estate Investors	544-8888	Longleaf Reality	445-9469
United Services	873-8637	Vanguard S.P. REIT Index	523-1154

The Federal Housing Tax Credit Act of 1993

Real estate investing gives rise to equity growth, tax sheltering, and social responsibility. In 1993, Congress underscored more than fifty years of federal government support for every citizen to have the opportunity to benefit from affordable housing. Congressional support targeted the elderly and citizens at the low end of the wage economic scale. Jointly, the government and tax payer can corporate through a partnership agreement while providing low and moderate income housing. The *Federal Housing Tax Credit Act* authorizes investor tax relief through a tax credit trust. The government, tax payer, elderly, handicapped, poor; and, low income citizens equally benefit by having affordable housing provided through a cooperative partnership between the investing public and the federal government. Operating through a Congress approved trust, investors can purchase, maintain, and manage selected rental properties. Renters pay the government while the government rewards investors year after year through tax credits. A tax credit reduces the investors personal annual income tax obligation down too but not below the alternative minimum tax for each year the investment meets the Trust guide lines.

Low income housing tax credits exempts personal income tax obligations annually on investments not exceeding $25,000 for up to 15 years. The actual exempted dollar value is dependent upon the initial investment value, the investors personal income tax bracket; and, the length of time it takes the property to meet occupancy requirements. Each tax credit dollar increases after-tax disposable income which becomes available for leveraging into even higher investment returns. Of course, as with any government sponsored program, there is always the "good news" (benefits) associated with the "bad news" (limitations). Let's discuss the limitations first. Limitations: (1) tax credit real estate investing is a long term investment strategy, (2) It generally has a very steep up front administrative fee that could exceed 25 percent of the initial investment, (3) there are no back-end guarantees, (4) tax credits generally do not begin until 60 percent of the property units are rented, (5) individual investments are limited to a maximum of $25,000, (6) tax credits will not reduce the alternative minimum tax, (7) there is no guarantee of a return of principle upon liquidation of the property, (8) tax is payable on all capital gains upon liquidation, (9) tax credits may represent the total investment return; and (10) there are no upper investment limits for corporations. Sounds like a bad investment choice, doesn't it! Not so for the savvy investor with a moderate net worth combined with a good upper level income. We agree it is not an investment alternative for the majority of Americans. We do; however, firmly believe information provided throughout this publication can aid investors reach important financial objectives necessary for them to benefit from this program. Now to the benefits: Low income housing tax credits should be considered a small single part of a well diversified investment portfolio. Benefits may well exceed what appears on the surface as very negative limitations. Consider the personal rewards and benefits associated with: (1) humanitarian response, (2) a tax credit on the investment every year for up to 15 years, (3) property capital appreciation potential, (4) increased after tax income, (5) the tax credit is awarded and budgeted by Congress up front before each project is approved, (6) tax credits are defined within IRS code section

42, (7) projects are usually diversified across several economic regions as well as properties within those regions, (8) a true tax savings, and (9) all unused credits may be carried forward or backward. Backward credits are limited to three years; however, forward credits can be taken annually; or, in a lump sum any time after they have been accrued. All credits must be claimed prior to the termination of the Trust. Finally, (10) the property is professionally managed by a general partner. To illustrate the tax benefit, consider a tax payer in the 28 percent tax bracket with an annual income of $45,000. On a $25,000 investment, once the property met the Trust requirement, the worker could eliminate the first $25,000 from taxable earnings for up to 15 years for a tax savings of $105,000: ($25,000 x 28%=$7000 x 15 yr. $105,000). Very few investments return 419 percent over a 15 year period. Assuming the worse case where the investor lost every cent of the initial investment, the investment return would still exceed $88,000. It is very important for investors to understand, THIS IS TAX FREE MONEY; except for the capitol gains upon liquidation.

Affordable housing is a basic human right. Society economically benefits through cooperation between the private investing sector and the government. Before committing funds long term, as with any investment, profits must be identified prior to entering into the deal. Always review the project prospectus. Request the general partner to provide a list of closed out projects they have participated in as the general partner, as well as, current projects; and, the annualized performance of each project. Consult with a tax advisor. Investors must never forget that real-estate investing is risky business regardless of how attractive it appears on the surface.

Property values generally rise at the end of a bullish stock market as investors who've enjoyed stock appreciation seek protection for their assets. The best time to consider real estate investments is before a bullish stock market turns bearish. Therefore, to maximize investment potential, knowledge of the stock market is correlated to successful real estate investing. A bullish stock market will generally be approaching a peak point when 80 to 90 percent of the New York Stock Exchange (NYSE) listed stocks trade above their 200 day arithmetic moving average. Market watchers would have noticed that on Wednesday, October 2, 1997, 84 percent of the listed NYSE stocks were trading above their 200 day moving average. Based on historical data, the end to the current bullish up trend is looming on the horizon. The *IBD* reports the figure daily. Another market topping indicator is when mutual fund excess cash reserves fall to less than 20 percent of the cash they need to meet normal daily redemption's. Low mutual fund reserve cash levels simply can not be a catalyst to push stock prices higher. Investors, being a greedy lot, seek fortunes elsewhere. Real estate and bonds are a natural target.

Capital appreciation is not the investment objective here! The objective is to benefit through a drastically reduced federal income tax liability. The *Federal Housing Tax Credit Act of 1993* is perhaps the last good deal Congress will ever pass along to the tax payer, as they panic to correct the social security and federal budget farce. Should investors elect to invest into a tax credit program? That depends on each individual situation. Before committing to a long term investing relationship, it is advisable to seek out an experienced general manager. Boston Capital Services, Inc., (1-800-866-2282), "the tax credit experts," are worthy of serious consideration. Boston Capital has been at the forefront of affordable housing legislation, development, management; and, financing for decades. Their record is impressive to say the least. Since 1974, they have raised over $1.5 billion from 53,000 investors to sponsor 350 programs consisting of 70,000 apartments on 1,800 properties in 48 states. The company offers professional management with true tax shelter opportunities. However, as we have stated over and over, never invest money unless it is fully understood why the investment is being made. In this instance, it's to cut taxes the humanitarian way.

The risk associated with real estate investing needs to be understood; and, investment skills developed before considering investing a single dollar. Local real estate agencies and Colleges often conduct courses on the subject.Additionally, there are mail order courses available. Mr. Carlton Sheets (1-800-770-2400) has advertised his real estate course through the television media for over thirteen years. Advertising any program for that long of time is a clear indication of success. Mr. Sheets has been reported to stress investors should always buy location-location-location, at wholesale. Wholesale buying, for remarketing at retail, has been a value investing approach for decades. Value investing does have pitfalls to negotiate around. We will help guide you.

VALUE INVESTING: Value occurs within the equity market when an investment is purchased at wholesale (discount) and resold at retail for a profit. Value investing into any commodity, including stocks is very risky. The risk is directly correlated to the accuracy of true book value estimates. True book value estimates are often at best a wild guess (WG). Wholesale stock evaluations emerge, as investors show lack of confidence in the free market, forcing the floating stock price to fall below the best "WG" breakup value of the corporation underlying net assets. For example, a company may have an estimated asset market value of $10 per share; but, for some unexplained reason, the stock is trading for a 20 percent discount a $8 per share. Investor confidence is often influenced by rumors, advice; and, negative news reported by individuals who may know actually very little about the company asset structure. Mr. Bert Dohmen, a noted economist and founder of the Dohmen Capital Research Institute (1-805-450-2243) website "dohmcap@aol.com" stated in a recent advertisement publication; "just say anything you want in a believable manner and the suckers will believe it." Mr. Dohmen's assessment emphasizes the importance of not following the crowd The crowd is generally always wrong. Every investor must learn how to select the proper investment not to exceed the recommended percentage of their net worth.

Investor assessment of a stock's true value is often influenced by negative news, analyst projected earnings short fall, labor strife; or, simply because the company's President is litigating a divorced. Regardless of the reason, an incorrect assessment of a stocks market value too its asset value can easily drive the stock price well below the companies "WG" asset book value. Almost without exception, current stock holders will incorrectly assume the lower stock price offers a better bargain and will purchase more stock as the price falls. The opposite is most likely true. Why? As the stock price drops, the overhead pressure increases. The further the price falls from its high point the greater overhead pressure. It could take years for the stock to fight its way back to an evaluation above the true corporate asset value. Stock shorting specialist often will squeeze the price even lower, as they purchase shares to cover their previous short selling position.

Another important point never to forget, is that corporate asset book value is always in a state of fluctuation, as corporate assets fight devaluation triggered by regulatory, depreciation; and, inflationary pressures. Value investing is like trying to hit a moving target in a house of mirrors. To be a profitable investment concept, investors must rely on the best information available, taken at a fixed snap shot during the corporate cycle. Stocks selling at, wholesale do offer long term wealth building opportunities for those lucky enough to have time to allow their selection to mature. The law of investing indicates that eventually the majority of undervalued stocks will eventually bottom in price and then trend toward book value. The price growth may be slow during the recovery phase until the overhead and short squeeze pressure is relieved through improved investor confidence. We know that value investing rarely benefits from the price movement action experienced with the new high price strategy discussed in the *Analytical Study* section of this chapter.

We understand many investors will follow a rocking chair approach to their portfolio management. There is nothing wrong with that investment management style. Investing should be relaxing, fun, stress free, lifestyle enhancing; but, more importantly, profitable. To aid our readership in reaching whatever personal investment objective they set for themselves, we have attempted to provide a wide array of investment strategies. Real estate, value investing and bonds are three strategies investors may consider avoiding until a solid positive net worth asset base has been built. As previously mentioned, the best personal investment strategy may actually be a combination of several strategies. The market is in a constant state of change and what is good for the market is good for the investor simply because the investor is the market Investors venturing into Value Investing must be committed to remaining in the investment 3 to 5 years. They must be willing to hang tough even when other opportunities may present themselves as having a higher profit potential. They must develop the analytical skills necessary to identify stocks selling at true wholesale to book value. We have provided for the Value investor the analytical points be which wholesale stocks are valued.

<u>Wholesale Valued Stock Analytical Points</u>

* Review the *Value Line Investment Survey* (1-800-833-0046). Weekly, the survey list stocks trading below corporate asset book value based upon a determination by Value Line analysts. Most public libraries make the survey available to investors.

* Stock book value can be quickly computed through a comparison between the stocks "market capitalization" (MC) and its "private value"(PV). Both pieces of information are published monthly within the *Standard and Poor's Stock Guide* (1-800-221-5277).

<u>Book Value Formula</u>

MC/PV = (X).

(X) less than 1 = wholesale value. (X) at 1 = book value. (X) greater than 1 = retail.
(MC) market capitalization = shares outstanding (x) current price. (PV) private value = assets less total liabilities.

For example: Company Wizbangitsme has 1,000 shares outstanding having a current trading price of $10 (MC) per share. The MC is $1,000 x $10 = $10,000. Current corporate assets equal $1,500. Current total liabilities are $1,000. PV equals $500. The stock is selling at 20 times book value ($10,000/ $500 = 20);and, fails to meet value investment qualifications. By contrast, should corporate assets equal $15,000 and the total liabilities outstanding equal $4,200, the PV would be $10,800. Therefore, $10,000/ $10,800 = .925 placing the stock at a 7.5 percent discount: (1.00- .925 = .075). The stock warrants further review, especially if the discount is off an historical high price point. Research into how much of a discount to book value is a good entry point has found the most profitable way to value invest is to purchase positions at a 20 percent discount and sell when the discount narrows to 15 percent.

Wizbangitsme should rise in stock price value by 8.1 percent in order to achieve book value (.075 / .925 = .081). A stock selling at a 30 percent discount; however, would need to rebound 42 percent in order to reach book value. Waiting a year or two for a 30 percent discounted stock to recover could be worth while, if the position is small when compared to the investors net worth. The wider the discount below book value generally the greater the risk. We suggest limiting the buy discount to a maximum of 20 percent and sell when the discount narrows to 15 percent. Wider discounts increases the overhead pressure to an extreme negative level. Overhead pressure is explained fully by William O'Neil in his excellent book *How to Make Money in Stocks.* For simplicity, (PV) assets are limited to corporate cash and cash equivalents. (PV) liability is limited to corporate long term debt. Things being equal, administrative and inventory assets are generally canceled out by short term debt liabilities.

The (PV) must always exceed the (MC). Negative net worth companies are just that: Worthless! Investors willing to reach for the golden value opportunity can spot opportunities by spending a few minutes at their public library. After a review of the *Value Line Investment Survey* (1-800-833-0046) and the *Standard and Poor's Stock Guide* (1-800-221-5277), investors can make logical investment decisions. Especially attractive are companies attempting to enhance shareholder equity through the elimination of long term debt, restructuring, spin-offs, legitimate stock repurchase programs, management insider buying; and, a Board of Directors not manipulated by management. Lets move out of equity investing into the purchasing of debt obligations issued by the U.S. Treasury Department. Before we do; however, we must reiterate that bills, notes, bonds; and, series EE bonds, typically drastically under-perform the total return of equity investments. Debt obligations are excellent for interest return and to use as a place to park equity funds until another equity investment is identified. Treasuries do provide an important shelter for the equity investor during stormy market conditions. To that end, effectively trading Treasury bonds, bills, and notes, requires an understanding the stock market.

It would be important, for example, to know the stock market has historically peaked when 80 to 90 percent of all listed New York Stock Exchange (NYSE) stocks are trading above their 200 day arithmetic moving average. If history repeats, and it generally does, perhaps the smart investor would have loaded up on 30 year Bonds when 83 percent of the NYSE stocks began to trade above their 200 day average during mid-day trading on August 6,1997. We at *Don't Die Broke* did! What did most investors do instead? They continued to pump billions of dollars into a market trending down off an historical high point. Eventually, the same investors will realize that a side moving market is a loosing market. When they do, they will jump out of stocks into debt obligations. The cycle repeats year after year. Because of that repetition, investors can create substantial wealth! Never purchase debt with a "bleeding heart" attitude that you are going to help good old Uncle Sam solve his budget problems. It an't gonna happen! Buy bonds to within net worth limits only to enhance personal wealth. Fact of the matter, the majority of Americans should never own a single bond including those bonds forced upon them through the forced socialist security system. Limit total bond holdings, including those held in the social security account, to a maximum percentage of net worth equal to 80 percent of the investors age.

BONDS, BILLS, and NOTES: Winning strategies discussed thus far have been related to equity investments. Bonds, bills, and notes are debt obligation investments. The investor loans money to the borrower at a fixed interest rate with the principle investment returned at some future date. The loan principle may or many not be secured by collateral. Bonds may be backed by corporate or government assets. Investment into corporate bonds require serious considerations. Corporations often seek out bond investors after reaching maximum share authorization and bank line of credit limits. Corporate bond collateral is often depreciating equipment. Smart investors avoid corporate bonds for a variety of reasons. For example, a bond is a debt which must be eventually retired by using either corporate earnings, assets, borrowed funds; or,. floating additional stock. Either way, equity value is removed from the company. Guess who the equity owners are? Yep, the stockholders! Therefore, our discussion will be limited to bonds, bills, and notes (treasuries) backed by the full faith of the US Government. Municipal bonds issued by local and state governments are eliminated from our recommendation due to the risk associated with complex tax considerations and the risk of bankruptcy. Local governments do file the big "B" word. Investors considering municipal and corporate bond investing should consult with a competent tax advisor prior to making a commitment.

Treasuries are backed by the full faith of the technically bankrupt federal government. However, risk of default is nil when supported by an ever ending deep pocket tax source. What's a couple of million dollars of wasted spending when spread out over 200 million tax supporters. Who should be concerned when the President is given a free ride aboard an Air Force Jet so he and his family can take a vacation? Investors should be very concerned! We suggest the Democratic National Convention reimburse the taxpayers for their boy joy riding at our expense! Do not take this comment in the wrong light. We are not picking on the first family. They have done a lot of good for not only the American people; but for the world as a whole. Look past human faults and poor personal business decisions they made have made prior to going to Washington. Considering the Presidential salary, he really deserves free transportation perks; but, only at the expense of those who hired him. That being his political party.

The point is simple. Default on United States treasury bonds, bill, and notes is nil dissipate wasteful spending.

However, the risk of long term negative net worth growth for American investors is very real. Phantom tax obligations on deferred treasury interest coupled with inflation nibbles away at future purchasing power. Bonds have historically under-performed equity investments by a wide margin. For that reason alone, except for diversification and interest income, they should be avoided. Rare special investment circumstances do occasionally arise. One such circumstance exist when a majority of stocks are priced above their 200 day moving average.

The United States federal government is the largest debt consumer on earth. Billions of dollars are borrowed monthly from people all over the earth to cover short term operational expenses. Let's review the big picture. The government levies dozens of tax categories ranging from income, social security, interstate telephone access, capitol gain, export, import, travel, highway, gas, special use, to consumer tax. The tax is then wasted through poor spending, to the benefit of a few and at the detriment of many. Next, the government seeks to justify poor management decisions by borrowing additional money from the over-taxed working population to pay for the waste. Purchasers of treasuries pay tax on the interest for the privilege of loaning money to a government who has been unable or unwilling to balance a simple budget. If the government were an individual seeking a loan from their local bank, the bank would almost surely deny the application. Ask yourself; Would I loan my dearest friend money if they were wasting their money and unable to balance their check book? Nay, Nay, Nay!

Investors interested in loaning money, only to have profits erode away through inflation and taxes; except in the rare instance of inflation adjusted bonds and stock market circumstances, should by all means consider bonds, bills and notes. We will assist investors who make that choice no differently than those who don't. Consider the following:

* Prior to the retirement years, treasury loans are best held through money market, mutual fund accounts; or social security. Limit holding values to 80 percent times age of total net worth. Social security should exempt folks from contributing if they do not have a positive net worth. That eliminates the majority of Americans!

* During retirement, individual bonds with a specific maturity date are preferred because mutual fund net asset values do fluctuate. A sell at a low NAV point can create loses. To its credit, the U.S. Treasury Department has realized the negative impact of inflation and has began to issue inflation indexed bonds. Time will only tell of the investing community will benefit during periods of low inflation; or, if the government will stick with the concept during periods of hyper inflation.

"Bills" are United States Government Treasury debt obligations issued at a discount to par value for a maturity period of less than one year. The discount equals the interest due at the end of the loan period.

"Notes" are intermediate debt obligations issued at a discount to par value maturing between one and five years hence. The interest rate is slightly higher than rates paid for bills.

"Bonds" are long term debt obligations issued at a discount to par value maturing between five and thirty years hence.

Bonds, bills, and notes purchased directly from the Treasury generally provide enhanced yields over bank accounts and Certificates of Deposits. Treasuries may be purchase through money market funds, mutual funds, brokerage firms, banks; or, directly from Federal Reserve Banks. Purchases not directly from the Treasury Department generally carry an administrative fee to compensate the "middleman" for their service. Investors wishing to avoid fees, and we recommend it, may purchase treasuries directly from their district Federal Reserve Bank. Contact the Bureau of Public Debt, Division of Customer Services, Washington DC 20239 (1-202-874-4000); or, (1-202-287-4133) for details. We have provided a telephone listing for most Federal Reserve Banks at the end of this section.

Do not confuse series EE Savings bonds offered through employers or the Federal Combined Campaign with treasuries. They are as different as night and day. Treasuries may be sold prior to maturity to other investors; whereas, EE savings bonds have no secondary market and must be sold back to the government. A substantial penalty is levied, if the EE bond is surrendered prior to the maturity date, except when certain exemptions apply. Education expenses for dependent children is an exception. Treasuries, on the other hand, sell at substantial discount to par value and are redeemable at maturity. The big difference; however; between EE Bonds and Treasuries is that until maturity, treasuries may change ownership thousands of times among speculators seeking capitol gains and not interest!

We previously alluded to research indicating opportunities where treasuries can return substantial capitol gains over a short time span. Long term 30 year bonds generally rise 10 percent for each ¼ point the Feds drop the bank discount rate. Additionally, when the stock market reaches over-evaluation, and the majority of stocks are selling above their 200 day arithmetic average, investors who understand how market stagnation loses money, will move into treasuries until stock evaluations correct. Demand for treasuries on the secondary market will generally push prices up as demand out runs supply while the government evaluated the economic impact.

EE savings bonds purchased prior to May 1, 1995 earn a minimum of 4 percent pretax annualized yield. However, if they are held for a minimum of five years, they earn an interest yield computed by the Bureau of the Public Debt. EE bonds purchased after May 1, 1995 earn a inflation indexed yield. Regardless of the date of purchase, investors pay ever increasing taxes to repay themselves a market rate only to be taxed on the gain. As a side note appropriate here, the government is not acting in the investors best interest; nor, that of America, by demanding taxes be paid on capitol gains or interest not adjusted for inflation. Under present tax codes, if an investment yields 4 percent with a 4 percent inflation, taxes are due on the yield even though the real purchasing power of the investment netted zero. Debt and equity investors are encouraged to address the unfairness to their congressperson without delay! The capitol gains tax overhaul of 1997 is a farce of the greatest magnitude. Investors who understand the market place are penalized for short term trading; whereas, the novice investor who holds an investment long term may save a few pennies in tax but loses out on the ability to reap benefits from other wealth building opportunities. We recommend treating investing as a business. Trade for after tax profits. Back to the subject at hand. Income from series EE Bonds may be completely tax-free if they are used to pay college tuition for children. Income limits do apply. Check with your tax advisor; or, the IRS for details.

To reiterate, debt securities should never be the 100 percent investment choice of investors seeking net worth growth. If they are, the American dream will escape many, leaving them only to die flat broke! Treasuries should; however, be considered as a short term holding within an investment portfolio. An asset parking spot, during equity asset management. For example, when opening a deep discount brokerage account, treasury holdings through a money market account may constitute the core investment, until the money is used to purchase a selected equity. Reserve funds from equity sell transactions can be parked in a money market position to earn interest until another equity is chosen. Brokerage money market rates generally far exceed returns offered from bank accounts and Certificates of Deposits.

How much of an investment portfolio should be earmarked for treasuries? Again, many formulas to answer this age old question have surfaced. Regardless of the formula used, limit total debt obligations (checking accounts, savings accounts, CDs, bonds, bills, notes, corporate bonds; and, the social security account value, to a maximum of 80 percent times the investors age. A 50 year old investor should limit total treasury debt exposure to a maximum of 40 percent of total net worth. The net worth is negative for the majority of Americans. Debt obligations should never be a part of their investment portfolio. The federal government is well aware of the sad state of personal net worth in America. Yet, poor and low income people having a negative net worth are forced to purchase government debt obligations through the Social Security system. What a disgrace to human dignity!

Investors with a positive net worth wishing to venture into debt instruments as a natural process for diversification should request form *SSA-7005 SM "Statement of Earnings"* from the Social Security Administration. Double check the reported earnings. To arrive at an estimated value of the treasury debt obligation already owned within the social security account, multiply the reported earnings by 15.7 percent. Factor the debt held in the account into the "80 percent times age" to net worth rule prior to obligating additional funds. If the market has topped out or the Fed.'s indicate they could lower the bank discount rate, purchase the maximum limit of 30 year bonds directly from the Treasury. As a service of convenience we offer the following telephone listing:

Federal Reserve Bank Branches

Atlanta	404-521-8653	Louisville	502-568-9236
Baltimore	410-576-3553	Memphis	901-523-7171
Birmingham	202-731-8702	Miami	305-471-6497
Boston	617-973-3810	Minneapolis	612-340-2075
Charlotte	704-358-2424	Nashville	615-251-7100
Chicago	312-322-5369	New Orleans	504-586-1505
Cincinnati	513-721-4787	New York City	212-720-7773
Cleveland	216-579-2490	Oklahoma City	405-270-8652
Dallas	214-922-6000	Omaha	402-221-5636
Denver	303-572-2477	Philadelphia	215-475-6675
Detroit	313-964-5657	Pittsburgh	412-261-7988
El Paso	915-544-4730	Portland	503-221-5921
Houston	713-659-4433	Richmond	804-697-8372
Jacksonville	904-632-1179	Salt Lake City	801-322-7911
Kansas City	816-881-2783	San Antonio	512-978-1330
Little Rock	501-372-5451	San Francisco	415-974-3491
Los Angeles	213-624-7398	Seattle	206-343-3605
		Saint Louis	314-444-8602

Investors are encouraged to review this chapter as many times as necessary to become proficient in the strategies outlined. As with any learned skill, don't expect to be an expert overnight. It takes time to mature into a winner.
It is important to complete the Appendix work sheets.

-----------------------------------NOTES-----------------------------------

CONCLUSION

We are confident *Don't Die Broke* can be a useful tool helpful in the developing of solid educational, financial, and investment strategies necessary to build net worth. We are confident it can guide motivated investors through the complex science of wealth building. Wealth is built upon a solid foundation based upon education, employment, debt reduction, controlled spending; and, the establishment of a personally tailored investment plan of action.

Readers have been exposed to concepts proven to be successful. They have been cautioned on the importance of breaking free of the so-called professionals plotting to fleece away their personal wealth. Investors have been encouraged to maintain a healthy body and mind. It has been strongly suggested, that common stocks have historically outperformed most other types of investments. We have emphasized, that it is more critical to know when to liquidate an investment to secure profits; than, perhaps knowing what type of investment to make. To that end, we have stressed the importance of conducting an individual analytical study, of any investment prior to commitment; and, that profits must be identified prior entering into the investment. Make no doubt about it, your financial security is serious business!

Food for thought! If the unmanaged Dow and S&P 500 Index have outperformed the total return performance of the majority of professional managers year after year for more than a decade, why hasn't your stockbroker put you into these investments. Why hasn't the brokerage business educated investors in the Motley Fool concept, O'Higgins study; or, any of the strategies we have discussed within *Don't Die Broke*? The answer is simple. They would lose their fat greedy commission supported lifestyle. We, on the other hand believe, every person has an individual right to education, happiness, peace of mind; and, financial security during their sunset years of life. We also believe in the ideology that each person is totally responsible for themselves; and, they can only be truly successful, by shaking themselves loose from the forces trying to financially; or, emotionally control them.

Stockbrokers, doctors, lawyers, ministers, psychiatrist; and, politicians, appear too many hard working folks, as the evil force undercutting the core of individualism. Too many, they have wiped away individual rights by making them immoral or illegal. Individualist are incorrectly categorized by these up-surgers as either crooks, fools, insane, or immoral sinners. Although each profession may serve society in very limited capacities of immeasurable degrees, many folks are convinced, it is their over-protectionism which destroys the wealth of society. Each person must determine for themselves how these groups fit into their wealth building plan. Alan Greenspan, the Fed Chairman himself, in the early 1960's eluded during a speech, that if a system was created to create wealth, the government would find a away to make it illegal. Greenspan has not been proven wrong often.

It was not until recent times, religious, business and government leaders began to take a positive stance toward encouraging individual wealth building. They have began to understand, the middle working class is being eroded through the increase of low paying jobs and the importation of immigrants who can not write their own name. Fear of loosing the middle class buffer between themselves and the poor has motivated the wealthy to help increase wealth building within the middle working class. Congratulations are extended to many private and government leaders for their stance on better education, increased employment of higher paying jobs, encouragement of personal savings; tax reduction; and, a balanced federal budget.

Throughout *Don't Die Broke* readers have been given reference material sources. Do not hesitate to contact them for additional information. "Never pay for something you can get for free." Review the Appendix for opportunities and critical work sheets. Thank you for your patronage. This publication has taken several years to research. I'll relax now and enjoy time with my wife, children and grandchildren. Don't worry, on your behalf, research will continue. God Bless.

APPENDIXES

MOTIVATIONAL PLEDGE

(Review Daily)

* I pledge to myself a commitment of maintaining a healthy body and mind both physically and spiritually. Wealth building will fail without considering a basic tool......ME!

* To seeking debt reduction on all loans where payments are scheduled to exceed ten months.

* To limit total debt to a maximum of 37 percent of my income.

* To control wasteful impulse spending while enhancing the probability of true financial freedom through continual education, improved employee performance; and, the development of a positive long term investment strategy.

* Not to surrender to short term setbacks associated with success.

* To accept responsibility for my personal wealth building objectives.

* To ignore those who will try to destroy my success with negative comments.

* To share with my family the prosperity realized from achieving my goals.

* To remind myself daily the importance of my objective; so I, **don't die broke**.

* To never forget that no one can manage my assets better than myself, once I develop the skills necessary to succeed.

Date:___/___/___

Signature____

BALANCE SHEET

Name:______________________________	Date:________________________
Current Net Worth:____________________	Net Worth Growth: ____________________
(-) Previous net worth:__________________	(/) Previous net worth: __________________
Net Worth Growth: ____________________	(=) % Net Worth Growth:_______________

(Assets)		(Liabilities)	
Cash on hand	___________	Rent	___________
Bank Accounts	___________	Mortgage	___________
Money Market	___________	Monthly Bills	___________
Stock market value	___________	Charge account	___________
T. Bonds, Bills, Notes	___________	Lay-a-way	___________
Mutual Funds Net Value	___________	Taxes owed	___________
Annuity net value	___________	Union dues	___________
Residential market value	___________	Pledges- charity	___________
Collectibles (stamps etc.)	___________	Transportation	___________
Whole Life Insurance Cash Value	___________	Allowances (Food, etc.)	___________
Auto Retail Value	___________	Entertainment	___________
IRA/FER'S/401K/Keogh, etc.	___________	Student loans	___________
Investment Real Estate	___________	Personal loans	___________
Precious Metals	___________	Auto note	___________
Other	___________	Other	___________
Total Assets	___________	Total Liabilities	___________

Total Assets	___________
(-) Total Liabilities	___________
(=) Net worth	___________

A *Balance Sheet* computation provides a snap shot of the investors current assets and the liability against those assets. The average person has no idea what they are truly worth; yet, they will obligate themselves to financial commitments often taking years to fulfill. We can not over emphasize the importance of computing net worth quarterly. All spending and investment diversification should take into consideration its effect on net worth growth.

Transportation cost per mile should be accounted for monthly. Failure to take transportation cost into consideration at the moment it occurs is a drastic mistake committed by practically every working American.

INCOME STATEMENT

Name:______________________	Date: ______________________
Current Net Income:______________	Net Income Growth:______________
(-) Previous Net Income: __________	(/) Previous Net Income:____________
(=) Net Income Growth: __________	(=) % Net Income Growth:__________

(Income)		(Expenses)	
Salary	________	Insurance	________
Interest	________	Federal Tax	________
Dividends	________	State Tax	________
Rental	________	FICA Tax	________
Royalties	________	Medicare	________
Sales	________	Retirement	________
Grants	________	Transportation	________
Gifts	________	Mortgage	________
Commissions	________	Personal	________
Directorship	________	Union Dues	________
Other	________	Other	________
Total Income	________	Total Expense	________

Total Income	________
(-) Total Expense	________
(=) Net Income	________

Personal income production, no differently than corporate income production, has associated expenses. Each employee is a production cost center unto themselves; and, accrue expenses rising out of that income production. Sad to say, the majority of workers fail to understand their personal expense relationship to their income production. The majority of workers labor their entire lives for a daily subsistence, only to die broke. Workers can rise above the "economic slave" syndrome, if they were better educated in asset management, they were allowed to express individual rights; and, the government went about its duty of national defense while refraining from meddling in the personal affairs of the citizenship. Each worker should strive to overcome obstacles put in their path of wealth building by those who fear losing the working class tax buffer between themselves and the nations poor. The "challenge of change" is an individual choice that will never materialize if expenses consistently exceed income. An Income Statement gives the investor a realistic view of their current relationship between income and expenses. It should be an on going review!

NOTICE

The publisher of *Don't Die Broke* is currently seeking readership input, by providing material of interest and worthy of public distribution. The material will be distributed via a proposed monthly news release to a subscribership and will be the primary method to provide updated material to owners of *Don't Die Broke*. The date and title of the subscription release will be finalized when enough interest is indicated. Through a consorted effort by our customers, we expect to become in effect their research committee.

Material submitted for distribution must be by original authorship, limited to a maximum of 500 words; and, be motivational, financial, investment, business, legal; or, health orientated toward net worth growth.

The publisher reserves the right to edit all submitted material for clarity, content; and, readership value. Rejection rights of all materials are retained by the publisher. No material will be returned to the author.

Full credit will be given to the author when the article is published. Articles will not be reviewed without a release signed and dated by the author.

This notice may be modified; or, canceled without prior notification.

A fee of $100, payable in United States currency, will be paid to the author of all selected material.

Due to the anticipated volume of articles in response to this notice, we request all correspondence be via mail. Please help spread wealth building information throughout America by submitting your works to:

G Howard Gunn
370 Lakeshore Drive: Swan Lake
Stockbridge, Georgia 30281-1709

---Cut Here---

<u>Release</u>

I, (Print Name)________________________________; hereby authorize the distribution, as edited by the Publisher of *Don't Die Broke,* the following article:____________________________________.

Accreditation Source:___________________________ Number of words:__________________________

I will receive full accreditation for my work upon release. I agree to accept as payment in full, a sum not to exceed $100 in United States currency. I retain full copyrights to my work.

Publisher G. Howard Gunn holds the sole authority, in the determination as to the release date of my material. I affirm my material is original; and, full accreditation is given to sources I used to compile the work.

Under no circumstance is the publisher into which this agreement is entered has the authority to resale my material, except through a monthly subscribership release, directly to clients of the publisher. No material will be returned.

Date: ______________________ Signature: ______________________
Telephone:______________________Address:____

INCOME OPPORTUNITY

THE PUBLISHER OF *DON'T DIE BROKE* IS ACTIVELY SEEKING 500 INDIVIDUALS, FUND RAISING ORGANIZATIONS, EDUCATIONAL INSTITUTIONS, CORPORATIONS, AND BOOK DEALERS, TO ASSIST IN THE DISTRIBUTION OF THIS BOOK.

A LIBERIAL DISCOUNT, OF UP TO 55 PERCENT OFF THE SUGGESTED RETAIL PRICE IS EXTENDED TO QUALIFIED ORDERS PLACED DIRECTLY WITH THE PUBLISHER. WE ACCEPT ADVANCED PAYMENT IN CASH, CHECK; OR, MONEY ORDERS. SORRY, NO COD'S. ALLOW FOUR WEEKS TO PROCESS ORDERS.

INTERESTED PARTIES, PARTICULARLY INVESTMENT CLUBS AND COMPANIES WISHING TO ASSIST THEIR WORKFORCE IN DEVELOPING AN INDIVIDUAL EMPLOYEE ASSET MANAGEMENT PLAN OF ACTION ARE ENCOURAGED TO CONTACT THE PUBLISHER VIA LETTER CORRESPONDANCE FOR SPECIFIC DISCOUNT DETAILS. WE WILL PROVIDE INFORMATION PROMPTLY. PLEASE INCLUDE A TELEPHONE CONTACT.

WHOLESALE ORDERS REQUIRE A TAXPAYER IDENTIFICATION NUMBER. ALL RETAIL ORDERS WILL BE ASSESED A 7% GEORGIA SALES TAX. SHIPPING AND HANDLING CHARGES MAY APPLY.

WE OFFER A **100 PERCENT GURANTEED REPURCHASE** OF ALL WHOLESALE BOOKS PURCHASED DIRECTLY FROM THE PUBLISHER AND RETURNED WITHIN 90 DAYS OF THE DATE OF PURCHASE, IN AN UNDAMAGED RESALEABLE CONDITION. WE WILL CHEERFULLY REFUND THE FULL PURCHASE PRICE. PROOF OF PURCHASE INCLUDING DATE, COST; AND, NAME OF SALES ORGANIZATION IS REQUIRED. SORRY! THERE ARE NO RETAIL REFUNDS. HOWEVER, WE WILL REPLACE BOOKS REPORTED DAMAGED IN SHIPPING IF A COPY OF THE DAMAGE CLAIM TO THE CARRIER ACCOMPANIES THE RETURNED MATERIAL.

WE WILL DROP SHIP SINGLE BOOKS DIRECTLY TO YOUR CUSTOMER ON YOUR PROVIDED MAILING LABEL. DEALERS ARE NEVER REQUIRED TO STOCK AN INVENTORY. WE DO THAT FOR YOU. THIS IS AN EXCELLENT OPPORTUNITY TO EARN EXTRA INVESTMENT INCOME.

NEED SALES MATERIAL? WE WILL PROVIDE SALES FLYERS, MAILERS, AND OTHER PROMPTIONAL MATERIAL AT OUR COST PLUS THE POSTAGE TO YOUR ADDRESS. REQUEST DETAILS.

PARTICIPANTS OF THIS OFFER ARE NOT EMPLOYEES OF THE PUBLISHER; AND, ARE RESPONSIBLE FOR COLLECTION AND PAYMENT OF RETAIL SALES TAXE TO THE APPROPRIATE AUTHORITIES. THIS OFFER MAY BE WITHDRAWN WITHOUT NOTICE.

DON'T DIE BROKE MAKES A GREAT GIFT. IT IS ONE GIFT THAT KEEPS GIVING THROUGHOUT LIFE!

SEND INQUIRES TO:

DON'T DIE BROKE
370 LAKESHORE DRIVE
STOCKBRIDGE, GA 30281-1709

INDEX